Learning Redux

Write maintainable, consistent, and easy-to-test web applications

Daniel Bugl

BIRMINGHAM - MUMBAI

Learning Redux

First published: August 2017

Production reference: 1260817

Published by Packt Publishing Ltd.
Livery Place
35 Livery Street
Birmingham
B3 2PB, UK.
ISBN 978-1-78646-239-8

www.packtpub.com

Credits

Author
Daniel Bugl

Reviewer
Sergii Shvager

Commissioning Editor
Wilson D'souza

Acquisition Editor
Shweta Pant

Content Development Editor
Roshan Kumar

Technical Editors
Akansha Bathija
Bharat Patil

Copy Editor
Dhanya Baburaj

Project Coordinator
Devanshi Doshi

Proofreader
Safis Editing

Indexer
Mariammal Chettiyar

Graphics
Jason Monteiro

Production Coordinator
Shraddha Falebhai

About the Author

Daniel Bugl is a developer, product designer and entrepreneur, focusing on web technologies. He currently lives in Vienna, Austria. He got into programming via game development as early as the age of 6. Later, at the age of 10, he first learned about web technologies such as HTML, CSS, PHP, and JavaScript.

During high-school, he contributed to the Ubuntu project, specifically the Ubuntu Beginners Team, supporting beginners with Linux and helping them get started with the community. He mentored some people who are full Ubuntu members now. He was also part of the Ubuntu-Youth council and leading the Ubuntu Austria LoCo (Local Community). Furthermore, he developed open source software, voluntarily translated software, and supported people on askubuntu.

He also did an internship as a researcher at the Vienna University of Technology, which would later become the university he studies at. Later on, he did an internship at Jung von Matt, an advertisement agency, where he collected practical experience in web development by developing a management panel.

He is now studying Business Informatics and Information Systems at the Vienna University of Technology (TU Wien) and is in the process of writing his bachelor thesis. At the university, he sometimes works as a tutor, on the Program Construction (entry-level programming), Usability Engineering, and Interface and Interaction Design courses.

Now, he is a contributor to many open source projects (including Redux and his own library, redux-undo) and a member of the React community on the Redux team. He also founded and still runs his own hardware/software startup TouchLay (touchlay), which helps other companies present their products and services. At his company, he constantly works with web technologies, especially React and Redux.

Acknowledgments

First of all, I would like to thank all of the people involved in the production of this book. The team at Packt was very nice and pleasant to work with. I would also like to thank Dan Abramov for creating Redux, helping me create redux-undo, and letting me create a recipe page in the Redux documentation. Him and his projects have been a great inspiration to me.

Furthermore, I would like to thank Nik Graf, Max Stoiber, and Andrey Okonetchnikov for organising the React Vienna Meetup, which deepened my interest in React and Redux. Special thanks for letting me give a talk on higher-order reducers! I would also like to thank my co-founder, Georg Schelkshorn, for running an amazing company with me – I would not get to use web technologies as much without it.

Finally, I would like to thank my family and friends for supporting me during the creation of this book. At this point, I would especially like to thank and send love to my girlfriend, Destiny Rebuck, for supporting me and caring for me during the most stressful part of the process--the weeks before publishing.

About the Reviewer

Sergii Shvager is a frontend developer who is passionate about React/Redux. He was born in Ukraine and is currently living in Berlin. He has worked on the frontend part of projects in different areas, such as e-commerce, game development, and services. He started his frontend experience with jQuery, Backbone.js, and Ext.js, and then switched to React/Redux stack.

He has had his own company that develops mobile applications. Currently, he is working at eBay Classified Group.

I would like to thank my wife, Anna, for her support.

www.PacktPub.com

For support files and downloads related to your book, please visit www.PacktPub.com. Did you know that Packt offers eBook versions of every book published, with PDF and ePub files available? You can upgrade to the eBook version at www.PacktPub.com and as a print book customer, you are entitled to a discount on the eBook copy. Get in touch with us at service@packtpub.com for more details.

At www.PacktPub.com, you can also read a collection of free technical articles, sign up for a range of free newsletters and receive exclusive discounts and offers on Packt books and eBooks.

https://www.packtpub.com/mapt

Get the most in-demand software skills with Mapt. Mapt gives you full access to all Packt books and video courses, as well as industry-leading tools to help you plan your personal development and advance your career.

Why subscribe?

- Fully searchable across every book published by Packt
- Copy and paste, print, and bookmark content
- On demand and accessible via a web browser

Customer Feedback

Thanks for purchasing this Packt book. At Packt, quality is at the heart of our editorial process. To help us improve, please leave us an honest review on this book's Amazon page at www.amazon.com/dp/1786462397.

If you'd like to join our team of regular reviewers, you can e-mail us at customerreviews@packtpub.com. We award our regular reviewers with free eBooks and videos in exchange for their valuable feedback. Help us be relentless in improving our products!

Table of Contents

Preface   1

Chapter 1: Why Redux?   7

    Defining the application state   10

    Defining actions   11

    Tying state and actions together   12

    Redux' three fundamental principles   13

        Single source of truth   13

        The read-only state   14

        State changes are processed with pure functions   14

    Introduction to the Redux ecosystem   16

    Summary   17

Chapter 2: Implementing the Elements of Redux   19

    The Redux cycle   20

        An action is dispatched   20

        The main reducer function gets executed   20

        Redux saves the new state   21

        Strictly unidirectional data flow   21

    Running code examples   22

        Setting up a new project   22

            Setting up Node.js   22

            Initializing the project   22

            Setting up webpack   23

            Setting up Babel   25

            Setting up the entry files   25

            Running webpack   26

            Setting up Redux   28

        The template code   28

    Implementing actions and action creators   28

        Separating action types   29

            ES2015 - import/export   29

        Introducing action creators   29

            ES2015 - arrow functions   30

            ES2015 - import/export   31

        Code example   32

    Implementing reducers   32

Defining/importing action types   33
Defining action creators   33
Writing the posts reducer   34
    The main structure of a reducer   34
    ES2015 - using destructuring and the rest operator to parse the action   35
    Handling CREATE_POST – creating a new post   36
    Handling EDIT_POST – editing posts   37
    Testing out our reducer   39
Writing the filter reducer   40
Combining reducers   40
    Testing out the full reducer   41
Code example   43
The store – combining actions and reducers   43
Creating the store   43
Subscribing to state changes   45
Dispatching actions   45
Rendering the user interface   46
    Creating sample data   47
    Handling the user input   47
Code example   49
Summary   49
Chapter 3: Combining Redux with React   51
Why React?   51
The principles of React   51
Setting up React   52
Rendering simple text   53
Rendering with JSX   54
    Setting up JSX   55
    Using JSX   55
Example code   55
First steps with React   56
Creating a simple React element   56
Creating a static React component   57
    Functional components   58
    Using components   58
    Example code   60
Class components – dynamic React components   61
    Creating a static class component   61
    Creating a dynamic class component   62
      Setting the initial state   62
      React life cycle methods   63
      Updating the state   64

Example – dynamic React component with timer	64
Example code	67
Connecting React to Redux	**67**
Presentational versus container components	68
Writing presentational components	69
Post component	69
PostList component	71
Example code	72
Writing container components	73
Implementing our own container component	73
Example code	76
Using React-Redux bindings to create a container component	76
Setting up React-Redux	77
Using React-Redux to create a container component	77
Using selectors	78
Example code	79
Building an application with Redux and React	**79**
The goal	80
Project structure	80
Defining the application state	82
Users state	82
Posts state	82
Filter state	83
Defining action types and action creators	83
Defining action types	83
Defining action creators	84
User action creators	84
Post action creators	85
Filter action creators	86
Implementing reducers	87
Users reducer	87
Posts reducer	88
Filter reducer	89
Root reducer	90
Setting up the Redux store	90
Code example – Redux-only application	92
Implementing the user interface	92
Implementing presentational components	92
User component	93
Post component	93
Timestamp component	94
PostList component	94
Filter component	95
FilterList component	95
Implementing container components	96

ConnectedPostList component	97
ConnectedFilterList component	98
Implementing the App component	100
Using <Provider>	100
Rendering the App component	101
Code example – React/Redux application	102
Further tasks	102
Summary	**103**

Chapter 4: Combining Redux with Angular — 105

Redux with Angular 1	**105**
Setting up Angular 1	105
Code example	107
Creating a basic Angular 1 application	107
Defining the module and controller	108
Code example	109
Setting up ng-redux	109
Redefining the controller	111
Dispatching actions from the user interface	112
Code example	112
Redux with Angular 2+	**113**
Setting up Angular 2+	113
Setting up @angular-redux/store	115
Code example	118
Summary	**119**

Chapter 5: Debugging a Redux Application — 121

Integrating Redux DevTools	**121**
Installing Redux DevTools	122
Creating a DevTools component	123
Connecting DevTools to Redux	124
Using the DevTools.instrument() store enhancer	125
Rendering DevTools	125
Implementing the persistState() store enhancer	127
Using multiple store enhancers	128
Implementing a simple session key provider	129
Do not re-dispatch on refresh	129
Using the store enhancer	130
Excluding Redux DevTools in production	130
Injecting the NODE_ENV environment variable with webpack	131
Adding new build scripts for production and development	132
Separating the production store from the development store	133
Implementing the development store	133
Implementing the production store	134
Importing the correct store	134

Importing and using configureStore()   134
Only loading the DevTools component in development mode   135
Running in production/development mode – example code   135

Setting up hot reloading   136
Hot reloading React components   136
Hot reloading other code with webpack   136
Hot reloading Redux reducers   139
Testing out hot reloading – example code   139
Using Redux DevTools   141
DockMonitor   141
Setup   142
Properties   142
LogMonitor   143
Setup   143
Usage   144
Properties   145
Inspector   145
Setup   146
Usage   146
Properties   148
SliderMonitor   148
Setup   149
Usage   150
Properties   150
ChartMonitor   150
Setup   151
Properties   152
Other monitors   152
Summary   153

Chapter 6: Interfacing with APIs   155
Setting up the backend   155
The backend API   156
GET /api   156
Example output   157
GET /api/posts   157
Example output   158
GET /api/posts/:id   158
Example output   158
POST /api/posts   159
Example request   159
Example output   159
POST /api/posts/:id   159
Example request   160
Example output   160

GET /api/users	160
Example output	161
GET /api/users/:username	161
Example output	161
POST /api/users	161
Example request	162
Example output	162
POST /api/users/:username	162
Example request	162
Example output	163
Handling asynchronous operations with Redux	**163**
Dispatching multiple actions from an action creator	163
Defining action types	164
Creating an asynchronous action creator	164
Handling asynchronous action creators via middleware	167
Setting up redux-thunk middleware	167
Pulling data from an API into the Redux store	**169**
Extracting boilerplate code	169
Pulling posts from the API	170
Pulling users from the API	172
Fetching a single user	172
Fetching users when fetching posts	174
Handling loading state	178
Implementing the reducer	178
Implementing the component	179
Using the component	181
Handling error state	181
Implementing the reducer	182
Implementing the component	183
Using the component	184
Example code	185
Sending notifications to an API via Redux	**185**
Using asynchronous action creators	185
Creating users via the API	185
Creating posts via the API	188
Example code	191
Summary	**192**
Chapter 7: User Authentication	**193**
JSON Web Tokens (JWT)	**193**
JSON Web Token structure	194
Header	194
Payload	195
Signature	196
Token	197

Using JSON Web Tokens   197
Implementing token authentication   198
Backend API   198
POST /api/login   199
Example request   199
Example output   199
POST /api/users   200
Example request   200
Example output   200
POST /api/posts   200
Example request   201
Example output   201
Secured routes   201
Storing the token in the Redux store   202
Defining the action types and action creator   202
Creating the reducer   203
Dispatching login action in the component   204
Testing out the login   204
Checking whether the user is logged in   206
Separating the header   206
Hiding/showing components when the user is logged in   208
Showing the currently loggedin user   208
Sending the token with certain requests   209
Example code   211
redux-auth   212
Summary   212
Chapter 8: Testing   213
Setting up Jest   213
Testing automatically on every file change   215
Checking code coverage   216
Example code   218
Using Jest   219
Using test and describe   219
Matchers   219
.toBe or .not.toBe   220
Truthiness   221
Numbers   221
Strings   222
Arrays   222
Exceptions   223
All matchers   223
Testing asynchronous code   223
Callbacks   224

Promises   225
   .resolves/.rejects   225
Setup and teardown   226
   Running every time before/after each test   226
   Running once before/after all tests   227
   Scoping   227
Mocking   228
   .mock property   228
   Return values   229
   Implementations   229
   Special matchers   230
Testing Redux   231
   Synchronous action creators   231
   Reducers   233
      Testing initial state   233
      Initializing state with beforeEach()   233
      Testing the setFilter action   234
      Testing the clearFilter action   235
   Reducers with async actions   235
   Asynchronous action creators   238
      Testing successful requests   239
      Testing failing requests   240
   Example code   241
   Other tests   241
Testing React components   242
Summary   243

Chapter 9: Routing   245

Creating a simple router   245
   Defining the action types and action creator   246
   Creating the reducer   247
   Creating the page components   248
      Creating the MainPage component   248
      Creating the AboutPage component   249
   Creating the Router component   250
      Connecting the Router component to Redux   251
      Using the Router component   251
   Creating the Navigation component   252
      Connecting the Navigation component to Redux   252
      Using the Navigation component   254
   Code example   255
Using a routing library   255
   Introducing react-router   256
      Static routing   256

Dynamic routing	256
Nested routes	257
More routing	257
Using react-router	258
Installing react-router	258
Defining the <Router> and <Route>	258
Defining the <Link>	259
Trying out the router	259
Marking the currently selected link	260
Using react-router with Redux	262
Do I need to connect my router to Redux?	262
Why deeply integrate my router with Redux?	263
Example code	263
Using react-router-redux	264
Installing react-router-redux	264
Using the routerMiddleware	264
Using the routerReducer	264
Using the ConnectedRouter	265
Testing out the router	266
Navigating by dispatching actions	266
Example code	267
Summary	267
Chapter 10: Rendering on the Server	269
Why render on the server?	269
Current process to load the page	269
Using server-side rendering	270
Preparing for server-side rendering	271
Using the isomorphic-fetch library	271
Implementing server-side rendering	272
Handling the request/routing	272
Emulating the Redux store and browser history	272
Initializing the Redux store	273
Using react-router to decide which page to render	274
Handling react-router redirects	275
Injecting rendered React components into the index.html template	275
Injecting the preloaded Redux store state	276
Rendering the template file	277
Using the preloaded Redux store state	277
Caching the index page	278
Performance improvements	279
Summary	281

Chapter 11: Solving Generic Problems with Higher-Order Functions   283

Making functions pure   284
  Simple side effects   284
  No side effects   284
  Other side effects   285
  Side effects and Redux   285
Creating higher-order functions   286
  Functions as arguments   286
  Functions as results   287
Solving generic problems with Redux   288
  Higher-order reducers   289
  Higher-order action creators   290
  Higher-order components   292
Implementing generic undo/redo Redux   294
  Setting up the counter application   294
  Looking at the counter reducer   295
  Implementing undo/redo in the counter application   295
    Defining the action types   296
    Defining the action creators   296
    Defining the new state   297
    Rewriting the counter reducer   298
      Handling the counter-related actions   298
      Handling the undo/redo actions   299
    Creating undo/redo buttons   300
    Trying out undo/redo   301
    Example code   303
  Implementing a generic undo/redo higher-order reducer   303
    Defining the undoable higher-order reducer   304
    Defining the initial state   304
      Problems with our previous solution   305
      A new kind of history   305
      Defining a generic initial state   307
    Handling generic undo/redo actions   308
      Defining the action types   309
      Defining the action creators   309
      Implementing the enhanced reducer   310
      Handling the undo action   310
      Handling the redo action   311
      Handling other actions (updating the present state)   312
      Removing undo/redo logic from the counter reducer   313
      Wrapping the counter reducer with undoable   314
      Problems with our simple undoable higher-order reducer   315
    Example code   315

Implementing redux-undo   316
    Installing redux-undo   316
    Wrapping our reducer with undoable   317
    Adjusting the state selector   317
    Importing the undo/redo actions   317
    Debug mode   318
    Example code   320
Summary   320

Chapter 12: Extending the Redux Store via Middleware   321

What is middleware?   321
Express middleware   322
Creating our own middleware pattern   323
    Sketching out the API   323
    Creating the Middleware class   323
      Defining the run method   324
      Defining the use method   325
    Using our own middleware pattern   325
Example code   327
Using the Redux store middleware   327
Implementing logging   327
    Manual logging   327
    Wrapping the dispatch function   328
    Monkeypatching the dispatch function   328
    Hiding monkeypatching   329
    Getting rid of monkeypatching   330
    Applying middleware   331
Implementing Redux middleware   332
    Creating a middleware folder   332
    Logging middleware   333
    Error reporting middleware   334
    Applying our middleware to the Redux store   335
Example code   335
Thunk middleware   337
Final tips and tricks   337
Designing the application state   337
    Using indices   337
    Normalized state   338
    Organizing data in the application state   339
Updating an application state   340
    Updating nested objects   340
      Common mistake 1 - New variables that point to the same objects   340
      Common mistake 2 - Only making a shallow copy   341
      Correct approach - Copying all levels of nested data   341
    Updating arrays   341

Inserting items   342
Removing items   342
Updating items   342
Mutating copies   343
Using libraries   343

Summary   344

Index   345

Preface

About the book

Redux is a predictable state container for JavaScript apps. It helps you write applications that run in different environments (client, server, and native) and are predictable and easy to test. Additionally, Redux provides a great developer experience, such as live code editing and time traveling debugging. Redux can be used together with a view library, like React and Angular.

This book will start out teaching you why and how Redux works. We are going to learn about principles and restrictions that make your application more predictable. Afterwards, we will implement the basic elements of Redux to create a blog application. Next, we will connect Redux to a user interface by combining it with a view library, like React and Angular. Then we move on by implementing common functionality in our Redux application, such as user authentication, interfacing with APIs, writing tests, and routing. Finally, we are going to discuss extending Redux itself, by solving common problems with state management (such as undo/redo functionality) through higher-order reducers and middleware.

After reading this book, you will be able to write maintainable, predictable, consistent, and easy-to-test applications with Redux and React.

What this book covers

Chapter 1, *Why Redux?*, will teach you about the principles that make Redux special, and why Redux should be used in a project. It starts out with the motivation behind Redux (complexity of state management), then briefly covers how Redux works in practice and how certain restrictions allow us to write maintainable, predictable, consistent, and easy-to-test applications.

Chapter 2, *Implementing the Elements of Redux*, explains how to set up a project that is ready for Redux and the new JavaScript ES2015 syntax. Then, you are going to implement the basic elements of Redux and put a full Redux project together.

Chapter 3, *Combining Redux with React*, covers what React is and why it makes sense to use it. Then you will learn how to set up a project with React and connect Redux to it.

Chapter 4, *Combining Redux with Angular,* covers using Redux in combination with Angular 1 and 2+ (compatible with Angular 4).

Chapter 5, *Debugging a Redux Application,* covers how to integrate and use Redux DevTools in an application. Then it covers various Redux DevTools monitors, explaining how to configure and use them in practice.

Chapter 6, *Interfacing with APIs,* teaches you how to handle asynchronous operations with Redux. Afterwards, this knowledge is used to pull blog posts and users from an API into the Redux store. Finally, you are going to learn how to dispatch actions that change the state in the frontend/client and the backend/server (creating users and posts).

Chapter 7, *User Authentication,* explains token authentication is and why using it over traditional cookie/session ID authentication makes sense. Next, you will learn how to use and implement an open standard of token authentication--**JSON Web Token (JWT)**.

Chapter 8, *Testing,* covers using Jest, a testing engine, to write tests for all the elements of Redux.

Chapter 9, *Routing,* covers how to implement routing with Redux and React, manually and by using libraries such as react-router and react-router-redux.

Chapter 10, *Rendering on the Server,* this chapter teaches you why server-rendering makes sense and what benefits we get from using this technique. Then, you are going to learn how to implement server-side rendering in a Redux/React application.

Chapter 11, *Solving Generic Problems with Higher-Order Functions,* explains about advanced patterns when developing JavaScript/Redux/React applications. It starts by teaching basic concepts such as pure functions, then moves on to higher-order functions. Next, you will learn how to use these concepts in a Redux/React application to implement generic undo/redo behavior.

Chapter 12, *Extending the Redux Store via Middleware,* teaches what middleware (specifically, Redux store middleware) is and how it can be used. To wrap up, this chapter ends with a section on general tips and tricks for developing Redux applications.

What you need for this book

- Node.js v6.11.1 LTS
- Needs to support nodejs (any Windows, macOS, Linux device)

Who this book is for

This book is for web developers who are already fluent in JavaScript, but want to extend their skills to be able to develop and maintain growing applications.

Conventions

In this book, you will find a number of text styles that distinguish between different kinds of information. Here are some examples of these styles and an explanation of their meaning. Code words in text, database table names, folder names, filenames, file extensions, pathnames, dummy URLs, user input, and Twitter handles are shown as follows: "The next lines of code read the link and assign it to the `BeautifulSoup` function."

A block of code is set as follows:

```
{
  "title": "Another test",
  "text": "Hello API!"
}
```

When we wish to draw your attention to a particular part of a code block, the relevant lines or items are set in bold:

```
{
  "username": "des",
  "realname": "Destiny",
  "password": "test123"
}
```

Any command-line input or output is written as follows:

```
npm install --save react react-dom
```

Warnings or important notes appear like this.

Tips and tricks appear like this.

Reader feedback

Feedback from our readers is always welcome. Let us know what you think about this book-what you liked or disliked. Reader feedback is important for us as it helps us develop titles that you will really get the most out of. To send us general feedback, simply e-mail feedback@packtpub.com, and mention the book's title in the subject of your message. If there is a topic that you have expertise in and you are interested in either writing or contributing to a book, see our author guide at www.packtpub.com/authors.

Customer support

Now that you are the proud owner of a Packt book, we have a number of things to help you to get the most from your purchase.

Downloading the example code

You can download the example code files for this book from your account at http://www.packtpub.com. If you purchased this book elsewhere, you can visit http://www.packtpub.com/support and register to have the files e-mailed directly to you. You can download the code files by following these steps:

1. Log in or register to our website using your e-mail address and password.
2. Hover the mouse pointer on the **SUPPORT** tab at the top.
3. Click on **Code Downloads & Errata**.
4. Enter the name of the book in the **Search** box.
5. Select the book for which you're looking to download the code files.
6. Choose from the drop-down menu where you purchased this book from.
7. Click on **Code Download**.

Once the file is downloaded, please make sure that you unzip or extract the folder using the latest version of:

- WinRAR / 7-Zip for Windows
- Zipeg / iZip / UnRarX for Mac
- 7-Zip / PeaZip for Linux

The code bundle for the book is also hosted on GitHub at
`https://github.com/PacktPublishing/Learning-Redux`. We also have other code bundles
from our rich catalog of books and videos available at
`https://github.com/PacktPublishing/`. Check them out!

Downloading the color images of this book

We also provide you with a PDF file that has color images of the screenshots/diagrams used
in this book. The color images will help you better understand the changes in the output.
You can download this file from
`https://www.packtpub.com/sites/default/files/downloads/LearningRedux_ColorImage`
`s.pdf`.

Errata

Although we have taken every care to ensure the accuracy of our content, mistakes do
happen. If you find a mistake in one of our books-maybe a mistake in the text or the code-
we would be grateful if you could report this to us. By doing so, you can save other readers
from frustration and help us improve subsequent versions of this book. If you find any
errata, please report them by visiting `http://www.packtpub.com/submit-errata`, selecting
your book, clicking on the **Errata Submission Form** link, and entering the details of your
errata. Once your errata are verified, your submission will be accepted and the errata will
be uploaded to our website or added to any list of existing errata under the Errata section of
that title. To view the previously submitted errata, go to
`https://www.packtpub.com/books/content/support` and enter the name of the book in the
search field. The required information will appear under the **Errata** section.

Piracy

Piracy of copyrighted material on the Internet is an ongoing problem across all media. At
Packt, we take the protection of our copyright and licenses very seriously. If you come
across any illegal copies of our works in any form on the Internet, please provide us with
the location address or website name immediately so that we can pursue a remedy. Please
contact us at `copyright@packtpub.com` with a link to the suspected pirated material. We
appreciate your help in protecting our authors and our ability to bring you valuable
content.

Questions

If you have a problem with any aspect of this book, you can contact us at questions@packtpub.com, and we will do our best to address the problem.

1
Why Redux?

If you have written a large-scale application before, you will know that managing application state can become a pain as the app grows. Application state includes server responses, cached data, and data that has not been persisted to the server yet.

Furthermore, the **User Interface** (**UI**) state constantly increases in complexity. For example, nowadays, routing is often implemented on the client so that we do not need to refresh the browser and reload the whole application in order to load a new page. Client-side routing is good for performance, but it means that the client has to deal with even more state (in comparison to using server-side routing).

As you can imagine, conflicts and inconsistencies in these various kinds of state can be hard to deal with. Managing all these states is hard and, if not managed correctly, application state can quickly grow out of control, like an untended garden.

If all of this was not bad enough, new requirements, such as optimistic updates and server-side rendering, become necessary to be able to keep up with the ever increasing performance demands.

State is difficult to deal with because we are mixing two concepts that can be very unpredictable when put together: **Asynchronicity** and **Mutation**.

Asynchronicity means that changes can happen anytime, in an asynchronous manner. For example, a user presses a button that causes a server request. We do not know when the server responds and, for performance reasons, we do not want to wait for the response. This is where Asynchronicity comes into play. We act on a response whenever it occurs, but it is unpredictable when this will happen.

Mutation means any change in the application state, such as storing the result from the server response in our application state or navigating to a new page with client-side routing, would change the value of the current route, mutating the application state.

When putting these two concepts together, bad things can happen. For example, the user might enter some new data and save it, while we are still persisting something else to the server, causing an inconsistent state.

This is where Redux comes in. Redux attempts to make state Mutations predictable, without losing the performance advantages of Asynchronicity. It does so by imposing certain restrictions on how updates can happen. These restrictions make applications predictable and easy to test.

As a result of these restrictions, Redux also provides a great developer experience. When debugging, you can *time travel* between previous application states, and pinpoint the exact time when a bug occurs. You can also use this functionality in production—when users report a bug, the whole application state can be transmitted. This means that you can load the exact state of the application when the bug occurred, making reproduction trivial:

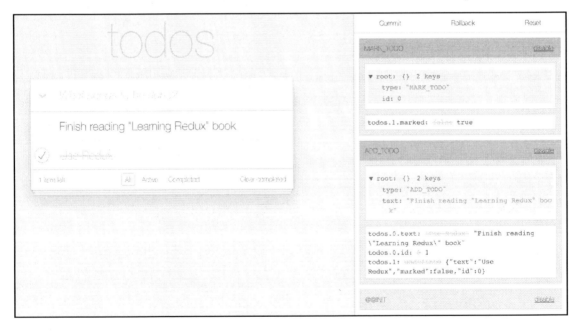

The Redux development experience (all state changes are visible, certain actions can be disabled, and the state will be recalculated)

Furthermore, Redux is very simple and uses plain JavaScript objects and functions. As a result, it can run in various different environments, such as a web client (browser), native applications, and even on the server.

To start out, we will cover the basic elements of a Redux application. Afterwards, we will also cover the restrictions mentioned earlier, resulting in the fundamental principles of Redux. Next, we will focus on how to use Redux with React, a library that shares similar principles and is used to generate user interfaces from the data maintained in Redux. Then, we will teach you how to use Redux with Angular, a framework that is also used to generate user interfaces. Next, we will dive deep into how to solve common problems in web development (such as debugging, user authentication, or interfacing with third-party APIs) with Redux:

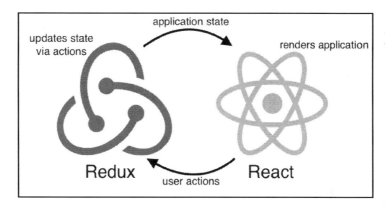

How Redux and React play together

Finally, we will discuss how to extend Redux by implementing generic solutions that work with all Redux applications. These generic solutions can be distributed as libraries and there are already many of these out there. For example, to implement undo/redo functionality in any application, you simply use a library, and it will work, regardless of how your application is structured.

In this book, we will develop a blog application with Redux. This application will keep getting extended throughout the chapters and help us practice concepts learned in the book.

In this chapter, we will cover:

- Defining the state of our application
- Defining actions
- Tying the state and actions together
- Learning about Redux's three fundamental principles
- Introducing the Redux ecosystem

Defining the application state

Before we start implementing a Redux application, we first have to think about the application state. The state of a Redux application is simply a JavaScript value (usually an object).

The application state includes all data needed to render the application and handle user actions. Later, we will use parts of the application state to render HTML templates and make API requests.

You might not know the full application state in the beginning; that's fine. We will make sure that we design our application state in an extendable way. In a Redux application, the state is usually represented as a JavaScript object. Each property of the object describes a substate of the application.

For example, a simple blog application state could consist of an array of posts (which are written by the user and contain some text):

```
{
  posts: [
    { user: 'dan', text: 'Hello World!' },
    { user: 'des', text: 'Welcome to the blog' }
  ]
}
```

Imagine that we want to add a category string to posts later—we can simply add this property to the objects in the posts array:

```
{
  posts: [
    { user: 'dan', category: 'hello', text: 'Hello World!' },
    { user: 'des', category: 'welcome', text: 'Welcome to the blog' }
  ]
}
```

Now, let's say we want to implement filtering posts by `category`; we could extend our state object with a `filter` property that stores the category as a string:

```
{
  posts: [
    { user: 'dan', category: 'hello', text: 'Hello World!' },
    { user: 'des', category: 'welcome', text: 'Welcome to the blog' }
  ],
  filter: 'hello'
}
```

We can reconstruct the whole application state from this object. Being able to do this is one of the things that makes Redux so awesome.

In a later chapter, we will observe how to add the logic that actually filters posts by making use of the application state.

You might think that the application state will become a very complicated object at some point, and that's true—but in a more advanced project; the state won't be defined in a single file. Application state can be split up and dealt with in multiple files (a separate file for each substate), then combined together.

To keep things simple, let's define our application state as an array of posts for now:

```
[
  { user: 'dan', category: 'hello', text: 'Hello World!' },
  { user: 'des', category: 'welcome', text: 'Welcome to the blog' }
]
```

Defining actions

Now that we have defined the state of our application, we also need a way to change the state. In Redux, we never modify the state directly. To ensure that the application is predictable, only **actions** can change the state. Redux actions are simply JavaScript objects, with a `type` property that specifies the name of the action. Let's say we want to create a new post in our blog, we could use an action like this:

```
{ type: 'CREATE_POST', user: 'dan', text: 'New post' }
```

Later on, we could define another action for setting the filter:

```
{ type: 'SET_FILTER', filter: 'hello' }
```

These action objects can be passed to Redux, resulting in a new state being calculated from the current state and the action. This process is called **dispatching** an action.

The way state changes are processed in Redux makes them very explicit, clear, and predictable. If you want to find out how a certain state change happened, just look at the action that was dispatched. Furthermore, you can reproduce state changes by reverting and redispatching actions (also known as *time traveling*).

Tying state and actions together

After defining the application state and actions, we still need a way to apply actions to change the application state. In Redux, the state is updated through special functions called **reducers**. Reducers contain the state changing logic of our application.

```
newState = reducer(state, action)
```

A reducer function takes the current `state` object and an `action` object as arguments. The reducer parses the `action` object, specifically, the `action.type`. Depending on the action type, the reducer function either returns a new state, or it simply returns the current state (if the action type is not handled in this reducer).

To write a function, we first have to think of the function signature (the head of the function). A reducer function takes the current `state` and an `action` argument. For the `state` argument, we set a default value, which is what the initial state is going to be.

In our example application, the initial state is an empty array of posts, so we can define the reducer function, as follows:

```
function postsReducer (state = [], action) {
```

Now, we will need to parse the `action` object. The most common way to handle actions in Redux is using a `switch` statement on `action.type`. That way, we can have separate cases for all the different action types that the reducer function is going to take care of:

```
switch (action.type) {
```

In the `switch` statement, we handle the CREATE_POST action we defined earlier using `Array.concat` to add the new post object to the state (an array of posts):

```
case 'CREATE_POST':
  return state.concat([{ user: action.user, text: action.text }])
```

For all other action types, we simply return the current state:

```
default:
   return state
 }
}
```

 Please note that the `default` branch is very important. If you do not return the current state for unhandled action types, your state will become `undefined`.

Redux' three fundamental principles

As mentioned earlier, Redux is based on certain principles and restrictions. The API of Redux is very small and only consists of a handful of functions. These principles and restrictions are what makes Redux so powerful, and you need to stick to them to be able to reap all the benefits of Redux.

We will now discuss the three fundamental principles of Redux:

- Single source of truth
- Read-only state
- State changes are processed with pure functions

Single source of truth

Redux consists of a single store, which is a JavaScript value containing the entire state of your application. A single source of truth comes with a lot of benefits:

- In traditional applications, the state is stored in different places across the whole application. With a single source of truth, debugging becomes easy, as you simply have one value to look at.
- It is easy to create universal apps, as you can serialize the application state on the server and send it to the client without much effort.
- Generalized functionalities, such as undo/redo, become easy to implement. For example, you can simply drop in a library that turns (a part of) your state into an *undoable* state.

To access the application state, Redux provides a `.getState()` function on the `store` object. You can view the full state, as follows:

```
console.log(store.getState())
```

The output of the preceding code will be the application state. In our example application, the output would be the post array we defined earlier:

```
[
  { user: 'dan', text: 'Hello World!' },
  { user: 'des', text: 'Welcome to the blog' }
]
```

The read-only state

In a Redux application, you cannot modify application state directly. The only way to change the state is by dispatching actions:

- This restriction ensures that state changes are predictable. If no action happens, nothing in the application changes.
- Because actions are processed one at a time, we do not have to deal with race conditions.
- Because actions are plain JavaScript objects, they can be easily serialized, logged, stored, and replayed. This makes debugging and testing easy.

A Redux action object (to create a new post) could look like this:

```
{ type: 'CREATE_POST', user: 'dan', text: 'New post' }
```

State changes are processed with pure functions

Given the same input, pure functions always return the same output. Because reducer functions are pure, given the same state and action, they are always going to return the same *new* state. This makes them predictable.

The following code defines an *impure function*, because subsequent calls with the same input result in different output:

```
var i = 0
function impureCount () {
  i += 1
  return i
}
```

```
console.log(impureCount()) // prints 1
console.log(impureCount()) // prints 2
```

As you can see, we are accessing a variable outside of the function which is what makes the function impure.

We could make the function pure by specifying `i` as an argument:

```
function pureCount (i) {
  return i + 1
}
console.log(pureCount(0)) // prints 1
console.log(pureCount(1)) // prints 2
```

Pure functions should only work with their input arguments and constants. For reducer functions, being pure means that all nontemporary data should be stored in the `state` object.

Reducers in Redux are always pure functions. They take the previous `state` and an `action` as arguments and return a *new* state object. The *new* part is important here. We never modify the passed state directly, because that would make the function impure. We always need to create a new `state` object based on the old state.

In our reducer function, we used `Array.concat` to create a new array from the old `state` array, adding the new post at the end:

```
function postsReducer (state = [], action) {
  switch (action.type) {
  case 'CREATE_POST':
    return state.concat([{ user: action.user, text: action.text }])
  default:
    return state
  }
}
```

You might think that such a reducer function will become very complicated, as it deals with the whole application state. Usually, you start out with a single simple reducer. As your application grows, you can split it up into multiple smaller reducers, each reducer dealing with a specific part of the application state. Because reducers are just JavaScript functions, it is easy to combine them, pass additional data, and even make reusable reducers for common functionality, such as undo/redo or pagination.

Introduction to the Redux ecosystem

As a result of Redux' small API and principles that make it very extensible, there is a huge ecosystem surrounding it. You will learn about some libraries throughout this book:

- **react-redux**: These are the official React bindings for Redux. They allow you to inject (parts of) the Redux store into your React components. Furthermore, they inject action creators (functions that return action objects), which can automatically dispatch actions to the Redux store. This allows you to communicate in both ways between React and Redux (`https://github.com/reactjs/react-redux`).

- **ng-redux**: This library lets you connect your Angular components with Redux. It works similar to React-Redux (`https://github.com/angular-redux/ng-redux`).

- **@angular-redux/store**: This library helps you to integrate the Redux store with Angular 2+ applications, similar to react-redux. It uses an approach based on RxJS Observables to select and transform data from the Redux store. It allows you to inject this data into your UI or side-effect handlers (`https://github.com/angular-redux/store`).

- **redux-devtools**: This is the official implementation of developer tools for Redux and allows watching state changes, live editing of actions, time traveling, and more. There are many monitor components available, each of them allowing you to debug your application in different ways. For a list of monitors, check out the redux-devtools repository on GitHub (`https://github.com/gaearon/redux-devtools`).

- **redux-promise**: This is middleware for Redux that allows you to dispatch JavaScript promises to the Redux store. These promises will be evaluated and can result in multiple actions, for example, a success and an error action as the result of a server request (`https://github.com/acdlite/redux-promise`).

- **redux-auth**: This library allows you to easily integrate token-based authentication into your Redux application. It supports various ways of authentication, such as OAuth2 and e-mail authentication. It also includes React components for common functionality—for example, registration, login, logout, password reset, updating passwords, and deleting accounts. These components include support for various themes, such as Material UI and React Bootstrap. Overall, this is a very extensive library that should simplify dealing with authentication a lot (`https://github.com/lynndylanhurley/redux-auth`).

- **react-router-redux**: This allows for additional communication between React Router and Redux. You can use React Router without this library, but it is useful to record, persist, and replay user actions using the time traveling. It also helps you keep the routing-related state in sync with your Redux store (`https://github.com/reactjs/react-router-redux`).
- **redux-UI-router**: This library is similar to react-router-redux, but for Angular. It maintains router state for your Angular application via Redux (`https://github.com/neilff/redux-ui-router`).
- **@angular-redux/router**: This is basically the same as redux-UI-Router, but for Angular 2. It maintains router state for your Angular 2 application via Redux (`https://github.com/angular-redux/router`).
- **redux-undo**: This is a higher-order reducer that allows you to make an existing reducer *undoable*. Basically, it is the easiest way to implement the undo/redo functionality with Redux (`https://github.com/omnidan/redux-undo`).
- **redux-logger**: This is middleware to log Redux actions and state changes in the console (`https://github.com/evgenyrodionov/redux-logger`).

You can find an official overview of the Redux ecosystem on the Redux website: `http://redux.js.org/docs/introduction/Ecosystem.html`.

There is also a community-maintained repository called *Awesome Redux*, which contains resources, libraries, boilerplates, and examples related to Redux: `https://github.com/xgrommx/awesome-redux`.

Summary

In this chapter, we covered the principles that make Redux special, and why it should be used in a project. We started out with the motivation behind Redux (complexity of state management), then briefly covered how Redux works in practice. We also discussed how certain restrictions allow us to write maintainable, consistent, and easy-to-test applications. Wrapping up, we took a look at the very extensive Redux ecosystem.

In the next chapter, we will discuss how to set up a Redux project. Afterwards, we will implement the basic elements of Redux and see how they work together in practice.

2
Implementing the Elements of Redux

After getting the first taste of Redux, we will now go into more detail on the elements that make up Redux:

- **Actions**: JavaScript objects, which describe state changes in the application
- **Action creators**: Functions that take some arguments and return an action
- **Reducers**: Functions that take the current state and an action, and return the new state
- **Store**: The heart of Redux, which actually stores and guards your application state; we can subscribe to state changes in the store and dispatch actions to it

In this chapter, we will discuss how to implement these elements and how to put them together. Furthermore, we will create our first small project using Redux. It will be a simple blog that lists posts and reacts to user input when we click on these posts.

The Redux cycle

Before we start implementing the elements of Redux, let's take a look at the data flow with Redux in one big picture—from an action getting dispatched to the updated application state:

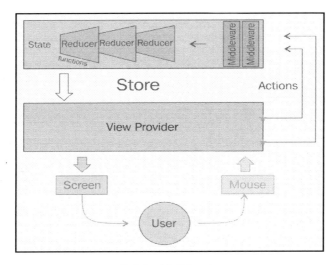

Illustration of the Redux cycle

http://staltz.com/unidirectional-user-interface-architectures.html

An action is dispatched

It all starts with a call to `store.dispatch(action)`, which means that some action happened (user action, request resolved, and so on). An action is a plain object that describes what happened:

```
{ type: 'CREATE_POST', user: 'dan', text: 'hello world' }
```

 It might help to think of the action as a kind of a log entry that tells we what happened, for example, *Post hello world created by user dan.*

Redux checks whether the dispatched action has a `type` property, then passes it on to the main reducer. This process is called *dispatching* an action.

The main reducer function gets executed

Redux executes the main reducer with the current state and the dispatched action. Usually, the main reducer function will pass substates and the action down to other reducers, which then process the action.

A reducer is just a function, and to get the next state, Redux calls it as follows:

```
let newState = reducer(previousState, action)
```

Keep in mind that the reducer function has to be pure. Pure means that it does not cause any side effects, such as modifying the `previousState` variable. Instead of directly modifying the previous state, a pure reducer function copies data from the previous state to create a new state object.

However, being pure also means that reducers should not perform any other side effects, such as API requests, either. Side effects should be handled by action creators, which then dispatch one or multiple actions.

Redux saves the new state

The main reducer function returns the new state, which is computed from the previous state and the action. The new state object is saved in the Redux store and all listener functions that are subscribed via `store.subscribe()` get called. This is when the user interface gets updated (re-rendered), but more about that in *Chapter 3*, *Combining Redux with React*, where we will discuss rendering user interfaces with React.

Strictly unidirectional data flow

One of Redux' principles is a **strictly unidirectional data flow**. This principle means that the whole cycle has to be completed to make changes in the application state. We cannot simply adjust the state without going through the whole cycle again. This restriction makes your application very predictable and easy to debug.

Running code examples

All examples in this book use the *new* JavaScript syntax ES6/ES2015. Newer browser and Node.js versions already support most of this syntax (at the time of this writing, import/export is not supported anywhere, except Babel). If we want to support older versions of browsers or Node.js, we will need to transpile your code to the older JavaScript version ES5 via a tool, such as Babel (`https://babeljs.io/`). In addition to transpiling, Babel also allows you to use JSX syntax (an extension of JavaScript used with React) and even the future JavaScript syntax, where the proposal is already finalized, but not implemented in any engines yet.

Setting up a new project

This section explains how to set up a complete project with the ES2015 JavaScript syntax and Redux library.

Setting up Node.js

If we do not already have Node.js and the npm tool installed (we can check this by running `npm -v` and seeing whether there is any version being output), go to the official Node.js website (`https://nodejs.org/`) and install the latest release. It is recommended to use at least node version 6 for this book. All code examples have been tested with node v6.11.1 LTS.

Initializing the project

When creating a new project, we will first need to create a `package.json` file. The easiest way to do this is to run the following command:

```
npm init
```

This command will ask you a few questions regarding the project name, version, and so on. Change the entry point to `src/index.js`. For everything else, we can simply press *Enter*. We can change these values in the generated `package.json` file later. If you already have an existing project, we can change the entry point by adjusting the `main` property in the `package.json` file.

For a complete list of configuration options in the `package.json` file, check out the NPM documentation at `https://docs.npmjs.com/files/package.json`.

Afterwards, create a `src` folder to store your JavaScript code in:

```
mkdir src
```

It is always a good idea to keep source files separate from your project configuration. Doing this ensures that when your project grows, the root folder structure does not get too messy. It also makes it easier to configure other tools, for example, configuring `babel-watch` to reload on file changes in the `src/` directory only.

Setting up webpack

Now, we will install webpack, which will be used to build your project. **Webpack** is a module bundler. It is used to bundle, transform, and package various files to be used in a browser. This includes JavaScript, JSX, HTML, and assets.

The advantages of using a module bundler, such as webpack, are listed as follows:

- It can bundle various kinds of JavaScript modules: ES Modules, CommonJS, and AMD.
- It works together with Babel to transpile newer JavaScript syntax, such as ES2015.
- Not just JavaScript, but various files can be preprocessed during compilation. For example, images can be converted to base64, or template files can be compiled into HTML.
- It can create a single bundle or multiple chunks. Splitting your code into multiple chunks can reduce initial loading time, by, for example, only loading certain code when it is needed.
- It resolves dependencies during compilation and removes unused code, thus reducing the code file size.
- It is extremely extensible and has a rich ecosystem with many plugins already available.

Webpack can be installed via npm. We will also install webpack-dev-server, which can run our project on a web server and provide live reloading; live reloading means that when files change, webpack automatically rebuilds the project and refreshes the website in your browser:

1. We start by installing webpack and webpack-dev-server:

```
npm install --save-dev webpack webpack-dev-server
```

2. Next, we will need to create a configuration file for webpack. This file is called webpack.config.js and contains the following code:

```
const path = require('path')
module.exports = {
  entry: './src/index.js',
  output: {
    path: path.resolve('dist'),
    filename: 'main.js'
  },
```

This configuration tells webpack where the entry and output files for our project are.

3. Now, we need to define loaders. Loaders tell webpack what to do with the entry file(s). Since we will be using Babel to transpile our JavaScript files, we will define the babel-loader for .js(x) files:

```
module: {
  loaders: [
    { test: /.jsx?$/, loader: 'babel-loader', exclude:
              /node_modules/
    }
  ]
}
}
```

That's all for the webpack configuration for now. If we want to find out more about webpack, we can check out its documentation at https://webpack.js.org/configuration/.

Setting up Babel

Now webpack knows that it should compile JavaScript files with Babel, but we haven't even set up Babel yet! To do so perform the following steps:

1. First, let's install the Babel-related libraries:

```
npm install --save-dev babel-core babel-loader babel-preset-es2015
npm install --save-dev babel-plugin-transform-object-rest-spread
```

   The preceding command includes `babel-core`, `babel-loader` for webpack, and the `babel-preset` for ES2015. We also installed the object rest/spread plugin, as it allows us to use rest/spread syntax with objects in addition to arrays. We will learn more about the rest/spread syntax later.

2. We still need to tell Babel which presets and plugins it should load. So, we will create a `.babelrc` file with the following content:

```
{
  "presets":[ "es2015" ],
  "plugins": [ "transform-object-rest-spread" ]
}
```

You can find more information about the Babel configuration on their API documentation page, at `https://babeljs.io/docs/usage/api/#options`.

Setting up the entry files

Now that we have webpack and Babel set up, we just need to create our entry point files:

1. First, let's create a very simple `src/index.js` file:

```
console.log('hello world!')
```

   The `src/index.js` file (including all imports and dependencies) will be transpiled into a `main.js` file by Babel.

2. Then, we create an `index.html` file, which will be the entry point for our web application:

```html
<!DOCTYPE html>
<html>
  <head>
    <meta charset="utf-8">
    <title>Learning Redux</title>
  </head>
  <body>
    <div id="root"></div>
    <script src="main.js"></script>
  </body>
</html>
```

Running webpack

The last step is adding scripts to our `package.json` file so that we can actually run our application via `npm start`.

Open `package.json` and find the `scripts` section, and replace it with the following:

```json
"scripts": {
  "start": "webpack-dev-server",
  "build": "webpack"
},
```

Finally, we can run our project by executing the following command:

```
npm start
```

Then open `http://localhost:8080/` in your browser. Open the **Console** to see the following **hello world!** message:

Output of our small project in the **Console** tab

 In Chrome and Firefox, you can open the console by right-clicking on the web page and selecting **Inspect** or **Inspect Element** from the context menu. Then, select the **Console** tab in the developer tools pane that opened.

Later, when setting up a production environment, you might want to rename the current start script to start:dev and define the start script as follows:

```
"scripts": {
  "start": "npm build && serve dist",
  "start:dev": "webpack-dev-server",
  "build": "webpack"
},
```

 serve is a simple NPM package/tool that hosts a small web server and serves all files from a certain directory. You first need to install it via npm install --save serve.

Note that for all custom scripts (such as start:dev), you will need to run npm run start:dev instead of just npm start:dev.

If we need to have some server-side code, for example, to implement server-side rendering, the `serve` tool can be replaced with a custom web server. Server-side rendering will be covered in *Chapter 10*, *Rendering on the Server*.

Setting up Redux

We will first need to use npm to install Redux:

```
npm install --save redux
```

Now that we have covered how to set up a full project with the ES2015 JavaScript syntax and Redux library, we can move on to implementing the basic elements of Redux.

In the next chapter, we will extend our project and render a user interface with React and React-Redux.

The template code

The template code can be found in the `chapter2_1.zip` attachment. Unpack the zip, change into the directory, and run `npm install` and `npm start`; then, open `http://localhost:8080` in your browser and check the console.

Implementing actions and action creators

In the first chapter, we learned how important actions are in Redux. Only actions can *change the state* of your application.

 Actions in Redux are valid if they have a `type` property. The rest of the object structure is totally up to you. If you prefer using a standard structure, check out `https://github.com/acdlite/flux-standard-action`.

Redux actions are simple JavaScript objects with a `type` property, which specifies the name of the action.

Let's define a simple action, in the `src/index.js` file:

```
const createPost = { type: 'CREATE_POST', user: 'dan', text: 'New post' }
console.log(createPost)
```

Now, save the file. Webpack should automatically refresh the page after modifying and saving a source file (such as `src/index.js`).

Separating action types

As we have learned in Chapter 1, *Why Redux?* reducers use the `type` property to check which action happened. That works fine, but there is a little problem with the value—it's a string. With string values, it is very easy to make mistakes, such as typos. Furthermore, we will need to know all possible string values (action types), which means that we need to consult the documentation or reducer source files—that's not good.

In Redux projects, we usually store the `type` property of the action in a constant, as follows:

```
const CREATE_POST = 'CREATE_POST'

const createPost = { type: CREATE_POST, user: 'dan', text: 'New post' }

console.log(createPost)
```

The first line defines what is called an **action type** in the Redux world. We then use this action type to define the `createPost` action.

ES2015 - import/export

As an added bonus of using webpack and Babel, we can put the action types in a separate `actionTypes.js` file and export them by performing the following steps:

1. Create a new `actionTypes.js` file and define and export the action type there:

   ```
   export const CREATE_POST = 'CREATE_POST'
   ```

2. Then, we can import the action types that we need in other files. Replace the `src/index.js` file with the following code:

   ```
   import { CREATE_POST } from './actionTypes'
   ```

Putting your action types in a separate file makes it very easy to figure out which actions are possible in the application—just look at the `actionTypes.js` file! As we are importing constants, your editor/IDE will also help by autocompleting the constant names.

Introducing action creators

There is another issue with actions—without documentation, we do not know which properties an action has. To solve this issue, we implement action creators. Action creators are functions that return actions. They can be thought of as an action factory. We tell the function what we want to do, and with which data. The function creates the action, which we can then dispatch to Redux. For example, we could replace our createPost action with a dynamic createPost(user, text) action creator:

```
function createPost (user, text) {
  return {
    type: CREATE_POST,
    user: user,
    text: text
  }
}

console.log(createPost('dan', 'New post'))
```

Now, we can reuse this function to create similar actions. Later, we will learn how to wrap action creators with the Redux dispatch() function. This means that we can simply execute createPost('dan', 'New post') in your UI, and it will create and dispatch a proper CREATE_POST action.

ES2015 - arrow functions

There is a new, more concise way to define functions in ES2015, called **arrow** function syntax. We could write the createPost(user, text) function in arrow function syntax, as follows:

```
const createPost = (user, text) => {
  return {
    type: CREATE_POST,
    user: user,
    text: text
  }
}
```

Additionally, ES2015 allows us to shorten property definitions where the object key and constant name are the same (for example, `user: user`):

```
const createPost = (user, text) => {
  return { type: CREATE_POST, user, text }
}
```

And we could return the object directly, by wrapping it with `()` brackets:

```
const createPost = (user, text) => ({ type: CREATE_POST, user, text })
```

The format that you use is mostly of your preference. However, there is one key difference between arrow functions and normal functions that you should be aware of: Arrow functions do not have their own `this` context; they inherit it from the parent. As a result, you do not need to write `var that = this` or `var _this = this` anymore. You can simply use an arrow function because it does not overwrite `this`.

ES2015 - import/export

With webpack and Babel, you can import/export action creators the same way as action types. Perform the following steps:

1. Create a new `actions.js` file. First, we import the `CREATE_POST` action type:

    ```
    import { CREATE_POST } from './actionTypes'
    ```

2. Then we define and export the `createPost` action creator:

    ```
    export const createPost = (user, text) => {
      return { type: CREATE_POST, user, text }
    }
    ```

3. Finally, we can import and use the `createPost` action creator in the `src/index.js` file. Replace the whole file with the following code:

    ```
    import { createPost } from './actions'

    console.log(createPost('dan', 'New post'))
    ```

Code example

The current state of the project can be found in the `chapter2_2.zip` attachment. Unpack the zip, change into the directory, run `npm install` and `npm start`, then open `http://localhost:8080` in your browser and check the console:

```
Object {type: "CREATE_POST", user: "dan", text:
"New post"}
  text: "New post"
  type: "CREATE_POST"
  user: "dan"
```

Output of our `createPost` action creator

Implementing reducers

In the first chapter, we learned about reducers, functions that take the current state and an action and return the new state of the application. As you now know, actions only describe what happened. Reducers use that information to compute the new state.

To be able to figure out state changes, we should first think about the state of our application. We have already done this in the first chapter, and our state looks as follows:

```
{
  posts: [
    { user: 'dan', category: 'hello', text: 'Hello World!' },
    { user: 'des', category: 'welcome', text: 'Welcome to the blog' }
  ],
  filter: 'hello'
}
```

As you can see, we have two separate sub-states in the main state object: `posts` and `filter`. This is a good hint for making two reducers: a `postsReducer` to handle the `posts` sub-state, and a `filterReducer` to handle the `filter` sub-state.

Try to structure your application state in such a way that each feature has its own sub-state of data to work on.

If we wanted to add more features, such as showing user information, we would make a new `users` sub-state, which stores all users. A separate `usersReducer` would then handle all actions related to that data set.

There are no generic rules on how to split up reducers and your application state. It depends on your projects' requirements and the existing structure. As a good rule of thumb, try not to make one reducer that handles all the actions, but also do not make a separate reducer for each action. Group them in a way that makes sense for the application structure. Throughout the following chapters, we will focus on how to structure a growing application in practice.

Defining/importing action types

First, we will define the action types; we have already covered how to do this in a previous section.

Edit `src/actionTypes.js` and define and export the following action types:

```
export const EDIT_POST = 'EDIT_POST'
export const SET_FILTER = 'SET_FILTER'
```

Defining action creators

As we have already learned about creating action creators, doing this is left as an exercise for the reader.

Or you can simply replace the contents of the `src/actions.js` file with the following code:

```
import { CREATE_POST, EDIT_POST, SET_FILTER } from './actionTypes'

export const createPost = (user, text) => {
  return { type: CREATE_POST, user, text }
}

export const editPost = (id, text) => {
  return { type: EDIT_POST, id, text }
}

export const setFilter = (filter) => {
  return { type: SET_FILTER, filter }
}
```

Then import the additional action creators we defined in the `src/index.js` file:

```
import { createPost, editPost, setFilter } from './actions'
```

Writing the posts reducer

We start with implementing the `postsReducer` function. First, we have to think about the function definition. This includes the initial/default state. In this case, we want to handle an array of posts, so the initial `state` is an empty array `[]`. The second argument is the `action`. The full function definition looks as follows:

```
function postsReducer (state = [], action) {
```

We set the initial state through a default value. If the `state` is `undefined` (which it is, when the Redux store gets initialized), the state will be set to the default value (in this case, `[]`). We will put our reducers into a separate file:

1. Create a new `reducers.js` file and import the action types we defined earlier:

    ```
    import { CREATE_POST, EDIT_POST, SET_FILTER } from './actionTypes'
    ```

2. Then, define and export the reducer function:

    ```
    export function postsReducer (state = [], action) {
    ```

In the next chapter, we will learn how to split this `reducers.js` file into multiple files and make a `reducers/` folder.

The main structure of a reducer

In the Redux world, it is best practice to use `switch` statements to handle multiple action types. Feel free to use `if/else` statements instead, especially when a reducer handles only a single action type:

1. In our case, we are handling multiple actions related to posts, so we `switch` on the `action.type`:

    ```
    switch (action.type) {
    ```

2. We will create a new scope by surrounding our `case` statement with { and } brackets. Creating a new scope ensures that constants with the same name declared in different action blocks do not conflict:

```
case CREATE_POST: {
  return ...
}
case EDIT_POST: {
  return ...
}
```

Note how we don't use a string (`'CREATE_POST'`), but the action type/constant (`CREATE_POST`).

3. Defining the `default` branch is *very* important: if you do not return the current state for unhandled action types, your state will become `undefined`:

```
default:
    return state
  }
}
```

ES2015 - using destructuring and the rest operator to parse the action

For action parsing, ES2015 syntax comes in handy. We can easily and declaratively parse an object using *destructuring*.

We can manually pull out properties from the `action` object, as follows:

```
case CREATE_POST: {
  const type = action.type
  ...
}
```

Instead of that, we can use destructuring, which would make the code look like this:

```
case CREATE_POST: {
  const { type } = action
  ...
}
```

It is a bit like pattern matching in other languages—you specify what the object looks like after `var`/`let`/`const`, and it gets parsed/destructured into that form.

In combination with destructuring, you can also use default assignments, as follows:

```
const { type, user = 'anon' } = action
// instead of
const type = action.type
const user = action.user || 'anon'
```

In this example, if `action.user` is `undefined`, it will be set to `'anon'`.

It is also possible to rename properties, as follows:

```
const { type: actionType } = action
// instead of
const actionType = action.type
```

The preceding code will store `action.type` in the `actionType` constant.

There is one more trick with destructuring—you can collect the rest of the properties into another object. This can be done with the `rest` operator. It works as follows:

```
const { type, ...post } = action
```

We can use the `rest` operator instead of manually collecting the rest of the properties:

```
const type = action.type
const post = {
  user: action.user,
  category: action.category,
  text: action.text
}
```

This is pretty cool! Using the `rest` operator, we can save a lot of code and keep the `post` object extensible. For example, if we want to add a title to posts later, we could simply add a `title` property to the action and it would already be in the `post` object when using the rest operator.

Handling CREATE_POST – creating a new post

Now that we know how to parse actions elegantly with ES2015 syntax, we can use that knowledge to parse the CREATE_POST action type:

1. First, we will pull out the data that we need from the action. In this case, we want to store everything—except for the `type` property—in a `post` object:

```
case CREATE_POST: {
  const { type, ...post } = action
```

2. Then, we will insert this `post` object into our array and return the new state. To insert the `post` object, we use something similar to the rest operator—the spread operator, which is basically the reverse of the `rest` operator. Instead of collecting all properties of an object/elements of an array, it spreads them out:

```
    return [ ...state, post ]
}
```

Using the spread operator achieves the same thing as using `Array.prototype.concat()`, which merges two arrays and returns a new one:

```
return state.concat([ post ])
```

 In Redux, all state is **immutable**. This means that you should never mutate the existing state, by, for example, using `state.push()`. Instead, you should create a new array with all the previous elements and the new element. It is very useful to use ES2015 spread syntax for this.

That's it for the `CREATE_POST` action. As you can see, the ES2015 JavaScript syntax makes state changes very explicit and easy to write.

Handling EDIT_POST – editing posts

Next, we will handle the `EDIT_POST` action type:

1. We start by parsing the action object:

```
case EDIT_POST: {
  const { type, id, ...newPost } = action
```

This time, we will pull out the `type` and `id` properties, because we will need the `id` later, and it should not be part of the `post` object.

We use the `Array.prototype.map()` function to return a new state array. If you do not know this function, it has the following signature:

```
const newArr = arr.map(
  (elem, index) => { ... }
)
```

As you can see, `map()` accepts a callback function. The `map` function executes the callback function on each element and creates a new array from the return values of that callback function. Basically, `map` lets us apply a function to all elements in an array.

For example, if we wanted to increase all numbers in an array by one, we could use the `map` function, as follows:

```
const numbers = [1, 2, 3]
const newNumbers = numbers.map(
  number => number + 1
)
console.log(newNumbers) // outputs: [2, 3, 4]
```

2. We can use `map` to edit a single post in the array, by going through all posts and returning the original post object, except for the one element that matches the `index`:

```
return state.map((oldPost, index) =>
```

3. First, we will make sure that the `id` value equals the `index` of the array because we want to edit only one of the posts:

```
action.id === index
```

4. Now, we can overwrite the `oldPost` properties with the `newPost` properties using the spread operator as follows:

```
    ? { ...oldPost, ...newPost }
    : oldPost
  )
}
```

When the `index` value matches the `id` specified in the action, the post object will be overwritten with all other properties from the action. When the `index` value doesn't match, we simply return the `oldPost`.

Imagine that we have the following `posts`:

```
posts: [
  { user: 'dan', category: 'hello', text: 'Hello World!' },
  { user: 'des', category: 'welcome', text: 'Welcome to the blog' }
]
```

We want to edit the first post, so we dispatch the following action:

```
{ type: 'EDIT_POST', id: 0, text: 'Hi World!' }
```

Our reducer would match the post with the 0 index in the array, which is the first one. Then, we have the following values:

```
const oldPost = { user: 'dan', category: 'hello', text: 'Hello World!' }
const newPost = { text: 'Hi World!' }
```

We use the `spread` operator to combine the objects:

```
{ ...oldPost, ...newPost }
```

This means that it will first spread out all properties from the `oldPost` object:

```
{ user: 'dan', category: 'hello', text: 'Hello World!', ...newPost }
```

Now, all properties from the `newPost` object will get spread out, overwriting some of the `oldPost` properties, and resulting in a new object:

```
{ user: 'dan', category: 'hello', text: 'Hi World!' }
```

Testing out our reducer

Now that we have written our reducer function, we can test it out by passing data directly to it. First, we will define the initial state, an empty array of posts:

```
const initialState = []
```

Now, we will need to define the action. To do this, we use the previously defined `createPost` action creator:

```
const action = createPost('dan', 'New post')
```

Finally, we execute the reducer and log the result:

```
const newState = postsReducer(initialState, action)
console.log(newState)
```

The preceding code should have the following output:

```
[
  {
    "user": "dan",
    "text": "New post"
  }
]
```

This means that we successfully inserted a new post into the application state.

Writing the filter reducer

Similar to the `postsReducer`, we could define a `filterReducer` function that takes care of handling the `filter` part of our state object. By default, we want to show all posts, so we set the default state to `'all'`.

The `filterReducer` only handles one action type, so an `if/else` statement can be used. If the reducer function grows and ends up handling more action types, it is a good idea to use a `switch` statement instead.

Define the `reducer` function in the `src/reducers.js` file:

```
function filterReducer (state = 'all', action) {
  if (action.type === SET_FILTER) {
    return action.filter
  } else {
    return state
  }
}
```

This `reducer` function is pretty simple—it sets the `filter` state to whatever is entered in `action.filter`.

 Note that we still need to take care of making use of the `filter` state when rendering our application, the reducer only takes care of state changes, not how they are applied to the user interface.

Combining reducers

Now, all that is left to do is combining these two reducers together to handle the whole state and all actions of the application:

```
function appReducer (state = {}, action) {
  return {
    posts: postsReducer(state.posts, action),
    filter: filterReducer(state.filter, action),
  }
}
```

The default state for our app is an empty object, `{}`. We create the state object by passing the substates and actions down to our other reducers. On initialization, these reducers get passed `undefined`, because `state.posts` and `state.filter` do not exist, yet. As a result, the default state defined in the subreducers will be used.

When the Redux store gets created from the appReducer function, Redux passes an @@redux/INIT action with an undefined state to the main reducer, which causes the state and substates to be set to the default values. This is how the state gets initialized in Redux.

Since an appReducer that combines other reducers is such a common function to write, Redux provides a combineReducers helper function, which creates a function that essentially does the same thing as the appReducer function we defined earlier:

1. Import the combineReducers helper function at the beginning of the src/reducers.js file:

   ```
   import { combineReducers } from 'redux'
   ```

2. Then call combineReducers with our reducer functions at the end of the src/reducers.js file. It returns an appReducer function:

   ```
   const appReducer = combineReducers({
     posts: postsReducer,
     filter: filterReducer,
   })
   ```

3. We export default the main reducer, by adding the following line at the end of the file:

   ```
   export default appReducer
   ```

4. Now, you can import the reducer in the src/index.js file, as follows:

   ```
   import appReducer from './reducers'
   ```

Testing out the full reducer

After combining our reducers, we can test them out by calling the appReducer:

1. First, we will initialize the reducers by passing an undefined state:

   ```
   let state = appReducer(undefined, { type: 'INIT_ACTION' })
   console.log('initial state:', state)
   ```

The resulting initial state looks as follows:

```
{
    "posts": [],
    "filter": "all"
}
```

2. Then, we will dispatch some actions by manually passing the current state and the action object to the `appReducer` function. We will start with a `createPost` action:

```
state = appReducer(state, createPost('dan', 'test'))
console.log('state after createPost:', state)
```

The state now looks like this:

```
{
    "posts": [
        {
            "user": "dan",
            "text": "test"
        }
    ],
    "filter": "all"
}
```

3. Then, we will edit the text of that post:

```
state = appReducer(state, editPost(0, 'edited post'))
console.log('state after editPost:', state)
```

This results in only the first post (index 0) getting changed:

```
{
    "posts": [
        {
            "user": "dan",
            "text": "edited post"
        }
    ],
    "filter": "all"
}
```

4. Finally, we will set the filter, which does not affect the posts array at all:

```
state = appReducer(state, setFilter('none'))
console.log('state after setFilter:', state)
```

The final state is as follows:

```
{
  "posts": [
    {
      "user": "dan",
      "text": "edited post"
    }
  ],
  "filter": "none"
}
```

Code example

The current state of the project can be found in the `chapter2_3.zip` attachment. Unpack the zip, change into the directory, run `npm install`, and `npm start`, then open `http://localhost:8080` in your browser and check the console.

The store – combining actions and reducers

By now, we might be wondering what exactly Redux is (besides a set of principles and some helper functions). Essentially, Redux brings actions and reducers together. It provides a **store**, which contains the application state and provides some functions to do the following:

- Access the application state: `store.getState()`
- Dispatch actions: `store.dispatch(action)`
- Register listeners: `store.subscribe(listener)`

According to the official documentation of Redux, *Redux is a predictable state container for JavaScript apps.*

The state container (store) is the heart of Redux: It contains your application state and does not allow external changes. Redux only allows changes through actions, which get passed to pure reducer functions. These restrictions that Redux enforces are what makes your application state predictable.

Creating the store

We will now cover how to use Redux to create a store from our `appReducer`, how to listen to changes in the store, and how to dispatch actions to the store:

1. First of all, we will need to import the `createStore` function from the Redux library. Add the following code at the beginning of the `src/index.js` file:

    ```
    import { createStore } from 'redux'
    ```

    The `createStore` function takes the following arguments:

    *   A reducer function (the main/root reducer, in our case, `appReducer`) as the first argument.
    *   An initial state as the second argument--if no initial state is specified, the store will be initialized by passing `undefined` to the reducer, and thus, using the default value returned by it.

    The `createStore` function returns the Redux store, which provides some functions to access the state (`store.getState()`), listen to state changes (`store.subscribe(listener)`), and dispatch actions (`store.dispatch(action)`):

    ```
    let store = createStore(reducer, initialState)
    ```

     You can specify a certain initial state as the second argument of the `createStore` function. This is useful to, for example, load an existing state and is used in server-side rendering (`Chapter 10`, *Rendering on the Server*).

2. We use the `createStore` function to create the store from our previously created `appReducer`. Instead of manually calling the reducer, we replace the rest of the code in `src/index.js` with the following:

    ```
    let store = createStore(appReducer)
    ```

3. That's basically all there is to it; now we can use the store. Let's try logging the initial state:

    ```
    console.log(store.getState())
    ```

The initial state looks exactly as we expected—it contains the default values specified in the reducers:

```
{
  "posts": [],
  "filter": "all"
}
```

Subscribing to state changes

To subscribe to changes in the store, we simply call `store.subscribe()` with a function that will be executed when the store changes. For example, we could log every state change:

```
const unsubscribe = store.subscribe(() => {
  console.log('state changed:', store.getState())
})
```

 The `store.subscribe()` function returns an `unsubscribe()` function, which can be executed to stop listening to state updates.

You might have noted that this code does not produce any output yet. The initialization process of the Redux store does not trigger a call to our subscribed function. We first need to dispatch an action to see the state change being logged.

Dispatching actions

Now, there is only one thing left to do—dispatching actions to the store. You can simply pass action objects to the `store.dispatch()` function:

```
store.dispatch({ type: 'CREATE_POST', user: 'dan', text: 'hello world' })
```

However, it is best practice to use action creators instead, as follows:

```
store.dispatch(createPost('dan', 'hello world'))
```

Dispatching an action will result in the state being changed (by executing the reducer), and thus, the subscribed function being called:

```
state changed:
▼ Object {posts: Array(1), filter: "all"}
    filter: "all"
  ▼ posts: Array(1)
    ▼ 0: Object
        text: "hello world"
        user: "dan"
```

Output of our subscribed function, after dispatching the createPost action

We can now dispatch any actions we want, have the state change accordingly, and then get notified about the new state.

Rendering the user interface

Now we can (re-)render our user interface every time the state changes. To keep it simple, we will not use a library yet. Perform the following steps and edit the src/index.js file, adding the following code:

1. First, we define a reference to the <div> root we created in the index.html file earlier:

    ```
    const root = document.getElementById('root')
    ```

2. Then, we define a render() function, which will be subscribed to the store:

    ```
    const render = () => {
    ```

3. In the render() function, we first clear the <div>:

    ```
    root.innerHTML = ''
    ```

4. Next, we get all posts from the current state of the store:

    ```
    const { posts } = store.getState()
    ```

5. Now that we have an empty container and an array of posts, we render all posts in a list:

```
posts.forEach((post) => {
    const item = document.createElement('li')
    const text = document.createTextNode(post.user + ' - ' +
post.text)
    item.appendChild(text)
    root.appendChild(item)
  })
}
```

6. Finally, we subscribe our `render()` function to state changes in the store:

```
const stopRender = store.subscribe(render)
```

Creating sample data

Let's dispatch some actions and see what happens.

Add the following code at the end of the `src/index.js` file:

```
store.dispatch(createPost('dan', 'hello world'))
store.dispatch(createPost('des', 'second post'))
```

These two posts will be inserted into the Redux store and rendered by our `render()` function.

Handling the user input

To add some interactivity (and show how to dispatch actions from the user interface), we will implement a feature that adds an exclamation mark to a post when it is clicked.

We just need to add a `click` event listener to each post. In this event listener, we `store.dispatch()` an `editPost` action that adds a ! to the post text. We can do this in our `render()` function:

```
const render = () => {
  root.innerHTML = ''
  const { posts } = store.getState()
  posts.forEach((post, index) => {
    const item = document.createElement('li')
    item.addEventListener('click', () =>
      store.dispatch(editPost(index, post.text + '!'))
```

```
    )
    const text = document.createTextNode(post.user + ' - ' + post.text)
    item.appendChild(text)
    root.appendChild(item)
  })
}
```

Note how we use the `index` (which `forEach` passes as a second argument to the callback function) and the current post text (`post.text`) to create the `editPost` action.

Try clicking on a post, and see how the exclamation mark gets added:

The result of our small Redux/JavaScript project after the first post is clicked

The `render()` function we created is actually already very similar to how React works. Given the current state of the application, we simply describe what needs to be rendered. When the state changes, `render()` gets called again, and the application gets re-rendered. However, React does this in a smart way—it only re-renders the parts of the interface that changed. It also offers a better way to describe your user interface using JSX syntax. We will learn more about React in the next chapter.

Code example

The current state of the project can be found in the `chapter2_4.zip` attachment. Unpack the zip and run `npm install` and `npm start`, then open `http://localhost:8080` in your browser and check the console.

Summary

In this chapter, we first learned how to set up a project that is ready for Redux and the new JavaScript ES2015 syntax. Then, we implemented the basic elements of Redux and learned how ES2015 syntax makes implementing them easier. Finally, you also learned how to put a full Redux project together, as well as subscribe to state changes and dispatch actions.

In the next chapter, we will discuss how we can render user interfaces with React and use it together with Redux. Afterwards, we will build a full application with Redux and React.

3
Combining Redux with React

Until now, we have only covered managing application state, which is what Redux focuses on. However, a web application also has a user interface, which Redux does not take care of. This is where React comes into play.

In this chapter, we are going to cover:

- What React is and why it is useful
- Setting up and using React
- Creating React components
- Connecting React components to Redux

Finally, we are going to create a small blog application with React and Redux, which will be further extended in the upcoming chapters.

Why React?

In the previous chapter, we manually rendered the user interface using **Document Object Model (DOM)** operations to generate HTML code with JavaScript. As you can imagine, it would be quite painful to have to manually do DOM operations to build your entire user interface. This is where React comes in. From React's official documentation: *React - A JavaScript library for building user interfaces*.

React takes a new approach to building user interfaces, by making use of functional programming principles—similarly to Redux!

The principles of React

Similarly to Redux, React also comes with a set of principles, as follows:

- **Declarative**: This means you write code of *what* you want and do not have to think about *how* to do it.
- **Component-based**: You can split your application into multiple modules and combine them to build complex user interfaces.
- **Learn once, write anywhere**: React is a library, not a framework. It is independent of your stack and you can use it in the browser, on the server, or even on mobile apps (using React Native).

These principles might remind you a bit of Redux—the reason for that is Redux being heavily inspired by React, and both libraries are inspired by functional programming principles.

Setting up React

Before learning how to use Redux with React, we should first get familiar with React itself. We are going to use the project template (the first code example) from *Chapter 2, Implementing the Elements of Redux*.

Firstly, we have to install React and ReactDOM via npm:

```
npm install --save react react-dom
```

React is the core library, which deals with user interface *components*.

ReactDOM renders React components to the DOM, which, in this case, means that HTML will get rendered in the browser.

 There are also other renderers for React, such as React Native. It allows you to render your application to native mobile apps, such as Android and iOS. You can find more information at https://facebook.github.io/react-native/.

Rendering simple text

Now, we can import both libraries and render simple text. Edit `src/index.js` and replace the contents with the following code:

1. Start by importing React and ReactDOM:

   ```
   import React from 'react'
   import ReactDOM from 'react-dom'
   ```

2. Then, we use `ReactDOM` to render our application to the HTML DOM:

   ```
   ReactDOM.render(
   ```

3. The first argument is a React component to be rendered. In this case, we create a new React component from the `h1` element, with the `hello world!` content:

   ```
   React.createElement('h1', {}, 'hello world!'),
   ```

   The function signature for `React.createElement` is as follows:

   ```
   React.createElement(type, props, children)
   ```

   The HTML equivalent for this would be:

   ```
   <type ...props>children</type>
   ```

4. The second argument of `ReactDOM.render` is the target. We select the `div` we defined in the `index.html` file, which has the ID `root`:

   ```
   document.getElementById('root')
   )
   ```

5. Save the file and start the webpack via:

   ```
   npm start
   ```

6. Then, visit `http://localhost:8080/` in your browser to see the h1 element being rendered!

Our first React application

Rendering with JSX

You might be thinking that for more complex user interfaces, you will have to use `React.createElement` a lot, which would be messy. React provides a JavaScript extension called **JSX**, which allows you to describe React components with HTML-like syntax. Remember the h1 element we created earlier?

```
React.createElement('h1', {}, 'hello world!')
```

With JSX, it would look like this:

```
<h1>hello world!</h1>
```

JSX is an HTML-like syntax, but not exactly HTML. You have to be careful in some cases because the attributes are named after the DOM property names. For example, you cannot write:

```
<h1 class="title">hello world!</h1>
```

You have to use `className` instead because that is the name of the DOM property:

```
<h1 className="title">hello world!</h1>
```

Thankfully, most HTML attributes have the same name as their DOM properties. `class` is special because it is a reserved keyword in the JavaScript language.

 The only other attribute that is renamed because of these conflicts is `for`, which got renamed to `htmlFor`.

Setting up JSX

To be able to use JSX, we need to install the React plugin for Babel. It will then compile JSX into proper calls to the React API. Firstly, we need to install the `babel-preset-react` package:

```
npm install --save-dev babel-preset-react
```

In addition to installing the preset, we also need to tell Babel to use it. Edit `.babelrc`, find the `"presets"` property, and add `"react"` to the array. It should look like this now:

```
{
  "presets":[ "es2015", "react" ],
  "plugins": [ "transform-object-rest-spread" ]
}
```

Using JSX

Now that we have JSX set up, let's use it! Edit `src/index.js` and replace the following line:

```
React.createElement('h1', {}, 'hello world!')
```

With the JSX version:

```
<h1>hello world!</h1>
```

The whole file should look like this now:

```
import React from 'react'
import ReactDOM from 'react-dom'

ReactDOM.render(
  <h1>hello world!</h1>,
  document.getElementById('root')
)
```

Restart the application and visit `http://localhost:8080/`; it should look the same way as before.

Example code

The example code can be found in the `chapter3_1.zip` attachment.

Unpack the zip, change into the directory, run `npm install` and `npm start`, and open `http://localhost:8080` in your browser.

First steps with React

In the previous section, you learned how to create simple HTML elements with React, through `React.createElement`. Toward the end, you learned how to do the same thing with JSX.

In this section, you are going to learn more about creating simple as well as more advanced React components.

Creating a simple React element

Just like other JavaScript values, you can store React elements in a variable/constant:

```
const greeting = <h1>hello world!</h1>
```

If you have JSX code that spans across multiple lines, you can wrap it in (and) brackets, as follows:

```
const greeting = (
  <h1>
    hello world!
  </h1>
)
```

There is something else that makes JSX special—you can embed JavaScript expressions in JSX by wrapping them in curly brackets { }. That way, you can display variables/constants, evaluate functions, show their result, and so on. Let's display a `name` constant instead of `world`:

```
const name = 'dan'
const greeting = (
  <h1>
    hello {name}!
  </h1>
)
```

ReactDOM escapes all values embedded in JSX before rendering. This means that it is totally safe to embed user input via JSX.

We could also show the name in uppercase, by calling `.toUpperCase()` on the constant:

```
const name = 'dan'
const greeting = (
  <h1>
    hello {name.toUpperCase()}!
  </h1>
)
```

In JSX, all JavaScript expressions are valid when written in curly brackets { }. They will be evaluated, and the result will be inserted in place of the expression. In our example, the following HTML code will be rendered:

```
<h1>hello DAN!</h1>
```

Creating a static React component

As you can see, we are storing JSX in a simple JavaScript constant. However, this constant is not a fully fledged React component yet. The idea of components is to split your user interface into multiple independent and reusable pieces. Then, you combine those pieces into a full application. The idea is to have simple components that are easy to create, extend, and reason about. The complexity of the application is contained by composing *simple components* into a *complex application.*

Now, you are going to learn how to create React components. There are two ways a React component can be defined:

- **Function:** This is called a *functional* component; for example, `MyComponent(props)`
- **Class:** This is called a *class* component; for example, `class MyComponent extends React.Component`

We will start by turning our constant into a *functional* React component because it is the easiest way to create React components.

Functional components

To turn our little snippet into a React component, we need to turn the simple constant into a function. We will pass a name to the function and then output `hello {name}!`:

```
const Greeting = ({ name }) => (
  <h1>
    hello {name}!
  </h1>
)
```

 It is best practice to name React components starting with an uppercase letter, to be able to distinguish them from simple HTML elements when they are used in JSX.

Note how instead of passing `name` as a single argument, we are expecting an object with a `name` property to be passed. React passes all properties as an object via the first argument. Then we use de-structuring to pull out the `name` from the object. If we wanted to process the input before rendering JSX (for example, to make the name uppercase), we could do the following:

```
const Greeting = ({ name }) => {
  const uppercaseName = name.toUpperCase()
  return (
    <h1>
      hello {uppercaseName}!
    </h1>
  )
}
```

While we could also put `.toUpperCase()` into the JSX expression, in most cases, it is much cleaner to carry out the processing outside of JSX.

 Do not put too much logic into your JSX code, as it can get very messy and hinders readability of your code. When deciding if you should put something into JSX versus processing the data in the function, you should always keep readability of your code in mind!

Note that functional React components have to be pure. As a result, properties are read-only and cannot be modified. Furthermore, the same input will always result in the same output. Of course, applications are not static and sometimes values do need to change. You will learn how to deal with state later in this chapter.

Using components

Now that we have a React component, we can render it via `React.createElement`. Putting everything together, our code should look as follows:

```
import React from 'react'
import ReactDOM from 'react-dom'

const Greeting = ({ name }) => {
  const uppercaseName = name.toUpperCase()
  return (
    <h1>
      hello {uppercaseName}!
    </h1>
  )
}

ReactDOM.render(
  React.createElement(Greeting, { name: 'dan' }),
  document.getElementById('root')
)
```

Here is the great thing about React and JSX: instead of rendering simple HTML elements, we can render our React component, as if it was an HTML element:

```
ReactDOM.render(
  <Greeting name="dan" />,
  document.getElementById('root')
)
```

Let's think about what happens here:

- We call `ReactDOM.render` with our `Greeting` component and a name property. It will be rendered to the element with `id="root"`, which we defined in our HTML template earlier.
- The `Greeting` function gets called as follows: `Greeting({ name: 'dan' })`.
- The `Greeting` function returns a simple HTML element: `<h1>hello DAN!</h1>`.
- ReactDOM (re-)renders the simple HTML element into the element with `id="root"`.
- In our browser, we should now see a heading with the text **"hello DAN!"**.

After learning how to define components and how to use them, you can put them together and reuse them to make a more complex application. The typical way to do this is to create an App component, which *composes* other components into the full application:

```
const App = () => (
  <div>
    <Greeting name="Daniel" />
    <Greeting name="Destiny" />
  </div>
)
```

 React components always have to have a *single* root element. If we want to return multiple components/elements, we need to wrap them in a <div> container.

Now, we can render the <App /> component instead of rendering the Greeting component directly:

```
ReactDOM.render(
  <App />,
  document.getElementById('root')
)
```

Our application should now look as follows:

Re-using React components

Example code

The example code can be found in the chapter3_2.zip attachment.

Unpack the zip, change into the directory, run `npm install` and `npm start`, then open `http://localhost:8080` in your browser.

Class components – dynamic React components

To deal with state, we are going to turn our functional component into a class component. As an example, we will make a timer that shows how many seconds a user has spent on the page. First of all, let's write this timer as a functional component:

```
const Timer = ({ seconds }) =>
  <h1>You spent {seconds} seconds on this page!</h1>
```

Creating a static class component

Now, we can turn this functional component into a class by performing the following steps:

1. We start with the definition:

   ```
   class Timer extends React.Component {
   ```

   Classes in ES2015 JavaScript work similar to classes in Java. They contain functions (methods) and variables/constants. Although you have to be careful, as there are some differences when it comes to inheritance. However, you should not have to deal with these differences, because when using React, you should favor composition (wrapping components in other components) over inheritance (extending components from other components).

2. Next, we need to define a `render` method, which will be called to render the component. It returns React elements, which means that we can use JSX here:

   ```
   render () {
   ```

3. With class components, properties are stored in `this.props` and not passed to the `render` method. We can also use de-structuring here to pull out the properties we need:

   ```
   const { seconds } = this.props
   ```

4. Now, we return the to-be-rendered content via JSX:

   ```
       return <h1>You spent {seconds} seconds on this page!</h1>
     }
   }
   ```

Creating a dynamic class component

However, our class component is still static. We are now going to add some state to our component. We start out by setting the initial state. Then, you will learn how to deal with side effects (such as timers or API requests) via React life cycle methods. Finally, you are going to learn how to update `this.state` with React, and thus create a dynamic component.

Setting the initial state

Firstly, we define the initial state by creating a `constructor` method. This method will be called when an instance of the class is created:

1. In our case, `constructor(props)` will be called when a React component is created from our class:

   ```
   class Timer extends React.Component {
     constructor (props) {
   ```

2. Because we are extending `React.Component`, which has its own `constructor(props)` method, we have to call `super(props)` to ensure that React's `constructor` also gets called, letting React know about the properties:

   ```
   super(props)
   ```

3. Now, we can define the initial state by writing to `this.state`:

   ```
   this.state = {
     seconds: 0
   }
   }
   ```

4. Then, we modify the `render()` method to pull `seconds` from `this.state` instead of `this.props`:

   ```
   render () {
     const { seconds } = this.state
     return <h1>You spent {seconds} seconds on this page!</h1>
   }
   ```

React life cycle methods

All that's left to do now is to update the state. React calls certain life cycle methods, which can be used to create side effects, such as timers or API requests. In our case, we will use two very commonly used React life cycle methods:

- `componentDidMount()`: This method is called when the component is *rendered* to the DOM for the first time. Note the difference to `constructor()`, which is called when the component is *created*. Creation happens much earlier than the actual *rendering*. `componentDidMount` offers a way to do something (creating timers, requests, and so on) when the component first appears.
- `componentWillUnmount()`: This method is called *before* the DOM produced by the component is *removed*. It is basically a way to clean up any side effects (timers, unfinished requests, and so on) before the component disappears.

We want to create a timer that triggers every second and calls a `this.tick()` method, where we are going to update the state:

1. We are going to use `setInterval` to create a timer that triggers every second (1000 milliseconds). Because we want this timer to be created when the component first appears (gets *mounted*), we use `componentDidMount()`:

```
componentDidMount () {
  this.timer = setInterval(
    () => this.tick(),
    1000
  )
}
```

2. Do not forget to clean up your timer before the component *unmounts*, via `componentWillUnmount()`:

```
componentWillUnmount () {
  clearInterval(this.timer)
}
```

Updating the state

Finally, we define the `tick()` method we referenced earlier. In this method, we will update the state by increasing `seconds` by one. React provides the `this.setState(state)` method, which works similarly to using *spread syntax* to update objects. Only the properties passed to `this.setState` will be updated/overwritten. For example, if we consider this snippet:

```
// in constructor() method:
this.state = { seconds: 0, somethingElse: true }

// in tick() method:
this.setState({ seconds: this.state + 1 })
```

The resulting state will be as follows:

```
{ seconds: 1, somethingElse: true }
```

It works similar to the following code using the spread operator:

```
const state = { seconds: 0, somethingElse: true }
const newState = { seconds: state.seconds + 1 }
const resultingState = { ...state, ...newState }
```

Now that we understand how updating state in React works, we can write our `tick()` method:

```
tick () {
  const { seconds } = this.state
  this.setState({
    seconds: seconds + 1
  })
}
```

 Do not update the state by writing to `this.state` directly—your component will not be re-rendered!

Example – dynamic React component with timer

Putting everything together, we have a `Timer` component that shows how many seconds we have been on the page:

```
import React from 'react'
import ReactDOM from 'react-dom'
```

```
class Timer extends React.Component {
  constructor (props) {
    super(props)
    this.state = {
      seconds: 0
    }
  }

  tick () {
    const { seconds } = this.state
    this.setState({
      seconds: seconds + 1
    })
  }

  componentDidMount () {
    this.timer = setInterval(
      () => this.tick(),
      1000
    )
  }

  componentWillUnmount () {
    clearInterval(this.timer)
  }

  render () {
    const { seconds } = this.state
    return <h1>You spent {seconds} seconds on this page!</h1>
  }
}

ReactDOM.render(
  <Timer />,
  document.getElementById('root')
)
```

The *best practice* structure for React components is defining the methods in the following order:

1. The `constructor()` method first.
2. Then, all life cycle methods.
3. Then, all your custom methods (like `tick()`).
4. And lastly, the `render()` method.

Let's think about what's going on in the preceding example:

1. We call `ReactDOM.render` with our `Timer` component. It will be rendered to the element with `id="root"`, which we defined in our HTML template earlier.

2. React calls the constructor of the `Timer` component, which initializes the state to be: `{ seconds: 0 }`.

3. Then, React calls the `render()` method and updates the DOM from the output. The component is now visible and shows **You spent 0 seconds on this page!** in the browser.

4. When the output is inserted into the DOM, React calls the `componentDidMount()` life cycle method. Our `Timer` component sets up a timer that triggers every second and updates the state.

5. After a second, the browser calls the `tick()` method, which calls `this.setState({ seconds: 1 })`. React now knows that the state has changed, and thus calls `render()` again.

6. React does a diff from the old output of the `render()` method and the new output, and then renders the change to the DOM.

7. If the component gets removed from the DOM, React calls the `componentWillUnmount()` life cycle method. This stops the timer we created earlier.

Because React components are independent of each other and, thus, can be composed, we could also render multiple `Timer` components and it will work just fine:

```
const timers = (
  <div>
    <Timer />
    <Timer />
  </div>
)

ReactDOM.render(
  timers,
  document.getElementById('root')
)
```

Example code

The example code can be found in the `chapter3_3.zip` attachment.

Unpack the zip, change into the directory, run `npm install` and `npm start`, and then open `http://localhost:8080` in your browser.

The timer should look as follows:

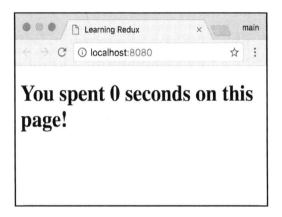

Initial state of our React timer application

Then, wait some time to see the counter change:

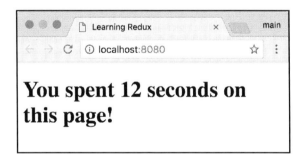

State of our React timer application after 12 seconds

Connecting React to Redux

Now that you learned how React works and how to write dynamic components with it, we will look into connecting React to our Redux store.

Connecting a component to Redux will allow us to replace React's internal state management with Redux' state management. Sometimes, it makes sense to use React's state. For example, when you have a local timer or form validation. In other cases, when state is used across multiple components, using Redux for state management makes more sense. Redux works especially well with React because they share a lot of principles. However, you can use Redux with any library: React, Angular, Ember, jQuery, or even vanilla JavaScript.

Presentational versus container components

In the React bindings for Redux, there is a principle of separating **presentational** from **container** components (sometimes also called **dumb** and **smart** components). It is best practice to put them in different folders.

Presentational components are:

- Concerned with *how things look*
- Usually written as functional components, because they are very simple; they only render a certain part of the user interface
- Not connected to the Redux store
- Contain both presentational and container components

Container components are:

- Concerned with *how things work*
- Usually written as class components or using React bindings, such as the React-Redux bindings, because they are usually stateful
- Data sources—they provide data and behavior to presentational or other container components

The idea behind separating components in such a way is *separation of concerns*. It is much easier to reason about presentational components, as they don't have complex state changes. Usually, they simply take properties as input, and render the output accordingly, without using React or Redux state.

It is also possible to re-use presentational components with different state sources. Furthermore, presentational components can be written and modified by designers, who just need to care about how the user interface elements look in different variations. They do not need to touch or look into the application logic, as it is contained in the container components.

 You can use React Storybook (`https://getstorybook.io/`) to create a development environment for your React components. In Storybook, you can visualize different states of your UI components and develop them interactively.

Most of your components will be presentational. You should use container components to connect certain presentational components to the Redux store.

Writing presentational components

We are now going back to our example from the previous chapter, where we built a way to create and edit posts with Redux, as well as setting a filter. We are going to need the following presentational components:

- **Post** component: To display a post
- **PostList** component: To display a list of posts

For this example, you can use the existing Redux code from `chapter2_4.zip`. We are going to replace the current `render` function with React components.

Post component

Let's start by writing the Post component as follows:

1. Create a new `src/components/` folder, and in this folder, create a `Post.jsx` file.
2. Remember, presentational components are concerned with *how things look*. The `Post` component will take a `user` and `text` as properties and display a username in bold next to the text. Put the following code in the `src/components/Post.jsx` file:

```
import React from 'react'

const Post = ({ user, text }) =>
  <span><b>{user}</b> – {text}</span>
```

```
export default Post
```

 In files that use JSX, it is important to import React at the beginning of the file. This is needed because JSX gets translated to calls to `React.createElement`.

3. In the `src/index.js` file, we can now import and render the `Post` component with `ReactDOM`. Replace the contents of the file with the following code:

```
import React from 'react'
import ReactDOM from 'react-dom'

import Post from './components/Post.jsx'

ReactDOM.render(
  <Post user="dan" text="hello world!" />,
  document.getElementById('root')
)
```

Our application should now look as follows:

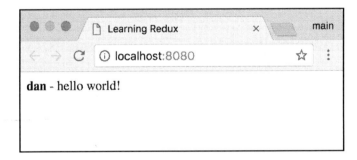

Rendering a single Post component

PostList component

The next step is writing a component that can display *multiple* posts:

1. Create a new `src/components/PostList.jsx` file.

2. The `PostList` component will take a `posts` array as a property and render multiple `Post` components. We will use the `map()` function you learned about earlier. Put the following code into the previously created file:

```
import React from 'react'
import Post from './Post.jsx'

const PostList = ({ posts }) =>
  <ul>
    {posts.map(
      (post, i) =>
        <li key={i.toString()}>
          <Post {...post} />
        </li>
    )}
  </ul>

export default PostList
```

Let's take a closer look at the `map()` function:

- We loop through all posts in the array and create and return a `<li>` element for each post. These `<li>` elements will be children of the `<ul>` element.

- In React, if you have a dynamic list, you need to provide a `key` property to help React identify which items have changed, are added, or removed. In this example, we simply use the index in the array as the key. If you forget to specify a key, you will get a warning about it in the console.

- In the `<li>` element, we use the `Post` component we defined earlier.

- To pass all properties from the `post` object to the component, we use the spread operator, which also works with JSX properties!

3. We can now render the `PostList` component to try it out. Replace `src/index.js` with the following code:

```
import React from 'react'
import ReactDOM from 'react-dom'

import PostList from './components/PostList.jsx'

const posts = [
  { user: 'dan', text: 'hello world!' },
  { user: 'des', text: 'hi!' }
]

ReactDOM.render(
  <PostList posts={posts} />,
  document.getElementById('root')
)
```

Our application should now look as follows:

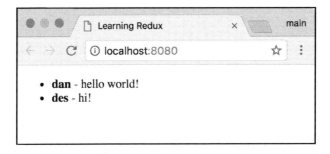

Rendering multiple Post components via the PostList component

Example code

The example code can be found in the `chapter3_4.zip` attachment.

Unpack the zip, change into the directory, run `npm install` and `npm start`, and then open `http://localhost:8080` in your browser.

Writing container components

Container components are concerned with *how things work*. They are usually data sources. To get a better feel for what the React-Redux bindings actually do, we will start by writing a container component by hand, without using the bindings. In our small example, we only have one container component: `ConnectedPostList`. This component will connect our `PostList` component to the Redux store. Afterward, you are going to learn how to accomplish the same things and more using the React-Redux bindings instead.

Implementing our own container component

In this small example, we only need one container component, `ConnectedPostList`:

1. Create a new folder `src/containers/` for our container components.
2. Create a new `src/containers/ConnectedPostList.jsx` file with the following contents:

   ```
   import React from 'react'
   import PostList from '../components/PostList.jsx'

   export default class ConnectedPostList extends React.Component {
   ```

   This component will actually be very similar to our `Timer` example. However, we use the life cycle methods to (un-)subscribe to the Redux store, instead of creating and removing a `setInterval` timer.

3. Again, we start with the `constructor()` method, where we set the initial state. In this case, we pull the initial state from the Redux store:

   ```
   constructor (props) {
     super(props)
     this.state = props.store.getState()
   }
   ```

4. We continue with the `componentDidMount()` life cycle method, where we subscribe to the store and call `this.setState` with the new Redux state:

   ```
   componentDidMount () {
     const { store } = this.props
     this.unsubscribe = store.subscribe(() =>
       this.setState({ ...store.getState() })
     )
   }
   ```

store.subscribe() returns an unsubscribe() function, which can be used to remove the subscription.

The fact that arrow functions don't have their own this context comes in useful here. We can use this.setState in the subscription function without having to worry about this getting overwritten by the function and not referencing the class anymore.

5. Now, we write the componentWillUnmount() life cycle method to make sure we clean up any side effects we caused. We simply call the this.unsubscribe() function that store.subscribe() created for us earlier:

```
componentWillUnmount () {
  this.unsubscribe()
}
```

6. Finally, we write the render() method, which will return our component, passing all state down to it as properties:

```
render () {
  return <PostList {...this.state} />
}
}
```

7. In the main file src/index.js, we now import everything that we need, including the ConnectedPostList component:

```
import { createStore } from 'redux'
import React from 'react'
import ReactDOM from 'react-dom'

import { createPost } from './actions'
import appReducer from './reducers'
import ConnectedPostList from './containers/ConnectedPostList.jsx'
```

8. Then, we create the Redux store:

```
let store = createStore(appReducer)
```

9. We dispatch a `createPost` action, so we can see a post:

```
store.dispatch(createPost('dan', 'hello world'))
```

10. After a second, we dispatch another `createPost` action:

```
setTimeout(() => store.dispatch(createPost('des', 'hi!')), 1000)
```

11. Finally, we render our `ConnectedPostList` component via `ReactDOM`:

```
ReactDOM.render(
  <ConnectedPostList store={store} />,
  document.getElementById('root')
)
```

Then, we start the `webpack-dev-server` via `npm start` and open `http://localhost:8080` in our browser, we should see the first post:

Initial state of our small React/Redux application

After a second, we will see the second post:

State of our small React/Redux application after one second has passed

We successfully connected React to Redux, without using bindings!

Example code

The example code can be found in the `chapter3_5.zip` attachment.

Unpack the zip, change into the directory, run `npm install` and `npm start`, and then open `http://localhost:8080` in your browser.

Using React-Redux bindings to create a container component

Writing a container component manually like that works fine. However, it is a bit tedious and there is a lot of boilerplate code. React-Redux makes connecting components to Redux a lot easier by providing a `connect()` function, which allows you to inject a part of the Redux store and bound action creators into the component. Furthermore, React-Redux also provides many performance optimizations for updating the state.

Setting up React-Redux

As mentioned previously, Redux is not tied to React in any way. As a result, the React bindings do not come with Redux. To be able to connect React to Redux, we need to install the React bindings for Redux:

```
npm install --save react-redux
```

Using React-Redux to create a container component

We are now going to use React-Redux to create a container component:

1. Rename your existing `containers/ConnectedPostList.jsx` to `containers/CustomConnectedPostList.jsx`.

2. Then, create a new `containers/ConnectedPostList.jsx` file. Let's start by importing the `connect` function from React-Redux, which will be used to connect our `PostList` component to Redux:

   ```
   import { connect } from 'react-redux'
   ```

3. We also need to import our `PostList` presentational component:

   ```
   import PostList from '../components/PostList.jsx'
   ```

   The `connect` function has the following signature: `connect(mapStateToProps, mapDispatchToProps)` This means that we need to pass two functions to the connect function:

   - `mapStateToProps(state, props)`: This function is used to pass *Redux state* as properties to the wrapped React component, similarly to our custom container component. It returns an object of properties that will be passed to the React component. You can decide to map the state to properties in any way and even do data processing (for example, for filter functionality) here.

   - `mapDispatchToProps(dispatch, props)`: This function is used to pass *Redux action creators* as properties to the wrapped React component. It returns an object of properties that will be passed to the React component. You can use this to pass functions that will dispatch actions to your React component. For example, to create a new post or change the filter when the user clicks a button/link.

   For this example, we only use the first function. Later in this chapter, we will extend the example and implement interactivity via `mapDispatchToProps`.

4. Now, we define our `mapStateToProps` function:

```
const mapStateToProps = (state, props) => {
  return { posts: state.posts }
}
```

5. Then, we create the container component by calling `connect` and exporting the resulting connected component:

```
const ConnectedPostList = connect(mapStateToProps)(PostList)

export default ConnectedPostList
```

Run the `webpack-dev-server` via `npm start` and open `http://localhost:8080` in your browser. You should see the same result as before, but with much less code!

Using selectors

Once you have more complicated behavior in your `mapStateToProps` function, you might want to consider writing **selector** functions. They take the state as an argument and return a certain part of the state.

Consider we have an object of posts stored by their IDs:

```
{
  "posts": {
    "0": {
      "id": 0,
      "author": "dan",
      "text": "hello world"
    },
    ...
  }
}
```

We could write a `getPosts` selector function, which returns a list of posts in an array:

```
const getPosts = ({ posts }) => {
  return Object.keys(posts).map(
    (id) => posts[id]
  )
}
```

Consider we have an array of selected post IDs and only want to get those from the state:

```
{
  "posts": { ... },
  "selectedPosts": ["0", "2"]
}
```

We could create another selector function to get all selected posts from the state:

```
const getSelectedPosts = ({ selectedPosts, posts }) => {
  return selectedPosts.map(
    (id) => posts[id]
  )
}
```

Now, we could use this selector function in the `mapStateToProps` function:

```
const mapStateToProps = (state, props) => {
  return { posts: getSelectedPosts(state) }
}
```

With selector functions, we can reuse code to process the state in certain ways before passing it down to a component. It is a very powerful pattern, especially in bigger Redux applications.

Example code

The example code can be found in the `chapter3_6.zip` attachment.

Unpack the zip, change into the directory, run `npm install` and `npm start`, and then open `http://localhost:8080` in your browser.

Building an application with Redux and React

In the previous chapters, you learned how Redux works. In the previous sections, you learned how React works and how to use React with Redux. Now, we will apply our knowledge to build a small blog application with Redux and React. This exercise will show you various problems that you may run into when writing a React/Redux application. We will go through best practice solutions to these problems. In the next chapters, we are going to extend this application with further functionality.

It might be tempting to simply run the code examples attached to this book to see the results. However, I strongly recommend writing the code yourself and trying to solve problems on your own, using the book as a guide. Feel free to extend the application if you have good ideas; it is important to practice the concepts you have learned. There is immense value in *learning by doing*, especially when it comes to programming, so make use of it and practice!

The goal

The goal of this section is to build a blog application with Redux and React. We will apply all the knowledge you have learned in this book so far. In the next chapters, we are going to extend this application with more features, to learn about more advanced concepts. The initial list of features for our blog application is as follows:

- **Users**: The blog should handle multiple user accounts. Every user can create posts.
- **Posts**: The essential part of every blog. Posts have an author (a user), a title, text, creation date/timestamp, last updated date/timestamp, and a category. Users can create new posts, which are displayed on the front page.
- **Filter**: The posts can be filtered by category.

To get an idea of what our application will look like, here is a screenshot of the result. At the end of this chapter, your application should look as follows:

What our application will look like after this chapter

Project structure

The project structure will be similar to the previous examples. To recap, we will go through the file/folder structure. You can use the code from the previous example in this book, where we connected React to Redux. The main difference to the previous examples is that we will split up our Redux actions, reducers, and action types into multiple files. That is why we are going to create separate folders for each of the Redux elements:

- `index.html`: The main HTML file of our application. This is where you would put meta tags and other stuff that should stay the same on every page.
- `package.json`: This file is used to manage dependencies via npm.
- `webpack.config.js`: The configuration file for webpack.
- `.babelrc`: The configuration file for Babel.
- `src/`: The main source code of our application:
  - `index.js`: The main entry point of our application. This is where we initialize the Redux store and render the main React component.
  - `actionTypes.js`: This is where we put our Redux action types.
  - `actions/`: This is where we put our Redux actions:
    - `index.js`: The main file for actions. Here we will re-export the actions from all other files in the folder.
    - `*.js`: Module-specific files for actions.
  - `reducers/`: This is where we put our Redux reducers:
    - `index.js`: The main file for reducers. Here, we will re-export the reducers from all other files in the folder.
    - `*.js`: Module-specific files for reducers.
  - `components/`: This is where we put our React presentational components:
    - `index.js`: The main file for components. Here, we re-export the components from all other files in the folder.
    - `*.js`: Module-specific files for components.
  - `containers/`: This is where we put our container components:
    - `index.js`: The main file for containers. Here, we re-export the containers from all other files in the folder.
    - `*.js`: Module-specific files for containers.

Defining the application state

The first thing to think about when developing a Redux application is the application state. You have already learned about this in the first chapter. You might not know the full state in the beginning—that's fine. We will make sure to design the state in an extendable way. Our blog consists of users, posts, and a filter.

The basic structure of our state is going to look as follows:

```
{
  users: [...],
  posts: [...],
  filter: ...
}
```

Users state

Let's start with the application state for `users`. Every user has a unique username and a full name. This means that a single user object could look like this:

```
{
  username: 'dan',
  realname: 'Daniel Bugl'
}
```

In our application state, we have an array of these objects. In the other parts of the state, we reference users by their unique username.

Posts state

Next is the application state for `posts`. Posts have an author (a user), a title, text, creation date/timestamp, last updated date/timestamp, and a category. A single post object could look like this:

```
{
  user: 'dan',
  title: 'Test Post',
  text: 'hello world!',
  category: 'test',
  created: 1491828725892,
  updated: 1491828725892
}
```

In the application state, we have an array of these post objects. In other parts of the state, we reference posts by their unique ID. As you can see, the `user` property here references the user object we defined earlier by username.

Filter state

Posts can be filtered by category. The filter state references a category, which means that it is simply a string:

```
filter: 'test'
```

In this case, we are referencing the `test` category from the post we defined earlier.

Defining action types and action creators

As you have learned previously, the next step is to define action types and action creators for our application. Keep in mind that, while we are always doing the steps in the same order in this book, in a real project you might start by defining your React components, and then later add logic to them. Since this is a Redux focused book, we start by thinking about the application logic, and then connect it to user interface elements.

Defining action types

We have already defined some action types in the previous chapters:

- CREATE_POST
- EDIT_POST
- SET_FILTER

In addition to these, we also define the following *new* action types:

- CREATE_USER
- DELETE_POST
- CLEAR_FILTER

We put all of our action types into the `src/actionTypes.js` file. You can use spacing and comments to separate the modules. If the project grows even more, you might want to consider splitting your action types into multiple files in a directory. We are going to do this for our action creators later. For now, define the following action types in the `src/actionTypes.js` file:

```
// users
export const CREATE_USER = 'CREATE_USER'

// posts
export const CREATE_POST = 'CREATE_POST'
export const EDIT_POST = 'EDIT_POST'
export const DELETE_POST = 'DELETE_POST'

// filter
export const SET_FILTER = 'SET_FILTER'
export const CLEAR_FILTER = 'CLEAR_FILTER'
```

Defining action creators

In the previous chapters, we already defined some action creators for our blog application. However, this time we are going to split up our action creators into multiple files in a directory.

Create a `src/actions/` directory. Afterward, delete the `src/actions.js` file to avoid conflicts when importing action creators.

User action creators

We start with the user actions, because there is only one action to be defined—creating users:

1. Create a `src/actions/users.js` file.
2. Because we are in a sub-directory now, we need to import action types from `../` instead of `./`:

   ```
   import { CREATE_USER } from '../actionTypes'
   ```

3. Creating a new user requires a username and a real name:

   ```
   export const createUser = (username, realname) => {
     return {
       type: CREATE_USER,
       username,
   ```

```
    realname,
  }
}
```

Now, all that's left to do is export the action creator from the directory.

4. Create a `src/actions/index.js` file and re-export everything from the `users.js` file:

```
export * from './users'
```

Now, we can import the `createUser` action creator as follows:

```
import { createUser } from './actions'
```

Note how the preceding statement looks the same as importing from an `actions.js` file. As a result, it is easy to split up a big file into multiple smaller files, stored in a directory with the same name as the original file.

Post action creators

Next, we define the post action creators:

1. Create a new `src/actions/posts.js` file.
2. We start by importing the action types we are going to use:

   ```
   import { CREATE_POST, EDIT_POST, DELETE_POST } from
   '../actionTypes'
   ```

3. Then, we define the `createPost` action creator. It takes two arguments—the username and all data for the post:

   ```
   export const createPost = (user, post) => {
   ```

4. For the second argument, we are going to use destructuring to pull out the data we need. Using destructuring, we can also set a default value for the category. By default, the category will be set to `'random'`:

   ```
   const { title, text, category = 'random' } = post
   ```

5. We throw an error if the title or text are not set:

   ```
   if (!title || !text) {
     throw new Error('invalid post, title and text required')
   }
   ```

6. Now, we can create and return the action:

```
return {
  type: CREATE_POST,
  post: { user, title, text, category },
}
}
```

7. Next, we define the `editPost` action creator, which edits a post by its `id` (index in the array). We simply pass the to-be-edited properties as a `post` object. A reducer will handle the actual editing:

```
export const editPost = (id, post) => {
  return {
    type: EDIT_POST,
    id,
    post,
  }
}
```

8. Finally, we define the `deletePost` action creator, which only takes an `id` as an argument:

```
export const deletePost = (id) => {
  return {
    type: DELETE_POST,
    id,
  }
}
```

9. Don't forget to export the posts action creators by editing `src/actions/index.js` and appending the following line:

```
export * from './posts'
```

Filter action creators

Finally, we define the filter action creators in `src/actions/filter.js`. These are pretty simple and straightforward:

```
import { SET_FILTER, CLEAR_FILTER } from '../actionTypes'

export const setFilter = (filter) => {
  return {
    type: SET_FILTER,
    filter,
```

```
    }
  }

export const clearFilter = () => {
  return {
    type: CLEAR_FILTER,
  }
}
```

Again, we need to export the action creators in our `src/actions/index.js` file:

```
export * from './filter'
```

Implementing reducers

Reducers describe how state changes happen. We are going to split up our reducers into multiple files in a directory.

Create a `src/reducers/` directory. Afterward, delete the `src/reducers.js` file to avoid conflicts when importing reducers.

Users reducer

Let's start with the users reducer.

1. Create a new file `src/reducers/users.js` and import the action type:

   ```
   import { CREATE_USER } from '../actionTypes'
   ```

2. Now, we define the function—the default state should be an empty array:

   ```
   export default function usersReducer (state = [], action) {
   ```

3. Since we are only handling one action here, we use an `if` statement instead of `switch`:

   ```
   const { type, ...user } = action
   if (type === CREATE_USER) {
     return [ ...state, user ]
   }
   ```

4. Don't forget to return the current state if the action isn't handled:

```
    return state
}
```

Posts reducer

Next we create the posts reducer, dealing with creating, editing, and deleting posts.

1. Create a new file `src/reducers/posts.js`.

2. We import the action types we need, and define the reducer function with the initial state being an empty array:

```
import { CREATE_POST, EDIT_POST, DELETE_POST } from
'../actionTypes'

export default function postsReducer (state = [], action) {
```

3. This time we use a `switch` statement, because we are handling multiple actions:

```
switch (action.type) {
```

4. We start by handling the `CREATE_POST` action. We need to set the `created` and `updated` values to the current timestamp here:

```
    case CREATE_POST: {
      const { type, post } = action
      const ts = Date.now()
      return [
        ...state,
        { ...post, created: ts, updated: ts },
      ]
    }
```

5. Then, we handle `EDIT_POST`, using `map()`, similar to how we did in *Chapter 2, Implementing the Elements of Redux.* However, this time we also need to update the `updated` value to the current timestamp:

```
    case EDIT_POST: {
      const { type, id, post } = action
      return state.map((oldPost, index) =>
        action.id === index
          ? {
              ...oldPost,
              ...post,
```

```
      updated: Date.now(),
    }
    : oldPost
  )
}
```

6. Next, we handle `DELETE_POST`, using `filter()`, which works similar to `map()`, but instead of transforming data, it returns a new array containing only elements where there function returned `true`. To delete a post, we always return `true`, except when the ID matches:

```
case DELETE_POST: {
  const { type, id } = action
  return state.filter((post, index) =>
    action.id === index
      ? false
      : true
  )
}
```

The preceding code can be shortened to:

```
case DELETE_POST: {
  const { type, id } = action
  return state.filter((post, index) =>
    action.id !== index
  )
}
```

7. Finally, we return the current state if none of the action types matched:

```
default:
  return state
  }
}
```

Filter reducer

This reducer function is quite simple; it simply sets and clears the `filter` value, which is set to `false` (show all posts) by default.

Create a new `src/reducers/filter.js` file with the following contents:

```
import { SET_FILTER, CLEAR_FILTER } from '../actionTypes'

export default function filterReducer (state = false, action) {
  switch (action.type) {
    case SET_FILTER:
      return action.filter
    case CLEAR_FILTER:
      return false
    default:
      return state
  }
}
```

Root reducer

This time we will do something a little different in the `src/reducers/index.js` file. Instead of re-exporting all reducers, we import all reducers, then export a single root reducer, which we create using the `combineReducers` helper from the Redux library:

1. Create a new `src/reducers/index.js` file.
2. First, we import the `combineReducers` helper function and all reducers:

   ```
   import { combineReducers } from 'redux'

   import usersReducer from './users'
   import postsReducer from './posts'
   import filterReducer from './filter'
   ```

3. Then, we use `combineReducers` to create a reducer for the whole application state and export it:

   ```
   const appReducer = combineReducers({
     users: usersReducer,
     posts: postsReducer,
     filter: filterReducer,
   })

   export default appReducer
   ```

Now, we could import the app reducer the following way:

```
import appReducer from './reducers'
```

Setting up the Redux store

Now that we implemented our action types, action creators, and reducers, we need to create the Redux store from our app reducer.

1. Open `src/index.js` and clear the contents of the file.

2. We start by importing the `createStore` function from the Redux library and our app reducer:

   ```
   import { createStore } from 'redux'

   import appReducer from './reducers'
   ```

3. We also import the `createUser` and `createPost` action creators, so we can populate our blog with some sample content:

   ```
   import { createUser, createPost } from './actions'
   ```

4. Now, we create the store and dispatch some actions:

   ```
   let store = createStore(appReducer)

   // create users
   store.dispatch(createUser('dan', 'Daniel Bugl'))
   store.dispatch(createUser('des', 'Destiny'))

   // create posts
   store.dispatch(createPost('dan', {
     title: 'First post',
     text: 'Hello world! This is the first blog post.',
     category: 'welcome',
   }))
   store.dispatch(createPost('des', {
     title: 'Another test',
     text: 'This is another test blog post.',
     category: 'test',
   }))
   ```

5. Let's log the current state of our store to see if the Redux part of our application works fine:

   ```
   console.log('initial state:', store.getState())
   ```

6. We can also subscribe to state changes, which will help us debug our application:

```
store.subscribe(() =>
  console.log('state changed:', store.getState())
)
```

Code example – Redux-only application

The current state of the project can be found in the `chapter3_7.zip` attachment.

Unpack the zip, change into the directory, run `npm install` and `npm start`, and then open `http://localhost:8080` in your browser and check the console.

Implementing the user interface

You might remember that before we looked into creating reducers, we first figured out what our application state will look like. With React, it is also a good idea to first think about what your component tree will look like.

We usually start with the smallest presentational components (for example, the `Post` component), then compose them into more complex components (for example, the `PostList` component). Finally, we think about container components, which connect our React components to Redux.

You should try to split your components in a way that maximizes reusability. This is why we start with the smallest components, then re-use them in other components.

Implementing presentational components

Let's start by thinking about our presentational components:

- Users module:
    - **User** component : To display a single user object (username and real name).
- Posts module:
    - **Post** component: To display a single post object.
    - **PostList** component: To display multiple post objects

- Filter module:
  - **Filter** component: To display a clickable link to change the filter
  - **FilterList** component: To display multiple links to change the filter and a special link to clear the filter

Create a `src/components/` directory for our presentational components.

User component

We start by creating a component that displays a user object (username and real name).

Create a `src/components/User.jsx` file, with the following contents:

```
import React from 'react'

const User = ({ username, realname }) =>
  <span>@{username} ({realname})</span>

export default User
```

Because we are going to import components directly, we do *not* need to create a `src/components/index.js` file that re-exports all components. We are going to import components as follows:

```
import User from './components/User.jsx'
```

Post component

Let's recap the structure of a post so that we can think about how to display all the data from it:

```
{
  user: 'dan',
  title: 'Test Post',
  text: 'hello world!',
  category: 'test',
  created: 1491828725892,
  updated: 1491828725892
}
```

To display the user property, we are going to use a container component to replace the username with a user object so that we can directly pass it down to the User component. Displaying the title, text, and category properties should be straightforward. For the created and updated properties, we will create a Timestamp component that displays the date/time later.

Create a src/components/Post.jsx file with the following contents:

```
import React from 'react'

import User from './User.jsx'
import Timestamp from './Timestamp.jsx'

const Post = ({ user, title, text, category, created, updated }) =>
  <span>
    <b>{title}</b>: {text}
    <i>{' ~ '}<User {...user} /></i><br />
    (Created at: <Timestamp data={created} />, Updated at: <Timestamp
data={updated} />)
  </span>

export default Post
```

Timestamp component

This component will actually be quite simple, but it still makes sense to make a separate component for it, because the code will be re-used multiple times in other components. Furthermore, if we want to change the date/time format later, we can simply change it once in the Timestamp component, and it will be consistent everywhere.

Create a src/components/Timestamp.jsx file with the following contents:

```
import React from 'react'

const Timestamp = ({ data }) => {
  const d = new Date(data)
  return <span>{d.toUTCString()}</span>
}

export default Timestamp
```

PostList component

We already implemented a PostList component earlier in this chapter. The code for this component will not change.

Create a `src/components/PostList.jsx` file with the following contents:

```
import React from 'react'
import Post from './Post.jsx'

const PostList = ({ posts }) =>
  <ul>
    {posts.map(
      (post, i) =>
        <li key={i.toString()}>
          <Post {...post} />
        </li>
    )}
  </ul>

export default PostList
```

Filter component

Our `Filter` component takes a `name` and an `onClick` function, which will be called when the link is clicked on.

Create a `src/components/Filter.jsx` file, with the following contents:

```
import React from 'react'

const Filter = ({ name, onClick }) =>
  <a href="javascript:void(0)" onClick={onClick}>{name}</a>

export default Filter
```

FilterList component

This component works similar to the PostList component. We pass an array of `categories`, and `setFilter` and `clearFilter` action creators. Additionally, we display a link to clear the filter:

1. Create a `src/components/FilterList.jsx` file, where we `map()` over all categories:

```
import React from 'react'
import Filter from './Filter.jsx'

const FilterList = ({ categories, setFilter, clearFilter }) =>
  <span>
    {categories.map(
```

```
(category, i) =>
  <span key={i.toString()}>
```

2. Then, we use the Filter component, passing the name of the category to it:

```
<Filter
  name={category}
```

3. We also pass an `onClick` handler to it, which calls the `setFilter` action creator with the category name:

```
onClick={() => setFilter(category)}
/>
{' - '}
</span>
)}
```

4. Finally, we create a link for the `clearFilter` action creator:

```
<a href="javascript:void(0)" onClick={clearFilter}>all
posts</a>
  </span>

export default FilterList
```

Implementing container components

Next, we think about which of the components we defined need to be connected to Redux, our container components:

- **ConnectedPostList** container: This displays all posts from the Redux store, with the filter applied
- **ConnectedFilterList** container: This displays all categories from the Redux store as filters, injecting the action creators for setting and clearing filters

Create a `src/containers/` directory for our container components.

ConnectedPostList component

We have already implemented this container component, so we can use the existing code. However, we still need to implement the filter functionality:

1. Create a `src/containers/ConnectedPostList.jsx` file, with the following contents:

```
import { connect } from 'react-redux'
import PostList from '../components/PostList.jsx'

const mapStateToProps = (state, props) => {
  return { posts: state.posts }
}

const ConnectedPostList = connect(mapStateToProps)(PostList)

export default ConnectedPostList
```

2. Now, we modify the `mapStateToProps` function to apply the filter, using the `filter` function:

```
const mapStateToProps = (state, props) => {
  const filteredPosts = state.filter
    ? state.posts.filter((post) => post.category === state.filter)
    : state.posts

  return {
    posts: filteredPosts,
  }
}
```

3. In addition to filtering, we also need to resolve the usernames to the full user object:

```
return {
  posts: filteredPosts.map((post) => {
    const { user, ...rest } = post
    const userObj = state.users.find(
      ({ username }) => user === username
    )
    return {
      user: userObj,
      ...rest,
    }
  }),
}
```

In a real-world application, you may prefer to store your data in objects with their database ID as the key. Such an object is called an index, and is similar to the hashmap pattern. Structuring state as an index makes it easy to select the data.

For example, if we stored our users in an index instead of an array, we could simply do `state.users[username]` to get the user object, instead of having to loop through the whole array via `.find()`.

ConnectedFilterList component

Next, we implement the `ConnectedFilterList` component. For this component, we need to use `mapDispatchToProps` to inject the action creators:

1. Create a `src/containers/ConnectedFilterList.jsx` file with the following imports:

   ```
   import { connect } from 'react-redux'
   import { bindActionCreators } from 'redux'

   import FilterList from '../components/FilterList.jsx'

   import { setFilter, clearFilter } from '../actions'
   ```

2. Then, we define the `mapStateToProps` function:

   ```
   const mapStateToProps = (state, props) => {
   ```

3. This time, we cannot directly return filters from the state; we need to figure out which filters are possible by going through all the posts and adding categories to an array:

   ```
   const categories = state.posts.reduce((acc, post) => {
   ```

4. We use `reduce(fn, init)` here, which goes through all the elements in an array, such as `map(fn)`. However, it allows you to have a custom result, which in our case is the `acc` argument. In the function, we check if `acc` already contains a category, and if not, add it and return the new `acc`:

```
if (!acc.includes(post.category)) {
  return [ ...acc, post.category ]
}
return acc
```

More information about the `reduce` function can be found on the **Mozilla Developer Network** (**MDN**) web docs:
`https://developer.mozilla.org/en-US/docs/Web/JavaScript/`
`Reference/Global_Objects/Array/Reduce.`

5. The second argument to `reduce` is the initial state, which in our case is an empty array:

```
}, [])
```

6. Now, that we have an array of categories, we can pass it to our `FilterList` component by returning it from `mapStateToProps`:

```
    return { categories }
}
```

7. The next step is defining the `mapDispatchToProps` function, which injects the `setFilter` and `clearFilter` action creators:

```
const mapDispatchToProps = (dispatch, props) => {
  return {
    setFilter: (category) => dispatch(setFilter(category)),
    clearFilter: () => dispatch(clearFilter()),
  }
}
```

To shorten that code, we can use the `bindActionCreators` helper function we imported from Redux earlier:

```
const mapDispatchToProps = (dispatch, props) =>
  bindActionCreators({ setFilter, clearFilter }, dispatch)
```

8. Finally, we call `connect()` and export the container component:

```
const ConnectedFilterList = connect(mapStateToProps,
mapDispatchToProps)(FilterList)

export default ConnectedFilterList
```

Implementing the App component

We now need to put all our other components together by writing an App component.

Create a `src/components/App.jsx` file:

1. First, we import React and our connected components:

```
import React from 'react'

import ConnectedPostList from '../containers/ConnectedPostList.jsx'
import ConnectedFilterList from
'../containers/ConnectedFilterList.jsx'
```

2. Then, we define the App component, which takes the Redux store as property:

```
const App = ({ store }) =>
```

3. In the App component, we render a header, then the connected FilterList and PostList components:

```
<div>
  <h1>React/Redux blog app</h1>
  <div><ConnectedFilterList store={store} /></div>
  <div><ConnectedPostList store={store} /></div>
</div>
```

4. Finally, we export the App component:

```
export default App
```

Using <Provider>

In our App component, we pass the Redux store manually to each connected component. While this method works, it is a bit tedious and might get complicated when we have to pass down the store over multiple levels of components.

React-Redux provides a `<Provider>` component, which passes the Redux store down to all child components (even deeply nested ones), via React context.

Edit the `src/components/App.jsx` file:

1. Add an import for the Provider component.

    ```
    import { Provider } from 'react-redux'
    ```

2. Then, wrap the root `<div>` of the `App` component with the `<Provider>` component, passing the store to it:

    ```
    const App = ({ store }) =>
      <Provider store={store}>
        <div>
          . . .
        </div>
      </Provider>
    ```

3. Finally, we can get rid of the manual passing of the `store` property to connected components. *Remove* the code marked in bold:

    ```
    const App = ({ store }) =>
      <Provider store={store}>
        <div>
          <h1>React/Redux blog app</h1>
          <div><ConnectedFilterList store={store} /></div>
          <div><ConnectedPostList store={store} /></div>
        </div>
      </Provider>
    ```

Rendering the App component

Now, all that is left to do is to import React and ReactDOM in the main `src/index.js` file and render the `App` component there:

1. At the beginning of the `src/index.js` file, add the following code:

    ```
    import React from 'react'
    import ReactDOM from 'react-dom'

    import App from './components/App.jsx'
    ```

2. At the end of the file, add the following code:

```
ReactDOM.render(
  <App store={store} />,
  document.getElementById('root')
)
```

Open the application in your browser. You should now see the blog application with our example posts and users. Click on the filter links to filter posts.

Code example – React/Redux application

The current state of the project can be found in the chapter3_8.zip attachment.

Unpack the zip, change into the directory, run npm install and npm start, and then open http://localhost:8080 in your browser.

Further tasks

There are still a few things you could implement in this project. These tasks are similar to what we have already gone through, and are left as an exercise for the reader:

- Display the category in the blog post.
- Add a form to create a new blog post.
- Use an existing design framework to make the blog look nicer. For example, you could use http://www.material-ui.com/, which provides React components for Google's Material Design UI elements.
- Display a list of all users.
- Allow switching users by clicking on a user in the list.
- Make the currently selected filter look non-clickable (by removing the href attribute).

We are going to look at implementing more advanced tasks, such as authentication and interacting with third-party APIs, in the next chapters.

Summary

In this chapter, you first learned what React is and why it makes sense to use it. Then, you learned how to set up a project with React. Next, we covered how to connect React to Redux, manually and using the official React-Redux bindings. Finally, we used all our existing knowledge to build a blog application with React and Redux.

In the next chapter, you will learn how to use Redux with Angular. The next chapter is intended for readers who are already familiar with Angular. If you are not familiar with it, or prefer using React, feel free to skip the next chapter.

4

Combining Redux with Angular

In the preceding chapter, we discussed how to combine Redux with React. In this chapter, we will cover using Redux with Angular. This chapter is intended for readers who are already familiar with Angular. If you are not, feel free to skip this chapter, as the next chapters will use our React/Redux project as the base.

In this chapter, we will cover:

- Creating a basic Angular 1 application
- Connecting the Angular 1 application to Redux
- Creating a basic Angular 2+ application
- Connecting the Angular 2+ application to Redux

Note that Angular 2 is compatible with newer Angular versions (at the time of writing this book, up to Angular 4).

Redux with Angular 1

We will use the template from the second chapter, `chapter2_4.zip`. It already has webpack, Babel, and Redux set up, so all we need to do is the following:

- Install Angular 1
- Setup a basic Angular 1 application
- Install ng-redux
- Use ng-redux to connect Redux to Angular

Setting up Angular 1

To set up Angular 1, perform the following steps:

1. First of all, we need to install Angular via `npm`:

   npm install --save angular

2. Do not forget to install the other dependencies by running the following command:

   npm install

3. Next, we need to import Angular into our `src/index.js` file. At the top of the file, add the following:

   ```
   import angular from 'angular'
   ```

4. Now, we need to tell Angular which element to use as a container. With React, we set `id="root"`, and then referenced this element when rendering with ReactDOM. In the Angular world, we will need to set the `ng-app` attribute on the container element. In the `index.html` file, find this:

   ```
   <div id="root"></div>
   ```

   Now, replace the preceding line with this:

   ```
   <div ng-app></div>
   ```

5. Similar to JSX, Angular allows you to put JavaScript expressions in your HTML code with *double* curly brackets:

   ```
   <div ng-app>
       1 + 2 = {{1 + 2}}
   </div>
   ```

To check whether Angular works, let's run `webpack-dev-server` by executing the following command:

npm start

Open `http://localhost:8080/` in your browser; you should see the following output:

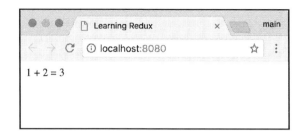

A very simple Angular application

Code example

The current state of the project can be found in the `chapter4_1.zip` attachment.

Unzip the file, run `npm install` and `npm start`, and then open `http://localhost:8080` in your browser.

Creating a basic Angular 1 application

Of course, there is much more to Angular than evaluating expressions in HTML. To connect Angular 1 with Redux, we will first need to set up a small application. In our template, we already have the code for a Redux blog application. We will use this existing code and replace our simple `render()` function with Angular 1.

For the sake of simplicity, we will put all our Angular code into the main HTML file:

1. Open `index.html` and replace the current `<div ng-app>` container with the following code:

   ```
   <div ng-app="blog" ng-controller="posts">
   ```

   This tells Angular that we want to use the `blog` module and the `posts` controller for this container.

2. Now, we will make a list and use `ng-repeat` to loop over all `posts`:

```
<ul>
  <li ng-repeat="post in posts">
```

3. We will display each `post` using expressions:

```
<b>{{post.user}}:</b> {{post.text}}
```

4. Finally, we close all tags:

```
    </li>
  </ul>
</div>
```

> In a real-world Angular project, you would split this code into multiple components. For the sake of simplicity, we will keep everything in the main HTML file in this example.

That's it for the HTML code of this example.

Defining the module and controller

Next, we will need to define the module and controller in our `src/index.js` file:

1. Remove the `render()` and `stopRender()` functions and replace them with the following code:

```
const app = angular.module('blog', [])
```

This tells Angular to attach (render the app) to the `ng-app="blog"` container element.

2. Now, we will define our controller:

```
app.controller('posts', ($scope) => {
```

3. In our controller, we first pull out the `posts` from our state:

```
const { posts } = store.getState()
```

4. Then, we add the `posts` to the Angular scope:

```
$scope.posts = posts
})
```

In your browser, you should now see a result similar to the previous `render()` function:

Manually connecting Angular to Redux

Code example

The current state of the project can be found in the `chapter4_2.zip` attachment.

Unzip the file, run `npm install` and `npm start`, and then open `http://localhost:8080` in your browser.

Setting up ng-redux

Although manually connecting Angular to Redux works, it is much easier and cleaner to do so using `ng-redux`.

1. As always, we first have to use `npm` to install `ng-redux`:

```
npm install --save ng-redux
```

2. Import `ng-redux` at the top of the `src/index.js` file:

```
import ngRedux from 'ng-redux'
```

3. You can *remove* the following import statement because `ng-redux` provides a special function that will create the store for us:

```
import { createStore } from 'redux'
```

4. Also, *remove* the lines that create the store and subscribe to it:

```
let store = createStore(appReducer)
const unsubscribe = store.subscribe(() => {
  console.log('state changed:', store.getState())
})
```

5. Now that we have removed our store definition, we also need to *remove* all lines that dispatch actions to the store:

```
store.dispatch(createPost('dan', 'hello world'))
store.dispatch(createPost('des', 'second post'))
```

You might have noted that we are passing an empty array to the `angular.module()` function. This is where we can pass `ngRedux` to load it for our `blog` app.

6. In `src/index.js`, take a look at the following:

```
const app = angular.module('blog', [])
```

Replace it with the following:

```
const app = angular.module('blog', [ ngRedux ])
```

7. Next, we will need to configure `ng-redux`; add the following code right after the preceding line:

```
.config(($ngReduxProvider) => {
  $ngReduxProvider.createStoreWith(appReducer)
})
```

Instead of passing the `appReducer` function to `createStoreWith`, you can also pass an object of reducers. It will combine them similar to the `combineReducers` helper.

As the second argument to `createStoreWith`, you can pass an array of middleware for the Redux store.

Redefining the controller

Now we can use `ng-redux` in our controller.

1. Replace the whole controller code with the following:

   ```
   app.controller('posts', ($ngRedux, $scope) => {
   ```

   In addition to `$scope`, we now also have `$ngRedux` available in our controller. `ng-redux` provides a `connect` function with the following signature:
   `$ngRedux.connect(mapStateToTarget, mapDispatchToTarget)(target)`

   Similar to calling `store.subscribe()`, the `ng-redux` connect function returns an unsubscribe function.

2. First, we will create the `mapState` function:

   ```
   const mapState = (state) => {
     return { posts: state.posts }
   }
   ```

3. The second argument accepts a function or an object of action creators. In our example, we simply pass an object of action creators. The `target` will be `$scope`.

   > If you are using a `class` to define your controller, use `this` as a target and the `this.mapState` method instead of a `mapState` function.

4. Let's use the `connect` function to connect our controller to Redux:

   ```
   let unsubscribe = $ngRedux.connect(mapState, { createPost,
   editPost })($scope)
   ```

5. We will need to make sure that we unsubscribe when the controller gets destroyed:

   ```
   $scope.$on('$destroy', unsubscribe)
   ```

ng-redux also provides all of Redux's store methods, so we can dispatch actions as follows:

```
$ngRedux.dispatch(createPost('dan', 'hello world'))
$ngRedux.dispatch(createPost('des', 'second post'))
```

You should see the same result as before.

Dispatching actions from the user interface

Finally, we will focus on how to dispatch an action to the Redux store when the user does something.

Edit the `<li>` element, and add the `ng-click` attribute:

```
<li
  ng-repeat="post in posts"
  ng-click="editPost($index, post.text + '!')"
>
```

When a user clicks on a blog post, we use the `editPost` action creator to add an exclamation point at the end of the text. To edit the current blog post, we pass the `$index` value of the array (which, in our example, is the ID of the blog post).

The application state after clicking three times on the first post, and one time on the second post

We successfully reproduced the functionality of our `render()` function with Angular 1.

Code example

The current state of the project can be found in the `chapter4_3.zip` attachment.

Unzip the file, run `npm install` and `npm start`, and then open `http://localhost:8080` in your browser.

Redux with Angular 2+

Angular 2+ makes extensive use of TypeScript, a typed superset of JavaScript. We will use the Angular 2+ command-line tool—ng (@angular/cli)—to create a new project, then copy over the Redux elements we already implemented earlier in the second chapter (chapter2_4.zip). After setting up a basic Angular 2+ application and copying the Redux application, we will combine them using @angular-redux/store to connect Redux with Angular 2+.

Setting up Angular 2+

We are now going to set up an Angular 2+ project:

1. First of all, we need to install the Angular 2+ command-line tool—ng via npm:

   npm install -g @angular/cli

2. Then, we create a new project with ng:

   ng new chapter44

   The preceding command will create a new directory, set up TypeScript, and install all dependencies via npm.

3. You can now go to the directory (cd chapter44) and launch the server:

   ng serve --open

 The --open flag means that the ng tool will try to open a browser window automatically. Feel free to omit the flag and open http://localhost:4200 manually.

You should now see the following page:

A basic Angular 2+ app, generated by the ng tool

The tool automatically created an App component for us. Open
`src/app/app.component.ts`. You can see that `app.component.html` is referenced as the
template. Further down, we define a title for our component. Edit the `title` to:

```
title = 'Redux <3 Angular';
```

The `ng` tool also sets up webpack for us, which means that the page will be automatically
refreshed once you save the file:

The base for our Redux and Angular application

Setting up @angular-redux/store

Now that we have an Angular 2+ project set up, it's time to connect it to Redux:

1. We start by copying over the following files from the second chapter (`chapter2_4.zip`) and pasting them into the `src/app/` directory. Ensure that you change the file ending to `.ts`. TypeScript is compatible with ES6 syntax, so our code will work fine. Copy over the following files from `chapter2_4.zip`:

   - `actionTypes.js` → `src/app/actionTypes.ts`
   - `actions.js` → `src/app/actions.ts`
   - `reducers.js` → `src/app/reducers.ts`

2. Then, we install `redux` and `@angular-redux/store` via npm:

   npm install --save redux @angular-redux/store

   Since we are using TypeScript, we first need to define our app state as an interface.

3. Create a new `src/app/types.ts` file. We start by defining a `Post` type:

   ```
   export type Post = {
     user: string;
     text: string;
   };
   ```

4. Now, we can use this `Post` type to define our app state interface:

   ```
   export interface IAppState {
     filter?: string;
     posts?: Array<Post>;
   }
   ```

5. Next, we need to import the `NgReduxModule` and add it to our application module as an `import` statement. Open `src/app/app.module.ts` and add the following import statements at the top of the file:

   ```
   import { NgReduxModule, NgRedux } from '@angular-redux/store';
   import appReducer from './reducers';
   import { createPost } from './actions';
   import { IAppState } from './types';
   ```

6. In the `@NgModule` decorator, add the module to the `imports` array:

```
@NgModule({
  ...,
  imports: [
    ...,
    NgReduxModule
  ],
  ...
})
```

7. In the class, add a `constructor` that calls `configureStore`:

```
export class AppModule {
  constructor (ngRedux: NgRedux<IAppState>) {
    ngRedux.configureStore(appReducer, {})
  }
}
```

The signature for `configureStore` is as follows:

```
ngRedux.configureStore(rootReducer, initialState,
middleware, enhancers)
```

We have successfully connected our Angular component to Redux. We can now access ngRedux (and thus the Redux store) from the component and use the `@select` decorator to access store state.

8. Open `src/app/app.component.ts`. First, we import the `@select` decorator and NgRedux:

```
import { select, NgRedux } from '@angular-redux/store';
```

9. We also import `Observable`, as we will use this to keep up with changes to the `posts` array:

```
import { Observable } from 'rxjs/Rx';
```

10. Then, we need to import our `Post` type and `IAppState` interface:

```
import { Post, IAppState } from './types';
```

11. Finally, we import the `createPost` and `editPost` action creators:

```
import { createPost, editPost } from './actions';
```

12. Now, we can use the `@select` decorator in the `AppComponent` class:

```
export class AppComponent {
    title = 'Redux <3 Angular';
    @select() posts$: Observable<Array<Post>>;
```

13. Next, we define a `constructor`, to access `ngRedux` from the component. Angular will pass the ngRedux instance when our component gets created:

```
constructor (private ngRedux: NgRedux<IAppState>) {
```

14. Here, we dispatch our `createPost` actions so that we have some posts to display:

```
this.ngRedux.dispatch(createPost('dan', 'hello world'))
this.ngRedux.dispatch(createPost('des', 'second post'))
}
```

15. Finally, we define an `editPost` handler method, which will dispatch an `editPost` action:

```
editPost (id: number, text: string) {
    this.ngRedux.dispatch(editPost(id, text))
}
}
```

16. After connecting our component to Redux, we can make use of the `posts` variable and the `editPost` method in the template file. Edit `src/app/app.component.html`:

```
<h1>{{title}}</h1>
<ul>
  <li
    *ngFor="let post of posts$ | async; let i = index;"
    (click)="editPost(i, post.text + '!')"
  >
    <b>{{post.user}}:</b> {{post.text}}
  </li>
</ul>
```

The `(click)` handler is similar to the Angular 1 example. Since we are using Observables now, we need to add `| async` after accessing our `posts$` variable.

You should now see a result similar as in the Angular 1 example:

The initial state of our Redux and Angular 2+ app

Click on one of the posts to see that the exclamation point is getting added:

The state of our app after the first post has been clicked on three times, and the second post has been clicked on once

Code example

The current state of the project can be found in the chapter4_4.zip attachment.

Unzip the file, run npm install and npm start, and then open http://localhost:4200/ in your browser.

Summary

In this chapter, you learned how to use Redux together with Angular 1 and 2+. The latest version, Angular 4, is compatible with Angular 2.

In the next chapter, you will learn how to debug a Redux application.

5
Debugging a Redux Application

In the preceding chapter, we discussed how to combine Redux with Angular. Before that, we focused on how to combine Redux with React.

As you learned, in order to develop a full application, it is not enough to learn Redux, as Redux only deals with the application state. We need to use a separate library/framework to render the user interface and handle interaction with the user. User actions then dispatch actions through action creators, which get processed by reducers. Afterward, the new state is reflected in the user interface by passing it to React or Angular. React and Angular complete the cycle by allowing the user to interact with our Redux application.

Previously, we built a small blog application with React and Redux. In subsequent chapters, we will add more advanced functionalities to our blog application. Before we get to that, however, in this chapter, we will first look into debugging Redux applications.

Learning how to debug will not only help us solve issues and fix bugs during development, but will also help us get a deeper understanding of what is going on in the background. As a user, we only see everything that goes on in the user interface (which is covered by a library such as React, or a framework such as Angular). Redux DevTools (developer tools) allows us, as a developer, to see what is going on in the background, that is, the state processing part of our application (which is covered by Redux).

In this chapter, we will cover the following topics:

- Integrating Redux DevTools into our application
- Using the `persistState()` store enhancer to save application states
- Excluding Redux DevTools in the production environment
- Setting up hot reloading for React components and Redux reducers
- Using Redux DevTools to debug an application

Integrating Redux DevTools

There are two different variants of Redux DevTools:

- **Redux DevTools**: The official implementation of developer tools for Redux, implemented and maintained by Dan Abramov (the creator of Redux)
  `https://github.com/gaearon/redux-devtools`
- **Redux DevTools Extension**: A browser extension that implements the same developer tools for Redux
  `https://github.com/zalmoxisus/redux-devtools-extension`

The main difference is that the first variant is integrated into your application and you can decide where to place the developer tools. For example, you can overlay a sidebar over your application. The second variant is a browser extension for Chrome and Firefox, which shows the developer tools in separate windows.

Both variants are compatible and offer various monitors that can be used to debug your application. For example, there is a `LogMonitor` to inspect the state and do time traveling debugging (going back and forth through the state changes). This monitor can be wrapped in a `DockMonitor`, which can be moved across the screen. New monitors can be implemented, and there are many official and unofficial (community maintained) monitors out there.

In this book, we will cover setting up the official implementation of Redux DevTools. However, using Redux DevTools Extension is very similar and should be easy to do once you know how to set up the official Redux DevTools.

Let's go over the features of using Redux DevTools:

- Inspect every state and actions that changed the state
- Go back and forth in time by reverting/reapplying actions
- Cancel a certain action that happened at any time and recalculate the state, excluding that action
- When you change the reducer code, all *staged* actions will be re-evaluated
- When a reducer throws an error, you will see which action caused the error and what the error was
- With the `persistState()` store enhancer, you can persist debug sessions even across page reloads

Installing Redux DevTools

Now that we have covered what Redux DevTools are and why they are useful, let's try them out by integrating them in our existing React/Redux project:

1. We start by copying the example code from the end of *Chapter 3*, Combining Redux with React, `chapter3_8.zip`. This is already a full React/Redux project, a small blog application.

2. Then, we install `redux-devtools` using `npm`:

    ```
    npm install --save-dev redux-devtools
    ```

 Note that `redux-devtools` only contains the core for Redux DevTools, we do not have any monitors yet.

3. Next, we install the `LogMonitor` and `DockMonitor` using the following commands:

    ```
    npm install --save-dev redux-devtools-log-monitor
    npm install --save-dev redux-devtools-dock-monitor
    ```

 We use the `--save-dev` flag to ensure that `redux-devtools` related packages do not get installed in a production environment.

Creating a DevTools component

We create a new DevTools container component, which will contain all the monitors that we want to use:

1. Create a new `src/containers/DevTools.jsx` file.

2. We first import React and the `createDevTools` helper function from `redux-devtools`:

    ```
    import React from 'react'

    import { createDevTools } from 'redux-devtools'
    ```

3. Next, we have to import our monitors, in this case, the `LogMonitor` and `DockMonitor`:

```
import LogMonitor from 'redux-devtools-log-monitor'
import DockMonitor from 'redux-devtools-dock-monitor'
```

4. Now, we can use the `createDevTools` helper function to create a DevTools component:

```
const DevTools = createDevTools(
  <DockMonitor
    toggleVisibilityKey='ctrl-h'
    changePositionKey='ctrl-q'
    defaultIsVisible={true}
  >
      <LogMonitor theme='tomorrow' />
  </DockMonitor>
)
```

 All monitors offer options via properties. We will take a closer look at each monitor later in the chapter. Consult the repository for the monitor to find out more about the options at https://github.com/gaearon/redux-devtools-dock-monitor and https://github.com/gaearon/redux-devtools-log-monitor.

In this example, we create a `LogMonitor`, which will allow us to debug state changes. Additionally, we wrap it into a `DockMonitor`, which will allow us to hide the monitor and change the position of the dock. Wrapping monitors into a `DockMonitor` is optional; we could also directly use the `LogMonitor`.

5. Finally, we export the `DevTools` component:

```
export default DevTools
```

Connecting DevTools to Redux

After creating our `DevTools` component, we will still need to connect it to Redux. The `createDevTools()` helper returns a special static method—`DevTools.instrument()`—a store enhancer, which can be passed to the Redux store.

A store enhancer is a function that is passed as the last argument to `createStore()`. It can extend (enhance) the behavior of our Redux store. However, we need to be careful to use only `DevTools.instrument()` in a development environment—never load the DevTools store enhancer in production.

Using the DevTools.instrument() store enhancer

In the Redux world, you can extend the functionality of the store via **store enhancers**. A store enhancer is a function that gets passed as the last argument to `createStore`. Let's take a look at the function signature:

```
createStore(reducer, [initialState], [enhancer])
```

The `createStore` function takes the following arguments:

- `reducer`: Required; the first argument is the root reducer
- `initialState`: Optional; the second argument is the initial state to use for the Redux store
- `enhancer`: Optional; the third argument is the store enhancer

We will pass the `DevTools.instrument()` store enhancer as the third argument.

Let's load the store enhancer when creating our Redux store:

1. Edit `src/index.js` and import the DevTools component at the top of the file:

   ```
   import DevTools from './containers/DevTools.jsx'
   ```

2. Then, replace the line where we create the store:

   ```
   let store = createStore(appReducer, {}, DevTools.instrument())
   ```

Rendering DevTools

Finally, we will need to include the DevTools component somewhere in our application to make sure that React displays it:

1. We already have a file that contains our whole application, `src/components/App.jsx`. Edit this file and import the DevTools component at the beginning of the file:

   ```
   import DevTools from '../containers/DevTools.jsx'
   ```

2. Now we can use our DevTools component in the `App` component:

```
const App = ({ store }) =>
  <Provider store={store}>
    <div>
      <h1>React/Redux blog app</h1>
      <div><ConnectedFilterList /></div>
      <div><ConnectedPostList /></div>
      <DevTools />
    </div>
  </Provider>
```

 Note that we have to pass our Redux store to the DevTools component via the `store` property or using `<Provider>`. Otherwise, the component will not have access to the Redux store.

If you haven't already, install all dependencies via `npm install` and start the application:

npm start

Then, navigate to `http://localhost:8080/` in your browser, and you should see DevTools being rendered as a sidebar:

Our React/Redux blog application with Redux DevTools

As you can see, the `LogMonitor` on the right side shows us a history of all actions and state changes.

You can press the *Ctrl + H* key combination to hide, and the Ctrl + Q key combination to move the `DockMonitor`:

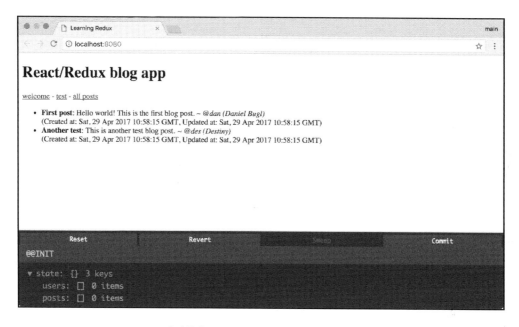

DockMonitor was moved to the bottom by pressing *Ctrl + Q*

Implementing the persistState() store enhancer

There is another store enhancer that Redux DevTools provides—the `persistState` store enhancer. It serializes the whole session, storing the session key in the URL, which means that when you copy the URL, all dispatched actions and the current state will be included.

This makes it very easy to reproduce bugs or provide an initial state to debug from. It is possible to automate debugging steps that way. For example, you can keep your test user logged in and on a certain page already. Persisting state and actions with the `persistState` store enhancer saves a lot of time, as you do not need to repeat these actions manually every time you change some of the code; Redux DevTools automatically recomputes the new state with the same actions.

Using multiple store enhancers

We are now going to learn how to compose store enhancers to be able to use multiple at once:

1. We first need to import the `persistState` function from the `redux-devtools` package. Add the import statement at the top of the `src/index.js` file:

   ```
   import { persistState } from 'redux-devtools'
   ```

2. Then, we pass the store enhancer to `createStore`. The signature of this function is as follows:

   ```
   createStore(reducer, [initialState], [enhancer])
   ```

   So, we need to pass `persistState` as the third argument. However, there is a problem—we have already passed the `DevTools.instrument()` store enhancer to it. Similar to the `reducer` argument, the store enhancer argument only accepts a single function.

   Thankfully, in functional programming, there is an easy way to combine multiple pure functions into one. We have already used `combineReducers` to combine an object of functions into a function that returns the whole state tree as an object. To compose the store enhancer functions, we will use the `compose` helper function from Redux.

   Functional composition, which is what the `compose` helper function implements, chains functions together from right to left. Assume the following function:

   ```
   const d = compose(a, b, c)
   ```

   Executing `d()`, in this case, would be the equivalent to executing `a(b(c()))`. We could compose functions manually using the spread operator:

   ```
   const d = (...args) => a(b(c(...args)))
   ```

3. We import the `compose` helper function from Redux. Edit the Redux import statement at the top of the `src/index.js` file:

   ```
   import { createStore, compose } from 'redux'
   ```

4. Now, we can use it to combine both store enhancers into one, as follows:

```
const enhancer = compose(
  DevTools.instrument(),
  persistState(getSessionKey())
)
```

Implementing a simple session key provider

The `persistState` store enhancer requires a session key as an argument. You can implement any functionality you want here. For the sake of simplicity, we will define a function to get it from the URL query parameters, like this:

```
http://localhost:8080/?debug=SESSION_KEY
```

Let's implement a session key provider that reads from URL query params:

1. We start by defining the function and regex matching for the query parameter:

```
function getSessionKey () {
  const matches =
  window.location.href.match(/[?&]debug=([^&#]+)\b/)
```

2. Then, we return the match if we got one, otherwise, we return `null`:

```
  return (matches && matches.length > 0)
    ? matches[1]
    : null
}
```

Do not re-dispatch on refresh

We still manually dispatch some actions in `src/index.js` to produce an initial state. When using `persistState()`, we need to make sure that we do not dispatch these actions again, as the state has already been initialised. Now we are going to ensure that we do not re-dispatch actions on refresh:

1. Edit `src/index.js`, find the line where the store gets created, and add the following code:

```
const initialState = store.getState()
```

2. Now, find the code where we dispatch the `createUser` actions and check whether we already have user objects in the store before creating them:

```
if (!initialState.users || initialState.users.length === 0) {
  // create users
  store.dispatch(createUser('dan', 'Daniel Bugl'))
  store.dispatch(createUser('des', 'Destiny'))
}
```

3. We will do the same for the `createPost` actions:

```
if (!initialState.posts || initialState.posts.length === 0) {
  // create posts
  store.dispatch(createPost('dan', {
    title: 'First post',
    text: 'Hello world! This is the first blog post.',
    category: 'welcome',
  }))
  store.dispatch(createPost('des', {
    title: 'Another test',
    text: 'This is another test blog post.',
    category: 'test',
  }))
}
```

Using the store enhancer

Now, we can use our previously created store enhancer:

1. Replace the following line:

```
let store = createStore(appReducer, {}, DevTools.instrument())
```

Replace the preceding line with this code:

```
let store = createStore(appReducer, {}, enhancer)
```

2. Finally, open `http://localhost:8080/?debug=filter_test` and do an action. For example, click on the **welcome** filter. Now, go to `http://localhost:8080/` to see the initial state again. When you go back to `http://localhost:8080/?debug=filter_test`, your debug session from earlier will be restored (the **welcome** filter should be active).

Excluding Redux DevTools in production

Now that we have Redux DevTools set up, when you:

- Change some of the reducer code, it should now automatically recompute the state
- Refresh in a debug session, it will persist the state across refreshes

However, we are now always loading Redux DevTools. In a production environment, that is not a good idea, as it will reduce performance immensely. We will now make sure that we exclude all DevTools-related code when building for production with webpack.

Injecting the NODE_ENV environment variable with webpack

Firstly, we will inject the NODE_ENV environment variable into our project, so that we know if we are in production or development mode:

1. Edit `webpack.config.js`; for that, first we will import `webpack` via `require()`. Put the following code at the top of the file:

   ```
   const webpack = require('webpack')
   ```

2. Then, we add a `plugins` property to the `module.exports` object:

   ```
   // ...
   plugins: [
   ```

3. We inject the NODE_ENV environment variable by setting `process.env.NODE_ENV` to the environment variable passed to webpack:

   ```
   new webpack.DefinePlugin({
     'process.env.NODE_ENV': JSON.stringify(process.env.NODE_ENV ||
   'development')
     })
   ],
   // ...
   ```

Now, we can use `process.env.NODE_ENV` anywhere in the project. The value will either be the NODE_ENV environment variable passed to webpack, or `'development'`.

Adding new build scripts for production and development

We will now add new `package.json` scripts for the production environment. To set environment variables, we will use the `cross-env` tool, which makes setting environment variables easier across various platforms. In production mode, we will serve the static `.html` and `.js` files through a simple web server. In this example, we will use the `serve` tool.

Let's get started adding build scripts:

1. Firstly, we install the required tools:

    ```
    npm install --save cross-env serve shx
    ```

     The **shx** tool lets us run Unix commands (like cp) on all platforms (Windows, Linux, Mac).

2. Then, edit `package.json` and replace the `scripts` section with the following code:

    ```
    "scripts": {
      "start": "npm run build:app && serve -p 8080 dist/",
      "build:app": "npm run build:webpack && npm run build:assets",
      "build:webpack": "cross-env NODE_ENV=production webpack",
      "build:assets": "shx cp index.html dist/",
      "start:dev": "webpack-dev-server"
    },
    ```

Note that, from now on, you have to execute `npm run start:dev` to start your application in development mode. `npm start` will build and run application in the production mode.

NPM defines some default scripts, such as `start` and `build`, which can be executed directly via `npm start` and `npm build`.

For all custom scripts, such as our `start:dev` script, you have to run `npm run <SCRIPT>`. In this case: `npm run start:dev`.

Separating the production store from the development store

Now all that's left to do is exclude DevTools from the production build. To achieve this, we will put our store creation logic into a separate file. Then, we will make two separate files: one for production, and one for the development environment.

Implementing the development store

We will start with the development store:

1. Create a `src/store/` directory, then a `src/store/index.dev.js` file. Remove all the store-specific logic from the `src/index.js` file and put it into this file. `src/store/index.dev.js` should look as follows:

```
import { createStore, compose } from 'redux'
import { persistState } from 'redux-devtools'

import appReducer from '../reducers'
import DevTools from '../containers/DevTools.jsx'

function getSessionKey () {
  const matches =
window.location.href.match(/[?&]debug=([^&#]+)\b/)
  return (matches && matches.length > 0)
    ? matches[1]
    : null
}

const enhancer = compose(
  DevTools.instrument(),
  persistState(getSessionKey())
)
```

2. Then, we will export a `configureStore(initialState)` function, in which we will create and return our store:

```
export default function configureStore (initialState) {
  return createStore(appReducer, initialState, enhancer)
}
```

Implementing the production store

The production store will be much simpler than the development store:

1. Create a `src/store/index.prod.js` file. First, we import everything we need:

   ```
   import { createStore } from 'redux'

   import appReducer from '../reducers'
   ```

2. Then, we define and export our `configureStore(initialState)` function:

   ```
   export default function configureStore (initialState) {
     return createStore(appReducer, initialState)
   }
   ```

Importing the correct store

Now, we create the `src/store/index.js` file, which will load the correct store depending on the value of the NODE_ENV environment variable we injected earlier:

```
if (process.env.NODE_ENV === 'production') {
  module.exports = require('./index.prod')
} else {
  module.exports = require('./index.dev')
}
```

Importing and using configureStore()

Finally, we need to import and use the `configureStore()` function in our main file:

1. Add the following code at the top of the `src/index.js` file:

   ```
   import configureStore from './store'
   ```

2. Then, add this code after the `import` statements:

   ```
   const store = configureStore()
   ```

Only loading the DevTools component in development mode

The last step is to not display the DevTools component when we are not running in development mode. Edit `src/components/App.jsx`, and consider the following line:

```
<DevTools />
```

Replace the preceding line with the following conditional expression, which only renders the component when the NODE_ENV environment variable is not set to `'production'`:

```
{ (process.env.NODE_ENV !== 'production') && <DevTools /> }
```

Running in production/development mode – example code

You can use the example code from the `chapter5_1.zip` attachment. Do not forget to install dependencies:

```
npm install
```

Then, we can build and run the app in production mode by executing the following command:

```
npm start
```

This command will build your application with webpack, then serve the static production files from a directory.

Alternatively, we can run our application in development mode by executing the following command:

```
npm run start:dev
```

The preceding command will run your application with `webpack-dev-server` and Redux DevTools.

Setting up hot reloading

Now that we have set up Redux DevTools, we will set up hot reloading. Hot reloading is a way to update code in a React/Redux project without having to refresh the page. At the moment, webpack automatically refreshes the page when some of the code changes (when we save a file). Hot reloading means that the code change will be applied when we save a file, **without a full browser refresh**.

Hot reloading React components

Let's set up hot reloading for our React components.

1. First of all, we install `react-hot-loader`, which implements hot reloading for React components:

   ```
   npm install --save react-hot-loader@next
   ```

2. Then, we edit our babel config; open the `.babelrc` file and add `react-hot-loader/babel` as a plugin. The file should look as follows:

   ```
   {
     "presets":[ "es2015", "react" ],
     "plugins": [
       "transform-object-rest-spread",
       "react-hot-loader/babel"
     ]
   }
   ```

Hot reloading other code with webpack

Now, we will configure webpack for hot reloading. We start by splitting our `webpack.config.js` into two files:

- `webpack.config.prod.js`: The production build, the content will mostly be copied over from our current config file
- `webpack.config.dev.js`: The development build, which enables hot reloading

We are now going to create those two files:

1. Rename the current `webpack.config.js` to `webpack.config.prod.js`, then edit `package.json`, specifying the new config file in the `build:webpack` script:

   ```
   "build:webpack": "cross-env NODE_ENV=production webpack --
   config webpack.config.prod.js",
   ```

2. While we are at it, let's also modify the `start:dev` script to use the `webpack.config.dev.js` config:

   ```
   "start:dev": "webpack-dev-server --config
   webpack.config.dev.js"
   ```

3. Create a new `webpack.config.dev.js` file that requires webpack and the production configuration:

   ```
   const webpack = require('webpack')
   const prodConfig = require('./webpack.config.prod')
   ```

4. Similar to using the spread operator, we can override some properties from the production configuration by combining the objects with `Object.assign`, as follows:

   ```
   module.exports = Object.assign(prodConfig, {
     // ...config...
   })
   ```

   This is similar to the following code (this won't work in the webpack config, as webpack does not support spread syntax):

   ```
   module.exports = {
     ...prodConfig,
     // ...config...
   }
   ```

5. We need to modify the `entry` property and load some other entry points before our main file. Write the following code instead of the `// ...config...` comment:

   ```
   entry: [
     'react-hot-loader/patch',
   ```

   Adding this entry point activates **Hot Module Replacement (HMR)** for React.

6. Next, we will bundle the client for `webpack-dev-server`, and connect it to our server:

```
'webpack-dev-server/client?http://localhost:8080',
```

7. Now, we will load the hot reloading extension from webpack:

```
'webpack/hot/only-dev-server',
```

The `only-` part means that webpack will only hot reload for successful updates.

8. Finally, we will load our main file:

```
    prodConfig.entry
],
```

9. We also need to specify a few other properties to enable hot reloading:

```
devtool: 'inline-source-map',
devServer: {
  hot: true,
  contentBase: prodConfig.output.path,
  publicPath: '/' // necessary for HMR to know where to load the
hot update chunks
},
```

10. Next, we need to include the `webpack.HotModuleReplacementPlugin()`. We will also include the `webpack.NamedModulesPlugin()` to print more readable module names in the browser console.

We cannot use spread syntax to extend the `plugins` array from the production configuration, so we will use `Array.concat`:

```
plugins: prodConfig.plugins.concat([
  new webpack.HotModuleReplacementPlugin(),
  new webpack.NamedModulesPlugin()
])
```

11. Finally, we need to enable hot reloading in our source code by adding the following code in the `src/index.js` file, right after the import statements:

```
if (module.hot) {
  module.hot.accept()
}
```

Hot reloading Redux reducers

Now that we have configured webpack and React to use hot reloading, there is just one thing missing—we need to integrate hot reloading into Redux. The idea is that, whenever the reducer code changes, the state will be recomputed. For this to be possible, Redux needs to know when the reducer code changes. We can give Redux a new reducer by calling `store.replaceReducer()`.

Edit `src/store/index.dev.js` and replace the `configureStore` function with the following code:

```
export default function configureStore (initialState) {
  const store = createStore(appReducer, initialState, enhancer)
  if (module.hot) {
    module.hot.accept('../reducers/index', () =>
      store.replaceReducer(require('../reducers/index').default)
    )
  }
  return store
}
```

 We need to use `require('./reducers/index')`**.default**, because `export default` actually exports an object with a `default` property.

Whenever webpack detects a change in the reducer code, we require the new reducer and use `store.replaceReducer()` to load the updated reducer code after webpack has hot reloaded it for us. Then, Redux DevTools re-computes the whole state with the new reducer code.

Testing out hot reloading – example code

The example code can be found in the `chapter5_2.zip` attachment.

Unpack the zip, change it into the directory, run `npm install` and `npm run start:dev`, and then open `http://localhost:8080` in your browser.

Your app should load with Redux DevTools open. In the console, you should see the following message:

```
[WDS] Hot Module Replacement enabled.
```

This means that hot reloading is active—let's try it out!

Keep the console open. Edit `src/components/App.jsx` and, for example, change the header. When you save the file, webpack will automatically rebuild the changed code and hot reload it without a refresh.

You should see the following output in the console:

```
[WDS] App updated. Recompiling...
[WDS] App hot update...
[HMR] Checking for updates on the server...
[HMR] Updated modules:
[HMR]   - ./src/components/App.jsx
[HMR]   - ./src/index.js
[HMR] App is up to date.
```

Whenever you save a file, **webpack-dev-server (WDS)** recompiles and triggers a hot update, then **hot module replacement (HMR)** replaces the code for the affected modules without a refresh:

Hot reloading in action, after removing "app" from the header text and saving the file

Using Redux DevTools

We have successfully set up Redux DevTools and webpack hot reloading. We can now run the app in production mode via `npm start` and in development mode via `npm run start:dev`:

- In **development mode** (`npm run start:dev`):
    - We can use Redux DevTools to debug our Redux application's state and actions.
    - Whenever we make a code change in a component, webpack will recompile and replace the code for that component (*hot reloading*). This happens automatically, without a refresh, whenever you save a file in the `src/` directory.
    - Hot reloading also works for reducers. In this case, the state is recomputed automatically, without a refresh.
    - We can store state in debug sessions by adding `?debug=SESSION_NAME` to the URL.
- In **production mode** (`npm start`):
    - We have the same app, without Redux DevTools and hot reloading.
    - We build the app first, then serve the static files with a simple web server. As a result, the application will load much faster.

We will now go over some Redux DevTools monitors and explain how to configure and use them to debug a Redux application.

DockMonitor

A container for other monitors, it provides a resizable and movable dock, which any other monitor can be wrapped in to make it dockable to screen edges.

It is possible to put more than one monitor inside a DockMonitor. There will be a single dock, and you will be able to switch between monitors by pressing the key combination specified via the `changeMonitorKey` property.

If the `persistState` store enhancer is used, the current size and position of the dock are persisted between sessions. For more information, refer to:

```
https://github.com/gaearon/redux-devtools-dock-monitor
```

Setup

You can install DockMonitor using `npm`:

```
npm install --save-dev redux-devtools-dock-monitor
```

Since `DockMonitor` only wraps other monitors and does not display anything on its own, we will use it to wrap a `LogMonitor`. Edit `src/containers/DevTools.jsx`, and import and use the monitor there:

```
import React from 'react'
import { createDevTools } from 'redux-devtools'

import DockMonitor from 'redux-devtools-dock-monitor'
import LogMonitor from 'redux-devtools-log-monitor'

export default createDevTools(
  <DockMonitor
    toggleVisibilityKey='ctrl-h'
    changePositionKey='ctrl-q'
  >
      <LogMonitor />
  </DockMonitor>
)
```

Properties

The `DockMonitor` always needs to have children, which can be any valid Redux DevTools monitor (or multiple monitors). In the example earlier, we passed a `<LogMonitor />` as a child.

The following properties can be passed to the `DockMonitor` component:

- `toggleVisibilityKey`: Required; the key or key combination that toggles the dock visibility, for example, *Ctrl + H*.
- `changePositionKey`: Required; the key or key combination that toggles the dock position, for example, *Ctrl + W*.
- `changeMonitorKey`: Required if there is more than one child; the key or key combination that switches the currently visible monitor, for example, *Ctrl + M*.
- `fluid`: Optional; the default is `true`; if set to `true`, the dock size is relative to the window size; fixed otherwise.
- `defaultSize`: Optional; default is `0.3`; a *float* if `fluid` is set to `true`, otherwise a width in pixels.

- `defaultPosition`: Optional; default is `'right'`; initial position of the dock on the screen—can be `'left'`, `'top'`, `'right'`, or `'bottom'`.
- `defaultIsVisible`: Optional; default is `true`; if set to `true`, the dock will initially be visible.

 Note that all key/key combinations must be recognizable by `parse-key` (`https://github.com/thlorenz/parse-key`).

LogMonitor

One of the most common monitors for Redux DevTools is the `LogMonitor`. It shows a history of states and actions, which you can explore with a tree view. You can also change the history by excluding/including actions. Refer to `https://github.com/gaearon/redux-devtools-log-monitor` for more information.

The LogMonitor looks as follows:

LogMonitor (in a DockMonitor) with an excluded action

Setup

As always, we first need to install the npm package:

```
npm install --save-dev redux-devtools-log-monitor
```

Like all monitors, you can use the LogMonitor in your DevTools component. Edit src/containers/DevTools.jsx, and import and use the monitor there:

```
import React from 'react'
import { createDevTools } from 'redux-devtools'

import DockMonitor from 'redux-devtools-dock-monitor'
import LogMonitor from 'redux-devtools-log-monitor'

export default createDevTools(
  <DockMonitor
    toggleVisibilityKey='ctrl-h'
    changePositionKey='ctrl-q'
  >
    <LogMonitor />
  </DockMonitor>
)
```

Usage

This monitor displays all actions in a log format. You can click on the action type to exclude a certain action. Redux DevTools will then recompute the state without this action (you can see this happening in the screenshot). We can make use of hot reloading by changing the reducer code and seeing what happens with/without the action by toggling it.

You can browse the action and state objects with a tree view to figure out which actions caused a certain state change. Set the markStateDiff property to true to visually highlight state changes.

There are four buttons at the top of the monitor (above the log):

- **Reset**: This resets the app to the initial state, without any actions dispatched.
- **Commit**: This removes all actions in the log and makes the current state the initial state. This is useful when you start debugging and want to remove the previous logs while keeping the state.
- **Revert**: After dispatching some actions, press this button to revert to the last committed state.
- **Sweep**: This removes all currently disabled actions from the log.

Properties

The following properties can be passed to the `LogMonitor` component:

- `theme`: Optional; default is `'nicinabox'`; can be a *string*, referring to one of the Redux DevTools Themes (`https://github.com/gaearon/redux-devtools-themes`) or an *object* with the same format.
- `select`: Optional; default is `state => state`; a *function* that selects a part of the state for DevTools to show, for example, `state => state.posts` to only debug posts.
- `preserveScrollTop`: Optional; default is `true`; if set to `true`, this will save the current scroll position and restore it on refresh. It only works when used together with the `persistState` store enhancer (which means you need to be in a `?debug=` session).
- `expandActionRoot`: Optional; default is `true`; if set to `true`, it expands the root tree views of all action objects.
- `expandStateRoot`: Optional; default is `true`; if set to `true`, it expands the root tree views of all state objects.
- `markStateDiff`: Optional; default is `false`; if set to `true`, it highlights state changes by comparing the new state with the previous state. Enabling this will significantly affect performance.
- `hideMainButtons`: Optional; default is `false`; if set to `true`, only shows logs without the buttons on top.

Inspector

The Inspector monitor shows a list of actions (similar to the `LogMonitor`) and a preview panel. You can filter the actions by entering text in a search field. It also shows the time between dispatched actions. In the preview, it is possible to *pin* a part of the state, which means the monitor will only show that subtree of the state object.

However, Inspector does not have any features to modify dispatched actions.

`https://github.com/alexkuz/redux-devtools-inspector`

Redux DevTools Inspector - filtering actions by POST, doing a diff, and pinning the posts part of the state

Setup

As always, we will need to install the npm package:

```
npm install --save-dev redux-devtools-inspector
```

Like all monitors, you can use the `Inspector` in your DevTools component. Edit `src/containers/DevTools.jsx`, and import and use the monitor there:

```
import React from 'react'
import { createDevTools } from 'redux-devtools'

import DockMonitor from 'redux-devtools-dock-monitor'
import Inspector from 'redux-devtools-inspector'

export default createDevTools(
  <DockMonitor
    toggleVisibilityKey='ctrl-h'
    changePositionKey='ctrl-q'
  >
    <Inspector />
  </DockMonitor>
)
```

Usage

You can select an action and toggle between showing the current state or a diff of the current and the previous state. This is useful to figure out how actions change the state. Instead of simply highlighting the change, this monitor shows the full diff of the previous and current state. If no action is selected, it will show the diff/state of the last action, which is the current state of the application.

If you have a very big application with many dispatched actions, the filter feature comes in very handy. You can filter the actions by entering a text in a search field.

It is also possible to pin a part of the state, which means the monitor will only inspect that part. You can do this by clicking on (pin) next to the key name in the tree view of the preview. For example, you can pin the posts key, and it will only show all posts in the preview window. Click on the **State** text (should now be a link) to show the full state again:

Redux DevTools Inspector showing the pinned posts part of the current state

The preview offers three different modes (click on the buttons to change the mode):

- **Action**: Shows the currently selected action object in a tree view (last action if nothing is selected)
- **Diff**: Shows a diff (difference) of the previous and current state, highlighting additions in green, and removal with red colors
- **State**: Shows the state after the currently selected action in a tree view (last action/current state if nothing is selected)

Properties

The following properties can be passed to the `Inspector` component:

- `theme`: Optional; default is `'inspector'`; can be a *string*, referring to one of the base16 themes (`https://github.com/chriskempson/base16`) or an *object* with the same format.
- `invertTheme`: Optional; default is `false`; inverts theme color luminance, turning a light theme into a dark theme, and vice versa.
- `supportImmutable`: Optional; default is `false`; improves rendering of `Immutable` in Diff mode—can affect performance if the state has big objects/arrays.
- `tabs`: Optional; overrides a list of tabs (check out `https://github.com/alexkuz/redux-devtools-inspector` for more information).
- `diffObjectHash`: Optional; callback for better array handling in diffs (check out `https://github.com/benjamine/jsondiffpatch/blob/master/docs/arrays.md` for more information).
- `diffPropertyFilter`: Optional; callback for ignoring particular properties in diff (check out `https://github.com/benjamine/jsondiffpatch/blob/master/docs/arrays.md` for more information).

SliderMonitor

The `SliderMonitor` shows a timeline of states and lets you step through time as if your application was in a video player.

```
https://github.com/calesce/redux-slider-monitor
```

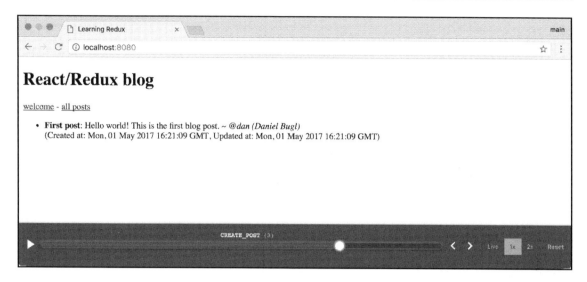

The Redux DevTools SliderMonitor in action!

Setup

As always, we first need to install the npm package:

```
npm install --save-dev redux-slider-monitor
```

Like all monitors, you can use the SliderMonitor in your DevTools component. Edit src/containers/DevTools.jsx, and import and use the monitor there:

```
import React from 'react'
import { createDevTools } from 'redux-devtools'

import DockMonitor from 'redux-devtools-dock-monitor'
import SliderMonitor from 'redux-slider-monitor'

export default createDevTools(
  <DockMonitor
    toggleVisibilityKey='ctrl-h'
    changePositionKey='ctrl-q'
    defaultPosition='bottom'
    defaultSize={0.15}
  >
      <SliderMonitor keyboardEnabled />
  </DockMonitor>
)
```

Usage

The `SliderMonitor` makes time traveling debugging as easy as playing a video. It records all actions that happen, and you can jump to any point in the history, then replay the rest of the actions by clicking on the play/pause button.

You can also step through actions by clicking on the arrow buttons. Furthermore, you can change the replay speed with the `1x` and `2x` buttons. **Live** will replay actions with the same time intervals as when the actions were originally dispatched.

Reset resets the application state to the initial state before any actions were dispatched.

If you pass the `keyboardEnabled` property, you can use the following keyboard shortcuts to control the `SliderMonitor`:

- *Ctrl + J*: Toggle play/pause button
- *Ctrl + [*: Step backward
- *Ctrl +]*: Step forward

Properties

The `SliderMonitor` component has only one property:

- `keyboardEnabled`: Optional; default is `false`; setting this property will enable the keyboard shortcuts for this monitor

ChartMonitor

This monitor shows the current state tree as a graphical tree structure. You can hover over parts of the state to show the contents.

```
https://github.com/romseguy/redux-devtools-chart-monitor
```

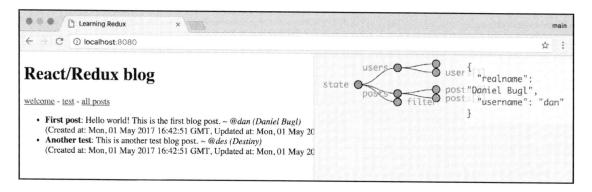

The ChartMonitor showing our application state, hovering over the first user.

Setup

As always, we first need to install the npm package:

```
npm install --save-dev redux-devtools-chart-monitor
```

Like all monitors, you can use the ChartMonitor in your DevTools component. Edit src/containers/DevTools.jsx, and import and use the monitor there:

```
import React from 'react'
import { createDevTools } from 'redux-devtools'

import DockMonitor from 'redux-devtools-dock-monitor'
import ChartMonitor from 'redux-devtools-chart-monitor'

export default createDevTools(
  <DockMonitor
    toggleVisibilityKey='ctrl-h'
    changePositionKey='ctrl-q'
  >
      <ChartMonitor />
  </DockMonitor>
)
```

Properties

The following properties can be passed to the `ChartMonitor` component:

- `theme`: Optional; default is `'nicinabox'`; can be a *string*, referring to one of the Redux DevTools Themes (`https://github.com/gaearon/redux-devtools-themes`) or an *object* with the same format.
- `invertTheme`: Optional; default is `false`; inverts theme color luminance, turning a light theme into a dark theme, and vice versa.
- `select`: Optional; default is `state => state`; a function that selects a part of the state for DevTools to show, for example, `state => state.posts` to only debug posts.
- `defaultIsVisible`: Optional; default is `true`; if set to `true`, the monitor will initially be visible.
- `transitionDuration`: Optional; default is `750`; time for a transition to a new state, in milliseconds.
- `heightBetweenNodesCoeff`: Optional; default is `1`.
- `widthBetweenNodesCoeff`: Optional; default is `1.3`.
- `onClickText`: Optional; callback function, called with a reference to the clicked node when clicking on the text next to a node.
- `style`: Optional; configure the style of the monitor. Refer to `https://github.com/romseguy/redux-devtools-chart-monitor#chartmonitor-props` for more information.
- `tooltipOptions`: Optional; configure the tooltip that appears when hovering over an element; refer to `https://github.com/romseguy/redux-devtools-chart-monitor#chartmonitor-props` for more information.

Other monitors

There are many other monitors out there, developed by the Redux community. Here is a short list of what else is out there:

- **DiffMonitor**: This is similar to the `LogMonitor`, but specifically shows changes in the store state. You can refer to `https://github.com/whetstone/redux-devtools-diff-monitor` for more information.

- **FilterableLogMonitor**: This is similar to the `LogMonitor`, but allows filtering actions with a search field. Plain text and regex search are supported. You can refer to `https://github.com/bvaughn/redux-devtools-filterable-log-monitor/` for more information.

- **FilterMonitor**: This is not a monitor, but a monitor container (like the `DockMonitor`). It allows you to filter out certain actions before they reach other monitors. You can refer to `https://github.com/zalmoxisus/redux-devtools-filter-actions` for more information.

- **Dispatcher**: This allows you to dispatch actions from Redux DevTools. You can refer to `https://github.com/YoruNoHikage/redux-devtools-dispatch` for more information.

- **MultipleMonitors**: They display multiple monitors at once, for example, a `LogMonitor` and a `Dispatcher`. You can refer to `https://github.com/YoruNoHikage/redux-devtools-multiple-monitors` for more information.

You can find a list of Redux DevTools monitors on the Ecosystem page of the official Redux documentation; `http://redux.js.org/docs/introduction/Ecosystem.html#devtools-monitors`.

Summary

In this chapter, we first discussed how to integrate and use Redux DevTools in an application. Then, we took a look at various Redux DevTools monitors, learning how to configure and use them in practice.

In the next chapter, we will cover how to interface with Application Program Interfaces (APIs) by pulling data from a server into our Redux application, as well as sending requests to an API from Redux action creators. As a result, our blog application will be connected to a backend (the code for the backend server is provided in the book). We will also cover handling asynchronous operations (such as API requests) with Redux in general.

6
Interfacing with APIs

In the preceding chapter, we covered how to debug a Redux application with Redux DevTools and the webpack **Hot Module Replacement (HMR)**. We started by integrating Redux DevTools and enabling hot reloading in our application. Afterward, we covered the configuration of various Redux DevTools monitors and how to use them to debug an application.

In this chapter, we will cover the following topics:

- Setting up the backend server for our application
- Extending our blog application by communicating with a backend server (through an API)
- Learning how to handle asynchronous operations with Redux
- Using our knowledge to make asynchronous API requests in our application

Setting up the backend

The backend will serve as a database and API for our blog. It will store user information and blog posts, and serve them to our application via a REST API.

The backend server code is provided by the book. You can find the template code for this chapter in `chapter6_1.zip` (which contains the server and our React/Redux application from the previous chapters).

Unpack the zip, change into the directory, and run `npm install` to install the dependencies. The backend server will also serve the frontend now. This means that it replaces the `serve` tool we used earlier. You can now:

- Use `npm start` to start the backend and frontend in production mode
- Use `npm run start:dev` to start the backend and frontend in development mode

Run `npm run start:dev` and open `http://localhost:8080/api/` in your browser to verify that the backend is available and working:

```
●  ●  ●    ▢ localhost:8080/api/         ×              main

←  →  C    ⓘ localhost:8080/api/                   ☆    ⋮

{
  "version": 1,
  "paths": {
    "GET /api": "Get API version and paths",
    "GET /api/posts": "Get all posts",
    "GET /api/posts/:id": "Get a single post",
    "POST /api/posts": "Create a new post",
    "POST /api/posts/:id": "Edit an existing post",
    "GET /api/users": "Get all users",
    "GET /api/users/:username": "Get a single user",
    "POST /api/users": "Create a new user",
    "POST /api/users/:username": "Edit an existing user"
  }
}
```

Accessing the backend API in the browser

Then, open `http://localhost:8080` in your browser to see the client.

Now that we have the backend server and frontend client running, we will focus on how to connect our Redux application to the backend.

The backend API

However, before we start connecting our application to the backend, let's take a look at the API it provides. This section serves as the documentation for the backend API.

GET /api

GET /api is the main entry point of the API. It returns the API version and all available paths. The resulting object has the following properties:

- **version**: The API version
- **paths**: All available paths of the API

Example output

The following is example output obtained by making an HTTP GET /api request to the backend server:

```
{
  "version": 1,
  "paths": {
    "GET /api": "Get API version and paths",
    "GET /api/posts": "Get all posts",
    "GET /api/posts/:id": "Get a single post",
    "POST /api/posts": "Create a new post",
    "POST /api/posts/:id": "Edit an existing post",
    "GET /api/users": "Get all users",
    "GET /api/users/:username": "Get a single user",
    "POST /api/users": "Create a new user",
    "POST /api/users/:username": "Edit an existing user"
  }
}
```

GET /api/posts

GET /api/posts returns all posts from the database as an array.

Each post object in the array has the following properties:

- id: Automatically generated ID of the post
- user: Username of the user that created the post
- title: Title of the post
- text: Content of the post
- category: Optional; category of the post
- created: Automatically set to the timestamp when the post is created
- updated: Automatically set to the timestamp when the post is last edited (or created if it was never edited)

Example output

The following is example output obtained by making an HTTP GET `/api/posts` request to the backend server:

```json
[
  {
    "id": "13b68488-5e02-46ea-84f3-612970175951",
    "user": "dan",
    "title": "First post",
    "text": "Hello world! This is the first blog post.",
    "category": "welcome",
    "created": 1494494448048,
    "updated": 1494494448048
  },
  {
    "id": "11b9b72f-342a-49ef-ba19-68b55fbe3e2c",
    "user": "des",
    "title": "Another test",
    "text": "This is another test blog post.",
    "category": "test",
    "created": 1494494448048,
    "updated": 1494494448048
  }
]
```

GET /api/posts/:id

GET `/api/posts/:id` returns a single post from the database. The ID of the post has to be passed in the URL; for example, `http://localhost:8080/api/posts/13b68488-5e02-46ea-84f3-6129701 75951`.

Example output

The following is example output obtained by making an HTTP GET `/api/posts/13b68488-5e02-46ea-84f3-612970175951` request to the backend server:

```json
{
  "id": "13b68488-5e02-46ea-84f3-612970175951",
  "user": "dan",
  "title": "First post",
  "text": "Hello world! This is the first blog post.",
  "category": "welcome",
  "created": 1494494448048,
```

```
    "updated": 1494494448048
}
```

POST /api/posts

POST /api/posts creates a new post. Data can be specified in the request body as application/json or URL-encoded (query string).

The following properties can be specified:

- user: Required; a username, referencing a user object, the username has to exist in the database
- title: Required; a title for the post
- text: Required; content for the post
- category: Optional; category of the post

Example request

URL: POST /api/posts

Body:

```
{
    "user": "dan",
    "title": "Another test",
    "text": "Hello API!"
}
```

Example output

The following is example output obtained by making the request described in the preceding *Example request* section:

```
{
    "user": "dan",
    "title": "Another test",
    "text": "Hello API!",
    "id": "e04ff961-9ddc-48cc-b8e6-5456d32bbc64",
    "created": 1494684775377,
    "updated": 1494684775377
}
```

POST /api/posts/:id

`POST /api/posts/:id` updates a post. The ID of the post has to be passed in the URL; for example, `http://localhost:8080/api/posts/13b68488-5e02-46ea-84f3-6129701 75951`.

The following properties can be updated:

- `title`: Title of the post
- `text`: Content of the post
- `category`: Category of the post

Example request

URL: `POST /api/posts/13b68488-5e02-46ea-84f3-612970175951`

Body:

```
{
  "category": "updated"
}
```

Example output

The following is example output obtained by making the request described in the preceding *Example request* section:

```
{
  "id": "13b68488-5e02-46ea-84f3-612970175951",
  "user": "dan",
  "title": "First post",
  "text": "Hello world! This is the first blog post.",
  "category": "updated",
  "created": 1494494448048,
  "updated": 1494685253795
}
```

GET /api/users

`GET /api/users` returns all users from the database as an array.

Each user object in the array has the following properties:

- username: The unique username of the user
- realname: The real/full name of the user

Example output

The following is example output obtained by making an HTTP GET /api/users request to the backend server:

```
[
  {
    "username": "dan",
    "realname": "Daniel Bugl"
  },
  {
    "username": "des",
    "realname": "Destiny"
  }
]
```

GET /api/users/:username

GET /api/users/:username returns a single user object from the database. The username has to be passed in the URL; for example, http://localhost:8080/api/users/dan.

Example output

The following is example output obtained by making an HTTP GET /api/users/dan request to the backend server:

```
{
  "username": "dan",
  "realname": "Daniel Bugl"
}
```

POST /api/users

POST /api/users creates a new user. Data can be specified in the request body as application/json or URL encoded (query string).

The following properties can be specified:

- `username`: Required; the unique username for the user
- `realname`: Required; the real/full name of the user

Example request

URL: `POST /api/users`

Body:

```
{
  "username": "des",
  "realname": "Destiny"
}
```

Example output

The following is example output obtained by making the request described in the preceding *Example request* section:

```
{
  "username": "des",
  "realname": "Destiny"
}
```

POST /api/users/:username

`POST /api/users/:username` updates a user. The username has to be passed in the URL; for example, `http://localhost:8080/api/users/dan`.

The following property can be updated:

- `realname`: The real/full name of the user

Example request

URL: `POST /api/users/dan`

Body:

```
{
  "realname": "Daniel B."
}
```

Example output

The following is example output obtained by making the request described in the preceding *Example request* section:

```
{
  "username": "dan",
  "realname": "Daniel B."
}
```

Handling asynchronous operations with Redux

In the preceding chapters, we were only dealing with synchronous operations—when a user interacts with the user interface (for example, clicks on a link), an action is immediately dispatched and the store is updated. However, we haven't yet covered how to dispatch actions that are asynchronous, such as requests to a server. Since the server does not respond immediately, we cannot block the whole application and wait for the result. That is the reason requests in JavaScript were designed in an asynchronous way.

Dispatching multiple actions from an action creator

For synchronous actions, we simply returned an action object from our action creator. A synchronous action creator to fetch posts could look like this:

```
export const fetchPosts = (posts) => {
  return {
    type: 'FETCH_POSTS',
    posts: posts
  }
}
```

Now, we will handle asynchronous operations by dispatching *multiple* actions from an action creator.

Defining action types

Let's think about which actions we need to dispatch while making a request to get all posts from the backend:

- FETCH_POSTS_REQUEST: We dispatch this action immediately when the request begins. The following action can be used to, for example, show a loading indicator while a request is in progress:
  ```
  { type: 'FETCH_POSTS_REQUEST' }
  ```

- FETCH_POSTS_SUCCESS: This action is dispatched once the server responds to our request, returning all posts. This action contains an array of posts, which we will store in our application state through a reducer:
  ```
  { type: 'FETCH_POSTS_SUCCESS', posts: [] }
  ```
- FETCH_POSTS_FAILURE: If the request fails or the server returns an error status code, we dispatch the following action and handle the error text in a separate reducer:
  ```
  { type: 'FETCH_POSTS_FAILURE', error: 'no permission to access posts' }
  ```

We will define these action types in our src/actionTypes.js file:

```js
// ...other action types...

// posts
export const FETCH_POSTS_REQUEST = 'FETCH_POSTS_REQUEST'
export const FETCH_POSTS_SUCCESS = 'FETCH_POSTS_SUCCESS'
export const FETCH_POSTS_FAILURE = 'FETCH_POSTS_FAILURE'
// ...other post related action types...

// ...other action types...
```

Creating an asynchronous action creator

Now that we know which actions we need to dispatch, let's try to implement an asynchronous action creator that dispatches them.

Instead of returning an action object, we will return a function that takes `dispatch` as an argument. Then, we can use the `dispatch` function to dispatch multiple actions. We can now define an *asynchronous* action creator function:

```
export const fetchPosts = () => {
  return function (dispatch) {
    // ...code...
  }
}
```

We can shorten the preceding code using arrow functions, as follows:

```
export const fetchPosts = () => (dispatch) => {
  // ...code...
}
```

Let's create the asynchronous `fetchPosts` action creator:

1. First, we adapt the import statement in `src/actions/posts.js` to import the new action types:

   ```
   import {
     FETCH_POSTS_REQUEST, FETCH_POSTS_SUCCESS, FETCH_POSTS_FAILURE,
     CREATE_POST, EDIT_POST, DELETE_POST
   } from '../actionTypes'
   ```

2. Then, we define a new *asynchronous* action creator:

   ```
   export const fetchPosts = () => (dispatch) => {
   ```

3. Let's dispatch an action that indicates that the request was started. Later on, this action will trigger the loading indicator mechanism:

   ```
   dispatch({ type: FETCH_POSTS_REQUEST })
   ```

4. Then, we make the API request. We will use the new `fetch` JavaScript API, which makes **Asynchronous JavaScript and XML (AJAX)** requests simple:

   ```
   return fetch('http://localhost:8080/api/posts')
   ```

 Note that at the time of writing this book, `fetch` is supported in *almost* all browsers. To ensure that it works on all browsers, you will need to use a polyfill such as `https://github.com/github/fetch`.

`fetch()` returns a **promise**. Promises are a new way to deal with asynchronous operations in JavaScript. They provide a `.then()` method, which will be triggered when the asynchronous operation is done. The `.then()` method returns another promise, which allows us to chain promises by subsequently calling `.then()`:

```
fetch(...)
  .then(... => ...)
  .then(... => ...)
  ...
  .catch(... => ...)
```

When chaining promises, the next handler function only gets triggered once the previous promise is resolved (which means the asynchronous operation was successfully completed). Promises also provide a `.catch()` method. If an error happens at any point, the handler function passed to `.catch()` gets triggered.

You might have heard about the JavaScript callback hell—when you're dealing with multiple asynchronous operations in a row, you end up with deeply nested callback functions. Promises provide a solution to callback hell—they are chainable via `.then()` and thus there is no need to nest callbacks.

5. When the `fetch()` promise gets resolved, it returns a response, which can be parsed as `.text()` or `.json()`. In our case, we are parsing JSON:

```
.then(response => response.json())
```

6. The preceding code will turn the raw JSON text into a JavaScript object (in our case, an array of posts), which we can dispatch now:

```
.then(json => {
  dispatch({ type: FETCH_POSTS_SUCCESS, result: json })
  return json
})
```

Returning the result in addition to dispatching it will allow us to chain action creators later.

7. If an error happens at any point, we will dispatch a failure action:

```
.catch(err =>
  dispatch({ type: FETCH_POSTS_FAILURE, error: err })
)
}
```

As you can see, we are now dispatching multiple actions from a single action creator. However, when we dispatch `fetchPosts()`, nothing will happen yet. This is because we are returning a function instead of an action object, and Redux does not know how to deal with *functions* being dispatched, yet. This is where middleware comes into play.

Handling asynchronous action creators via middleware

Middleware allows us to modify the behavior of the store. We will discuss middleware in `Chapter 12`, *Extending the Redux Store via Middleware*.

redux-thunk is a middleware that checks whether an object or a function is dispatched to the store:

- If an **object** is dispatched, forward it directly to the root reducer.
- If a **function** is dispatched, call it with the `dispatch` function as an argument. The dispatched function does not need to be pure; it can have side effects, such as asynchronous API calls and dispatching multiple actions by calling `dispatch`.

Setting up redux-thunk middleware

We are now going to set up the redux-thunk middleware:

1. As with all libraries, we first need to install `redux-thunk` with `npm`:

   ```
   npm install --save redux-thunk
   ```

2. Now, we need to import and load the middleware when creating our store. As we will use the same middleware for our development and production store, we create a new `src/store/middleware.js` file and import `redux-thunk` there:

   ```
   import thunkMiddleware from 'redux-thunk'
   ```

3. We also import the `applyMiddleware` helper function from Redux:

   ```
   import { applyMiddleware } from 'redux'
   ```

4. Then, we can create and export our middleware:

```
const middleware = applyMiddleware(
  thunkMiddleware
)

export default middleware
```

5. Now, all that's left to do is use the middleware while creating our store. Let's start with the production store. Edit `src/store/index.prod.js` and import our middleware at the top of the file:

```
import middleware from './middleware'
```

6. Then, replace the `createStore` line in `src/store/index.prod.js` with the following:

```
return createStore(appReducer, initialState, middleware)
```

7. Finally, we need to use our middleware in the development store. Edit `src/store/index.dev.js` and import our middleware at the top of the file:

```
import middleware from './middleware'
```

8. Then, we add our middleware to the enhancer. We are using `compose()` to be able to apply multiple enhancers (including our middleware). Make sure that you list our middleware *first*, before `DevTools.instrument()` and `persistState()`; edit `src/store/index.dev.js`:

```
const enhancer = compose(
  middleware,
  DevTools.instrument(),
  persistState(getSessionKey())
)
```

In this section, we discussed how to set up Redux to allow us to dispatch multiple actions from an action creator. This means that we can now handle asynchronous operations. In the next section, we will discuss how to make use of this knowledge to fetch data from an API and store it in our application state.

Pulling data from an API into the Redux store

Now that we have covered how asynchronous action creators work, it will be easy to pull data from an API into the Redux store.

Extracting boilerplate code

You may have noticed that we are writing a lot of boilerplate code to dispatch the three different actions. We can write a function to be able to reuse this behavior. We will pass an `action` object, which looks as follows, to this function:

```
{
  types: [ FETCH_POSTS_REQUEST, FETCH_POSTS_SUCCESS, FETCH_POSTS_FAILURE ],
  promise: fetch('http://localhost:8080/api/posts')
          .then(response => response.json())
}
```

We are now going to write a generic function that contains all the boilerplate code:

1. Create a `src/actions/utils.js` file and parse the `action` object:

   ```
   export const thunkCreator = (action) => {
     const { types, promise, ...rest } = action
     const [ REQUESTED, RESOLVED, REJECTED ] = types
   ```

2. Next, we will return a function that takes a `dispatch` argument, with similar code as before. We start by dispatching the REQUESTED action:

   ```
   return (dispatch) => {
      dispatch({ ...rest, type: REQUESTED })
   ```

3. Then, we will return the `promise` (in our case, a call to `fetch`). If the `promise` resolves successfully, we will dispatch the result. Otherwise, we will dispatch the error:

   ```
   return promise
     .then(result => {
   ```

4. Here, we also need to ensure that we catch API errors, which will look like this: `{ error: 'something bad happened!' }`. If an API error happens, we are going to `throw` an error, which will be caught by the handler function passed to `.catch()`:

```
if (result.error) throw new Error(result.error)
```

5. Otherwise, we dispatch the result:

```
        dispatch({ ...rest, type: RESOLVED, result })
        return result
    })
```

6. Finally, we use `.catch()` to catch all errors that happen in the promise. We also re-throw the error in case we want to chain promises later on:

```
        .catch(error => {
            dispatch({ ...rest, type: REJECTED, error })
            throw error
        })
    }
}
```

Pulling posts from the API

Now that we have a `thunkCreator` utility function, let's use it instead of manually handling the promise:

1. First, import the `thunkCreator` utility function at the top of the `src/actions/posts.js` file:

```
import { thunkCreator } from './utils'
```

2. Then, replace the `fetchPosts` action creator in `src/actions/posts.js` with the following code:

```
export const fetchPosts = () => thunkCreator({
    types: [ FETCH_POSTS_REQUEST, FETCH_POSTS_SUCCESS,
FETCH_POSTS_FAILURE ],
    promise: fetch('http://localhost:8080/api/posts')
              .then(response => response.json())
})
```

3. Edit the import statement in `src/index.js`, importing our new `fetchPosts` action creator:

```
import { createUser, fetchPosts } from './actions'
```

4. Now, we can replace the example actions we dispatched in our `src/index.js` file with the `fetchPosts()` action, find the following code:

```
if (!initialState.posts || initialState.posts.length === 0) {
  // create posts
  store.dispatch(createPost('dan', {
    title: 'First post',
    text: 'Hello world! This is the first blog post.',
    category: 'welcome',
  }))
  store.dispatch(createPost('des', {
    title: 'Another test',
    text: 'This is another test blog post.',
    category: 'test',
  }))
}
```

Now, replace it with our new action creator:

```
store.dispatch(fetchPosts())
```

5. Finally, we need to handle our new action type in a reducer. Edit `src/reducers/posts.js`; we start by importing the action type:

```
import {
  CREATE_POST, EDIT_POST, DELETE_POST, FETCH_POSTS_SUCCESS
} from '../actionTypes'
```

6. Then, we add a new `case` for this action type in the reducer function. This part will be really simple. After successfully fetching posts from the backend, we replace the whole `posts` part of the state with the result of the API:

```
export default function postsReducer (state = [], action) {
  switch (action.type) {
    case FETCH_POSTS_SUCCESS: {
      return action.result
    }

    // ...other cases...
  }
}
```

Run the application via `npm start` or `npm run start:dev`, and then visit `http://localhost:8080/` in a browser. You should see the same result as before, but this time we are fetching posts from the backend API:

Posts being fetched from the backend API

Pulling users from the API

After successfully pulling all posts from the API into our Redux store, we can almost display the main page. However, we still need to resolve the usernames from the posts to user objects.

We could pull users the same way we pulled posts; that is, by pulling all users into the Redux store. However, this approach will get problematic as our application scales. Imagine our blog having over 1000 users, but only a handful of them actually writing blog posts.

To solve this issue, we only pull the user objects we *need* to display the posts. After pulling all the posts, we iterate over the post objects and request the user objects for all usernames that appear in the posts.

Fetching a single user

We start by writing an action creator that fetches a single user object by username; we can use our `thunkCreator` utility function here:

1. We start by defining action types in the `src/actionTypes.js` file:

```
// ...other action types...

// users
export const FETCH_USER_REQUEST = 'FETCH_USER_REQUEST'
export const FETCH_USER_SUCCESS = 'FETCH_USER_SUCCESS'
export const FETCH_USER_FAILURE = 'FETCH_USER_FAILURE'
// ...other user related action types...

// ...other action types...
```

2. Then, we import the utility function at the top of the `src/actions/users.js` file:

```
import { thunkCreator } from './utils'
```

3. We also edit the other import statement to import the new action types:

```
import {
    FETCH_USER_REQUEST, FETCH_USER_SUCCESS, FETCH_USER_FAILURE,
    CREATE_USER
} from '../actionTypes'
```

4. Now, we create a new `fetchUser(username)` action creator. This action creator looks very similar to the `fetchPosts` action creator, except that this time, we will pass a *single* argument: the `username`:

```
export const fetchUser = (username) => thunkCreator({
```

5. Just like before, we pass our action types in an array via the `types` property:

```
    types: [ FETCH_USER_REQUEST, FETCH_USER_SUCCESS,
FETCH_USER_FAILURE ],
```

6. Next, we pass our `promise`. Again, we make an API request via `fetch`. However, this time we add the username to the URL:

```
    promise: fetch('http://localhost:8080/api/users/' + username)
             .then(response => response.json())
})
```

We can also use **template strings**, a feature of the new JavaScript syntax that makes dealing with strings easier. Let's take a look at the following line:

```
fetch('http://localhost:8080/api/users/' + username)
```

Replace it with a template string, like this:

```
fetch(`http://localhost:8080/api/users/${username}`)
```

Note how we are using ` instead of '. This is the way to define template strings. We can access variables or write any JavaScript expression in a template string by wrapping it with ${ }.

The preceding two code examples have the same effect; that is, they append the username to the URL. In this case, it makes almost no difference, but when dealing with more complicated string combinations, template strings come in really handy. Furthermore, it is possible to override the default behavior of putting together the string, by prefixing the template string with a function name. That way, you could, for example, escape all values before merging the string.

7. Import the new action type at the top of the `src/reducers/users.js` file:

```
import { CREATE_USER, FETCH_USER_SUCCESS } from '../actionTypes'
```

8. Lastly, we will handle the new action type in our `usersReducer` in the `src/reducers/users.js` file. Simply add a new `if` statement that adds a user on the `FETCH_USER_SUCCESS` action type:

```
if (type === FETCH_USER_SUCCESS) {
  return [ ...state, action.result ]
}
```

Fetching users when fetching posts

Now that we have an action creator to pull a single user from the API, we just need to modify our `fetchPosts` action creator to call the `fetchUser` action creator for every username:

1. We start by creating a new function, which will pull all usernames from an array of posts. Edit `src/actions/posts.js` and create a new function:

```
const getUsernamesFromPosts = (posts) =>
```

 Note that we do not `export` this function because it's not an action creator. It is simply a helper function for other action creators.

2. Here, we will make use of `.reduce()` to end up with an array of usernames (without duplicates):

```
posts.reduce((usernames, post) => {
  if (!usernames.includes(post.user)) {
    return [ ...usernames, post.user ]
  }
  return usernames
}, [])
```

 It is important not to put too much functionality in one function. If a function gets too big, you might want to consider splitting it up into multiple smaller functions, each dealing with just one thing. Then, combine them together in a function that accesses the other functions.

3. Next, we create a function that fetches user objects from an array of usernames. We will put this into `src/actions/users.js`:

```
export const fetchUsersByUsernames = (usernames) => (dispatch) =>
```

4. Here, we make use of `Promise.all()`, which returns a single promise that resolves when all promises passed to it in an array resolve:

```
Promise.all(usernames.map(username =>
  fetchUser(username)(dispatch)
))
```

 Note that we still need to pass `dispatch` down to the `fetchUser` action creator. Otherwise, our actions won't get dispatched to the Redux store.

5. We import the `fetchUsersByUsernames` function in `src/actions/posts.js`:

```
import { fetchUsersByUsernames } from './users'
```

6. After defining an action creator to fetch users for an array of usernames, we can create a *new* `fetchPostsAndUsers` action creator, which will make use of the `fetchPosts` action creator:

```
export const fetchPostsAndUsers = () => (dispatch) =>
    fetchPosts()(dispatch)
```

7. Then, we get the usernames from all posts:

```
.then(posts => getUsernamesFromPosts(posts))
```

This code can also be shortened as follows:

```
.then(getUsernamesFromPosts)
```

8. Finally, we fetch user objects for these usernames using the `fetchUsersByUsernames` action creator we implemented earlier:

```
.then(usernames => fetchUsersByUsernames(usernames)(dispatch))
```

9. It is important to *always* handle the error case when dealing with promises, by adding a `.catch()` handler function:

```
.catch(err =>
    console.error('could not fetch posts and users:',
err.message)
    )
```

We combined a few simple functions into much more complicated behavior (pulling only user objects for visible posts into the Redux store). Combined with promises, doing this allows us to write every declarative code. We don't even need to write comments for this function because the code itself already explains what it does:

```
export const fetchPostsAndUsers = () => (dispatch) =>
    fetchPosts()(dispatch)
        .then(getUsernamesFromPosts)
        .then(usernames =>
fetchUsersByUsernames(usernames)(dispatch))
        .catch(err =>
            console.error('could not fetch posts and users:',
err.message)
        )
```

Since we split up the functionality into multiple functions, we can reuse some of them in other features. For example, we could later have an action creator that fetches the posts with the most views only. Then, you could simply reuse the `getUsernamesFromPosts` and `fetchUsersByUsernames` functions there. Functional composition is a really neat pattern, and because Redux reducers and action creators are simply functions, we can easily compose the elements of Redux.

10. We import the new `fetchPostsAndUsers` action creator instead of `createUser` and `fetchPosts` in the `src/index.js` file:

    ```
    import { fetchPostsAndUsers } from './actions'
    ```

11. Finally, we replace the code in `src/index.js` that calls the `fetchPosts()` action creator, with the new `fetchPostsAndUsers()` action creator:

    ```
    store.dispatch(fetchPostsAndUsers())
    ```

12. Now, we can get rid of the code that manually dispatches the `createUser` actions. Remove the following code from `src/index.js`:

    ```
    if (!initialState.users || initialState.users.length === 0) {
      // create users
      store.dispatch(createUser('dan', 'Daniel Bugl'))
      store.dispatch(createUser('des', 'Destiny'))
    }
    ```

Open `http://localhost:8080` in your browser—the application should behave the exact same way as before, but now we are not creating the data in the client. Instead, we are using an API to pull blog posts and the necessary user objects.

You can see the API requests in the **Network** tab of the inspector in your browser, or in the logs of the backend (which should be printed to the console that you ran `npm run start:dev` in):

```
prod mode: serving client static assets
serving frontend on: http://localhost:8080/
serving backend on:  http://localhost:8080/api/
GET / 200 10.585 ms - 192
GET /main.js 200 2.858 ms - 1230744
GET /api/posts 200 5.393 ms - 487
GET /api/users/dan 200 3.146 ms - 52
GET /api/users/des 200 1.274 ms - 48
```

API requests sent to our backend while opening the client in production mode

Handling loading state

Until now, we only handled the _SUCCESS action types of our FETCH actions. Now, we will make use of the _REQUEST action types and show a loading indicator while requests are pending. We will accomplish this by storing pending requests in an object, as follows:

```
{
  FETCH_USER: 2,
  FETCH_POSTS: 1
}
```

The preceding state would mean that there are two FETCH_USER and one FETCH_POSTS request pending. If the object is empty or all values are 0, we are not waiting for anything. Otherwise, we will show the loading indicator.

Implementing the reducer

We start by creating a new reducer:

1. Create a `src/reducers/loading.js` file and define the reducer function:

   ```
   export default function loadingReducer (state = {}, action) {
   ```

2. We will make use of the fact that our action types for requests are standardized. For every action that ends with _REQUEST, we will increase the counter accordingly:

   ```
   if (action.type.endsWith('_REQUEST')) {
   ```

3. Next, we get the request name by removing the _REQUEST suffix from the action type:

   ```
   const requestName = action.type.replace('_REQUEST', '')
   ```

4. Then, we increase the counter and return the new state:

   ```
   const counter = state[requestName] || 0
   return { ...state, [requestName]: counter + 1 }
   }
   ```

5. Next, we handle the _SUCCESS and _FAILURE action types, and decrease the counter accordingly:

```
if (action.type.endsWith('_SUCCESS') ||
action.type.endsWith('_FAILURE')) {
    const requestName = action.type.replace('_SUCCESS',
'').replace('_FAILURE', '')
    const counter = state[requestName] || 0
    return { ...state, [requestName]: counter - 1 }
}
```

6. Finally, we return the current state for all other action types:

```
return state
}
```

7. We still need to include the new reducer in our root reducer. Edit src/reducers/index.js and import the loadingReducer:

```
import loadingReducer from './loading'
```

8. Finally, we include the reducer in the object we are passing to combineReducers:

```
const appReducer = combineReducers({
  users: usersReducer,
  posts: postsReducer,
  filter: filterReducer,
  loading: loadingReducer,
})
```

Implementing the component

The next step is implementing the React component, which will display the loading indicator:

1. Create a new component by creating the src/components/Loading.jsx file, with the following contents:

```
import React from 'react'

const Loading = ({ isLoading }) =>
    isLoading && <span>Loading...</span>

export default Loading
```

2. Next, we will create a container component, which connects the loading component to Redux. Create a new `src/containers/ConnectedLoading.jsx` file. We start by importing the `connect` helper function and the loading component:

```
import { connect } from 'react-redux'

import Loading from '../components/Loading.jsx'
```

3. Now, we need to define the `mapStateToProps` function, in which we determine whether we should display the loading indicator or not. To loop through the object of all pending requests, we will use `.reduce()` on the keys of the object:

```
const mapStateToProps = (state, props) => {
  const { loading } = state
  const isLoading = Object.keys(loading).reduce((result,
requestName) => {
```

4. If at least one request turns out to be pending, we are still loading, so we can skip checking the rest of the object:

```
    if (result === true) return true
```

5. Then, we check whether any of the keys in the loading object have a value greater than zero; if yes, we return `true`; otherwise, `false`:

```
    if (loading[requestName] > 0) return true
    return false
  }, false)
```

6. Now, we can return the `isLoading` property:

```
  return { isLoading }
}
```

7. Finally, we call `connect()` and export the resulting container component:

```
const ConnectedLoading = connect(mapStateToProps)(Loading)

export default ConnectedLoading
```

Using the component

We have successfully implemented the loading indicator. Now, all that's left to do is use it in our App component so that it actually gets shown in the client:

1. Edit `src/components/App.jsx` and import the container component:

```
import ConnectedLoading from '../containers/ConnectedLoading.jsx'
```

2. Then, display it after the `FilterList`:

```
const App = ({ store }) =>
  <Provider store={store}>
    <div>
      <h1>React/Redux blog</h1>
      <div><ConnectedFilterList /></div>
      <div><ConnectedLoading /></div>
      ...other components...
    </div>
  </Provider>
```

Open the client in your browser, and you should see the loading indicator briefly pop up and then disappear once the posts and users are loaded. If it happens too quickly, you can use Redux DevTools to deactivate the _SUCCESS action and see the loading indicator in action:

The loading indicator in action

Handling error state

Now we are handling the _SUCCESS and _REQUEST action types. However, there is still one possible result: _FAILURE. When an error happens, we want to display it in the interface so that the user knows something went wrong.

We start by producing an error so that we can see what happens while we implement error handling. Edit `server/api/posts.js` and replace the first route (GET `/api/posts`) with the following code:

```
app.get('/api/posts', (req, res) => {
  throw new APIError('something went wrong!')
  res.send(db.getPosts())
})
```

Implementing the reducer

Now we are going to implement the error reducer, which is going to handle error-related actions:

1. Create a new `src/reducers/error.js` file. We will make use of our standardized action types again and handle all action types that end with _FAILURE:

    ```
    export default function errorReducer (state = {}, action) {
      if (action.type.endsWith('_FAILURE')) {
    ```

2. Then, we simply return the whole error object:

    ```
        return action.error
      }
    ```

3. Finally, we return the current state if no error has happened:

    ```
      return state
    }
    ```

4. Do not forget to import and include the reducer in the root reducer. Edit `src/reducers/index.js`:

    ```
    // ...other imports...
    import errorReducer from './error'

    const appReducer = combineReducers({
      // ...other reducers...
    ```

```
    error: errorReducer,
})
```

Implementing the component

Next, we need to create the component that will display the error object:

1. Create a new file `src/components/ErrorMessage.jsx` with the following contents:

```
import React from 'react'

const ErrorMessage = ({ message }) =>
  message
    ? <span style={{ color: 'red' }}>Error: {message}</span>
    : null

export default ErrorMessage
```

2. Then, we will create the container component. Create a new file—`src/containers/ConnectedErrorMessage.jsx`. The code here is pretty straightforward:

```
import { connect } from 'react-redux'

import ErrorMessage from '../components/ErrorMessage.jsx'

const mapStateToProps = (state, props) => {
  return {
    message: state.error && state.error.message
  }
}

const ConnectedErrorMessage =
connect(mapStateToProps)(ErrorMessage)

export default ConnectedErrorMessage
```

Using the component

Finally, we need to display the `ConnectedErrorMessage` container component in our App component:

1. Edit `src/components/App.jsx` and import the container component:

```
import ConnectedErrorMessage from
'../containers/ConnectedErrorMessage.jsx'
```

2. Then, display the component after the loading indicator:

```
const App = ({ store }) =>
  <Provider store={store}>
    <div>
      <h1>React/Redux blog</h1>
      <div><ConnectedFilterList /></div>
      <div><ConnectedLoading /></div>
      <div><ConnectedErrorMessage /></div>
      ...other components...
    </div>
  </Provider>
```

Restart the backend server (it does not hot reload) by running `npm start` or `npm run start:dev` again. You should now see the error message when you open the frontend client in your browser:

The error message we produced on the server is displayed in the client

Do not forget to remove the error in the server code. Edit `server/api/posts.js` and replace the first route (`GET /api/posts`) with the following code:

```
app.get('/api/posts', (req, res) =>
  res.send(db.getPosts())
)
```

Restart the backend server by running `npm start` or `npm run start:dev`, and everything should work fine again.

Example code

The current state of the project can be found in the `chapter6_2.zip` attachment.

Unpack the zip, change into the directory, run `npm install` and `npm start`, and then open `http://localhost:8080` in your browser.

Sending notifications to an API via Redux

In the preceding section, we focused on how to access an API and pull its data *into* the Redux store. In this section, we will focus on how to send data *from* our Redux application to an API.

Note that in this section, we will only cover the Redux implementation. Additional React components need to be created to implement these features. If you want to practice using React with Redux, feel free to implement these yourself; otherwise, you can use the template in `chapter6_3.zip`. Unpack the zip, change into the directory, and run `npm install` to install the dependencies. You will see that the template already works. However, all changes are only made on the client and not persisted to the backend server/database.

Using asynchronous action creators

The most common way to send data from a Redux application to an API is by dispatching an asynchronous action creator directly with the user input. We have already discussed how to dispatch asynchronous actions. Sending data from our application to an API works similar to the way we fetched posts and users.

Creating users via the API

We will replace our synchronous `createUser` action creator with an asynchronous action creator that sends a request to the API. Instead of returning the action object, we will use the `thunkCreator` utility function we created earlier. We are now going to define the `createUser` action creator:

1. We start by turning our `CREATE_USER` action type into three action types. Edit `src/actionTypes.js`; find the following line:

   ```
   export const CREATE_USER = 'CREATE_USER'
   ```

   Replace it with these three action types:

   ```
   export const CREATE_USER_REQUEST = 'CREATE_USER_REQUEST'
   export const CREATE_USER_SUCCESS = 'CREATE_USER_SUCCESS'
   export const CREATE_USER_FAILURE = 'CREATE_USER_FAILURE'
   ```

2. Then, we import the new action types in `src/actions/users.js`:

   ```
   import {
     FETCH_USER_REQUEST, FETCH_USER_SUCCESS, FETCH_USER_FAILURE,
     CREATE_USER_REQUEST, CREATE_USER_SUCCESS, CREATE_USER_FAILURE
   } from '../actionTypes'
   ```

3. Next, we will replace the code for the `createUser` action creator in `src/actions/users.js`; the function definition stays the same, but we will use `thunkCreator` now:

   ```
   export const createUser = (username, realname) => thunkCreator({
     types: [ CREATE_USER_REQUEST, CREATE_USER_SUCCESS,
   CREATE_USER_FAILURE ],
     promise: fetch('http://localhost:8080/api/users', {
   ```

4. This time we are passing the second argument to `fetch`—an object of options. Here, we define the `method` (POST), `headers` (application/json), and `body` of the request:

   ```
   method: 'POST',
   headers: {
     'Accept': 'application/json',
     'Content-Type': 'application/json'
   },
   ```

5. The body is sent as a raw string, so we need to manually turn it into a JSON string:

```
body: JSON.stringify({
```

6. Then, we pass the `username` and `realname` (which get passed as arguments to the action creator):

```
        username, realname
      })
    })
    .then(response => response.json())
  })
```

7. Finally, we update the action type in the `usersReducer` from `CREATE_USER` to `CREATE_USER_SUCCESS`; edit `src/reducers/users.js`:

```
import { CREATE_USER_SUCCESS, FETCH_USER_SUCCESS } from
'../actionTypes'

export default function usersReducer (state = [], action) {
  const { type } = action
  if (type === CREATE_USER_SUCCESS) {
    return [ ...state, action.result ]
  }

  return state
}
```

In the template code, the action creator is already connected to the component. If you are implementing the components on your own, you need to make sure that you create a container component that connects the action creator via `mapDispatchToProps` (as we learned in *Chapter 3, Combining Redux with React*).

The component does not care whether the action creator is synchronous or asynchronous. Action creators are simply functions that get called and passed to `dispatch()`. This makes it easy to replace and extend action creators later.

Open the client in your browser. You should now be able to select **Register** and create a new account:

State of the client after creating a new user

If the username is already taken, you will see an error message (via the ErrorMessage component we implemented earlier):

State of the client after creating a user with an already taken username

Creating posts via the API

Creating posts will work very similar to creating a user. We will replace our synchronous `createPost` action creator with an asynchronous action creator that sends a request to the API. Instead of returning the action object, we will use the `thunkCreator` utility function we created earlier:

1. We start by turning our `CREATE_POST` action type into three action types. Edit `src/actionTypes.js`, and find the following line:

   ```
   export const CREATE_POST = 'CREATE_POST'
   ```

   Replace it with these three action types:

   ```
   export const CREATE_POST_REQUEST = 'CREATE_POST_REQUEST'
   export const CREATE_POST_SUCCESS = 'CREATE_POST_SUCCESS'
   export const CREATE_POST_FAILURE = 'CREATE_POST_FAILURE'
   ```

2. Then, we import the new action types in `src/actions/posts.js`:

   ```
   import {
     FETCH_POSTS_REQUEST, FETCH_POSTS_SUCCESS, FETCH_POSTS_FAILURE,
     CREATE_POST_REQUEST, CREATE_POST_SUCCESS, CREATE_POST_FAILURE,
     EDIT_POST, DELETE_POST
   } from '../actionTypes'
   ```

3. Next, we will replace the code for the `createPost` action creator in `src/actions/posts.js`:

   ```
   const _createPost = (user, post) => thunkCreator({
     types: [ CREATE_POST_REQUEST, CREATE_POST_SUCCESS,
   CREATE_POST_FAILURE ],
     promise: fetch('http://localhost:8080/api/posts', {
       method: 'POST',
       headers: {
         'Accept': 'application/json',
         'Content-Type': 'application/json'
       },
       body: JSON.stringify({
         ...post, user
       })
     })
     .then(response => response.json())
   })
   ```

4. After creating a post, we will also need to fetch the user (in case it wasn't loaded yet). We will do this in a separate function:

```
export const createPost = (user, post) => (dispatch) =>
  _createPost(user, post)(dispatch)
    .then(result => fetchUser(result.user)(dispatch))
    .catch(err =>
      console.error('could not create post:', err.message)
    )
```

5. Finally, we update the action type in the postsReducer from CREATE_POST to CREATE_POST_SUCCESS\ and edit src/reducers/posts.js:

```
import {
 CREATE_POST_SUCCESS, EDIT_POST, DELETE_POST, FETCH_POSTS_SUCCESS
} from '../actionTypes'

export default function postsReducer (state = [], action) {
  switch (action.type) {
    // ...reducer code...
    case CREATE_POST_SUCCESS: {
      const { type, result } = action
      return [ ...state, result ]
    }
    // ...reducer code...
  }
}
```

In the template, the action creator is already connected to the component. If you are implementing the components on your own, you need to make sure that you create a container component that connects the action creator via mapDispatchToProps (as we discussed in Chapter 3, *Combining Redux with React*).

Open the client in your browser. You should now be able to select **New post** and create a new post:

State of the client after creating a new post

Since we have not implemented authentication yet, make sure that you enter a username that exists. Otherwise, an error will be shown (via the `ErrorMessage` component we created earlier):

State of the client after trying to create a post with an invalid username

Example code

The current state of the project can be found in the `chapter6_4.zip` attachment.

Unpack the zip, change into the directory, run `npm install` and `npm start`, then open `http://localhost:8080` in your browser.

Summary

In this chapter, we covered how to handle asynchronous operations with Redux. We then used this knowledge to pull blog posts and users from an API into the Redux store. Furthermore, we covered how to dispatch actions that change the state in the frontend/client *and* the backend/server (creating users and posts).

In the next chapter, we will discuss how to authenticate users and handle their sessions in the Redux store. This means that our blog application will have a way to log in and we won't need to manually enter the username when creating a post anymore.

7
User Authentication

In the preceding chapter, we discussed how to interface with an API to do the following through a backend server:

- Fetch posts
- Fetch users
- Create user accounts (registration)
- Create posts

We got one step closer to a fully functional blog application. However, there is still an essential feature missing: login and authentication of users.

After creating a user account, there should be a way to login. Only after being logged in should the user be able to access the **New post** form. In this chapter, we will remove the username field from the form and instead use authentication to automatically use the currently loggedin user.

In this chapter, we will cover the following topics:

- Learning what **JSON Web Tokens (JWT)** are and how they can be used
- Implementing token authentication via JWT in our application

JSON Web Tokens (JWT)

To authenticate users, we need to store something on the client that identifies the user. Often, this is implemented through a session ID, which is sent via the cookie header. JWT (pronounced **jot**) works similar—it is also a string that can be sent via a header (or through a URL or POST parameter). However, since JWT does not make use of cookies, it can be easily used across multiple domains.

JWT are JSON objects, which can be signed using a secret key pair (with the HMAC algorithm) or a public/private key pair using RSA. This signature ensures that the tokens do not get forged.

In addition to authentication, JWT also allows for information exchange. For example, we could store information on user roles (is the user an admin or not?) in the token. Since the tokens are signed, we can be sure that this information is correct. As a result, we do not need to keep querying the database to verify that a user is an admin.

JSON Web Token structure

JWT consist of three parts, which are Base64 encoded and separated by dots (.):

```
header.payload.signature
```

If you want to play around with JWT, head over to `https://jwt.io/` for a token debugger. You can use this tool to generate your own tokens or debug existing tokens:

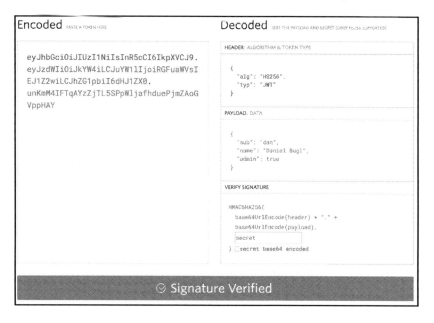

Generating/debugging a JSON Web Token via jwt.io

Header

The header typically consists of two parts:

- `typ`: The type of the token (`JWT`).
- `alg`: The hashing algorithm used, for example, HMAC SHA256 (`HS256`) or RSA.

 Note that official key names in JWT are only three characters long. This ensures that the token string stays compact.

Each part of the JWT is stored in JSON format and is Base64Url encoded. For example, consider the following header:

```
{ "alg": "HS256", "typ": "JWT" }
```

The preceding header becomes this, after encoding:

```
eyJhbGciOiJIUzI1NiIsInR5cCI6IkpXVCJ9
```

Payload

The payload is the main part of the token. It contains **claims** (statements about an entity, such as the user) and additional **metadata**.

The JWT standard defines the following three types of claims:

- **Reserved claims**: A set of predefined claims, which are not required but recommended. Here are some of the most common reserved claims (for a complete list, check out the standard `RFC 7519`):
  - `iss`: This indicates the issuer of the token. This can be set to the name of the service, domain, or URL, for example, `reduxblog`.
  - `sub`: This indicates the subject of the token. This can be set to, for example, a unique user ID. In our case, we will use the unique username, for example, `dan`.
  - `exp`: This indicates the expiration time of the token. After this timestamp, the token expires and will not be accepted anymore.
- **Public claims**: In addition to the reserved claims, any custom claims can be added, for example, `{ name: 'Daniel Bugl', admin: true }`.
  Some public claims are standardized. You can find a list of JWT public claim assignments at `https://www.iana.org/assignments/jwt/jwt.xhtml`.

- **Private claims**: Custom claims created to share information between parties that agree on using them.

We could create a payload that identifies an admin in our blog, as follows:

```
{
  "sub": "dan",
  "name": "Daniel Bugl",
  "admin": true
}
```

Just like the header, the payload also gets Base64Url encoded:

eyJzdWIiOiJkYW4iLCJuYW1lIjoiRGFuaWVsIEJ1Z2wiLCJhZG1pbiI6dHJ1ZX0

Signature

The last part of a JWT is the signature. It is created from the encoded header, the encoded payload, a secret, and the algorithm specified in the header.

The signature is used to verify that the JWT is valid. Since nobody except you (usually, the backend server) knows the secret, it is impossible to forge tokens. The signature also ensures that the claims were not modified.

Note that the secret should only be defined in the backend—you need to make sure that it *never* leaks. If it does, you have to set a new secret (which will invalidate all existing user sessions).

Using the HMAC SHA256 algorithm, the signature will be created as follows:

```
HMACSHA256(
  base64UrlEncode(header) + '.' + base64UrlEncode(payload),
  secret
)
```

With our secret set to `secret` (not a good secret; use a random string instead!), the signature would be as follows:

unKmM4IFTqAYzZjTL5SPpWljafhduePjmZAoGVppHAY

Token

Now that we have all three parts of the token, we can put them together to create a full JWT:

```
header.payload.secret
```

In our example, the token would look like this:

```
eyJhbGciOiJIUzI1NiIsInR5cCI6IkpXVCJ9.eyJzdWIiOiJkYW4iLCJuYW1lIjoiRGFuaWVsIE
J1Z2wiLCJhZG1pbiI6dHJ1ZX0.unKmM4IFTqAYzZjTL5SPpWljafhduePjmZAoGVppHAY
```

Using JSON Web Tokens

After learning what a JWT token looks like and how to generate them, we will cover how to use them. The most common method is to pass tokens via the `Authorization` header (of an HTTP request), as follows:

```
Authorization: Bearer <token>
```

With our example token, the header would look like this:

```
Authorization: Bearer
eyJhbGciOiJIUzI1NiIsInR5cCI6IkpXVCJ9.eyJzdWIiOiJkYW4iLCJuYW1lIjoiRGFuaWVsIE
J1Z2wiLCJhZG1pbiI6dHJ1ZX0.unKmM4IFTqAYzZjTL5SPpWljafhduePjmZAoGVppHAY
```

Just like session IDs being stored in cookies, JWT is a stateless authentication mechanism. The server does not need to handle sessions besides handing out and verifying tokens. In addition to that, JWTs are self contained, so there is no need to query the database multiple times for frequently needed information about the user. Furthermore, **Cross-Origin Resource Sharing** (**CORS**) will not be an issue, because JWT does not use cookies.

We will implement JWT authentication as follows (the parts that we need to handle are given in bold):

1. A user enters credentials in a form and clicks on the **Login** button.
2. **We send a request with the username and password via** POST /login.
3. The backend server returns a JWT token.
4. **We save the JWT token in the Redux store.**
5. **On the next request, we send the token via the** Authorization **header.**

6. The backend server verifies the JWT signature and gets user information from the JWT.

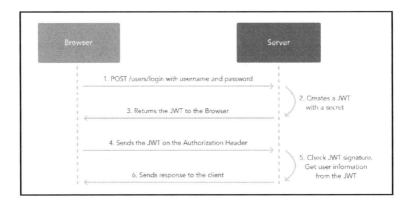

A diagram showing the JWT authentication process

Implementing token authentication

After learning why JWT make sense, how tokens look and work, and how to use JWT to authenticate users, we will manually implement token authentication in our Redux application.

The backend server code is provided by this book. You can find the template code for this chapter in `chapter7_1.zip` (this contains the server and our React/Redux application from the previous chapters).

Unpack the zip file, change into the directory, and run `npm install` to install the dependencies.

For the sake of simplicity, the JWT tokens that the server generates do not expire, and the secret is set to `secret` (so that we can use the debugger on `jwt.io` to generate valid tokens for testing purposes).

You can change the secret by setting the `JWT_SECRET` environment variable when starting the server.

Backend API

Before we start implementing authentication in our application, we will take a look at the changes in the backend API.

POST /api/login

The POST /api/login **API is new**. Log in as a user. This returns a JWT token. Data can be specified in the request body as application/json or URL encoded (query string).

The following properties can be specified:

- username: Required; the username of the user
- password: Required; the password of the user

Example request

URL: POST /api/login

Body:

```
{
    "username": "dan",
    "password": "password123"
}
```

Example output

The following is an example output obtained by making the request described in the preceding *Example request* section:

```
{
    "username": "dan",
    "realname": "Daniel Bugl",
    "token": "eyJhbGciOiJIUzI1NiIsInR5cCI6IkpXVCJ9.
            eyJzdWIiOiJkYW4iLCJuYW1lIjoiRGFuaWVsIEJ1Z2wifQ.
            AHRJsSR6Sii_Pfrc1_PgFO9y8l6LXVPuVJzeeWSgO14"
}
```

POST /api/users

This API changed. It now requires a password to create/register a new user. This creates a new user. Data can be specified in the request body as `application/json` or URL encoded (query string).

The following properties can be specified:

- `username`: Required; the unique username for the user
- `realname`: Required; the real/full name of the user
- `password`: Required; password for the user

Example request

URL: `POST /api/users`

Body:

```
{
    "username": "des",
    "realname": "Destiny",
    "password": "test123"
}
```

Example output

The following is example output obtained by making the request described in the preceding *Example request* section:

```
{
    "username": "des",
    "realname": "Destiny",
    "token": "eyJhbGciOiJIUzI1NiIsInR5cCI6IkpXVCJ9.
              eyJzdWIiOiJkZXMiLCJuYW1lIjoiRGVzdGlueSJ9.
              lSD8VGWRd3b26tkAX4aXYE5XgKmcmXAm2A7BAU2uvQ"
}
```

POST /api/posts

This API has changed. You no longer need to pass the username as the `user` property, because the username will be pulled from the token.

This creates a new post. Data can be specified in the request body as `application/json` or URL encoded (query string).

The following properties can be specified:

- `title`: Required; a title for the post
- `text`: Required; a content for the post
- `category`: Optional; a category of the post

Example request

URL: `POST /api/posts`

Body:

```
{
  "title": "Another test",
  "text": "Hello API!"
}
```

Example output

The following is example output obtained by making the request described in the preceding *Example request* section:

```
{
  "user": "dan",
  "title": "Another test",
  "text": "Hello API!",
  "id": "e04ff961-9ddc-48cc-b8e6-5456d32bbc64",
  "created": 1494684775377,
  "updated": 1494684775377
}
```

Secured routes

The following routes require the user to be authenticated, which means that we will need to send the `Authorization: Bearer <token>` header in order to make the request succeed:

- **POST /api/posts**: For creating a new post
- **POST /api/posts/:id**: For updating an existing post (you can only update your own posts)

- **POST /api/users/:username**: For updating a user (you can only update the currently loggedin user)

Storing the token in the Redux store

The first step to implementing authentication is the login functionality. When the user logs in via a form on the client, we will send a login action and store the result (user information and token) in our application state. Then, we can make use of this token in other parts of our application.

Defining the action types and action creator

As always, we start by defining action types and the action creator. The action creator will be used to create (and dispatch) the login request from the client:

1. Edit `src/actionTypes.js` and add the following lines:

```
// users
// ...other user related action types...
export const LOGIN_REQUEST = 'LOGIN_REQUEST'
export const LOGIN_SUCCESS = 'LOGIN_SUCCESS'
export const LOGIN_FAILURE = 'LOGIN_FAILURE'

// ...other action types...
```

2. Then, we import these action types; edit `src/actions/users.js`:

```
import {
  FETCH_USER_REQUEST, FETCH_USER_SUCCESS, FETCH_USER_FAILURE,
  CREATE_USER_REQUEST, CREATE_USER_SUCCESS, CREATE_USER_FAILURE,
  LOGIN_REQUEST, LOGIN_SUCCESS, LOGIN_FAILURE
} from '../actionTypes'
```

3. Next, we will create a new action creator. Edit `src/actions/users.js` and define a `login` function. We will use the `thunkCreator` helper function and pass our action types:

```
export const login = (username, password) => thunkCreator({
  types: [ LOGIN_REQUEST, LOGIN_SUCCESS, LOGIN_FAILURE ],
```

4. Now, we make the request to `POST /api/login`, with the username and password in the request body:

```
promise: fetch('http://localhost:8080/api/login', {
  method: 'POST',
  headers: {
    'Accept': 'application/json',
    'Content-Type': 'application/json'
  },
  body: JSON.stringify({
    username, password
  })
})
.then(response => response.json())
})
```

Creating the reducer

After defining our action types and action creator, we need to handle the action in a reducer:

1. We will introduce a new `session` substate. Create a new file, `src/reducers/session.js`. We start by importing the `LOGIN_SUCCESS` action type:

```
import { LOGIN_SUCCESS } from '../actionTypes'
```

2. Then, we define the reducer function. The default state will be `false` (no session):

```
export default function sessionReducer (state = false, action) {
```

3. Next, we handle the `LOGIN_SUCCESS` action type and store the result in our `session` substate by returning it from the reducer:

```
const { type, result } = action

if (type === LOGIN_SUCCESS) {
  return result
}

return state
}
```

4. Finally, we need to import and use our `sessionReducer` in the root reducer. Edit `src/reducers/index.js` and import it:

```
import sessionReducer from './session'
```

5. Then, pass it to the `combineReducers` helper function:

```
const appReducer = combineReducers({
  users: usersReducer,
  posts: postsReducer,
  filter: filterReducer,
  loading: loadingReducer,
  error: errorReducer,
  session: sessionReducer,
})
```

Dispatching login action in the component

The last step to implement login functionality is actually dispatching the action in the Login component:

1. First, we need to make the action creator available in the component. Edit `src/containers/ConnectedLogin.jsx` and import the action creator:

```
import { login } from '../actions'
```

2. Then, edit the `mapDispatchToProps` function:

```
const mapDispatchToProps = (dispatch, props) =>
  bindActionCreators({ login }, dispatch)
```

3. Finally, edit the `handleSubmit` method in the component. Edit `src/components/Login.jsx` and call the `login` function, then display a `Login successful!` message:

```
handleSubmit (evt) {
  evt.preventDefault()
  this.props.login(this.state.username, this.state.password)
  this.setState({ message: 'Login successful!' })
}
```

Testing out the login

Run the application via `npm start` or `npm run start:dev`, then visit `http://localhost:8080/` in a browser.

Try to log in with the following details:

- Username: `dan`
- Password: `password123`

You will see that logging in succeeds, and the user information (including the token) is stored in the `session` substate:

Successful login in our Redux application

If you enter the wrong username and/or password, the backend will return an error, which our error handling feature will show in the application:

Wrong password entered when logging in

Checking whether the user is logged in

Now that we have the session in our Redux store, we can use it to check whether the user is logged in. We will hide the **New post** link if the user *is not* logged in, and hide the **Registration** and **Login** components when the user is logged in. Furthermore, we will show some information about the currently loggedin user in the header.

Separating the header

First of all, we will put the header in a separate component. That way, we can connect the `Header` component and inject the `session` substate as a property.

Let's take a look at our `App` component. The parts in bold will be put into a separate `Header` component:

```
const App = ({ store }) =>
  <Provider store={store}>
    <div>
      <h1>React/Redux blog</h1>
      <div><ConnectedLoading /></div>
```

```
    <div><ConnectedErrorMessage /></div>
    <hr />
    <div><ConnectedRegistration /></div>
    <div><ConnectedLogin /></div>
    <br />
    <div><ConnectedCreatePost /></div>
    <hr />
    <div><ConnectedFilterList /></div>
    <div><ConnectedPostList /></div>
    { (process.env.NODE_ENV !== 'production') && <DevTools /> }
  </div>
</Provider>
```

We are now going to start separating out the Header component:

1. Create a new src/components/Header.jsx file, and move the imports and bold parts in the preceding code to this new component:

```
import React from 'react'

import ConnectedRegistration from
'../containers/ConnectedRegistration.jsx'
import ConnectedCreatePost from
'../containers/ConnectedCreatePost.jsx'
import ConnectedLogin from '../containers/ConnectedLogin.jsx'

const Header = ({ session }) =>
  <div>
    <div><ConnectedRegistration /></div>
    <div><ConnectedLogin /></div>
    <br />
    <div><ConnectedCreatePost /></div>
  </div>

export default Header
```

2. Next, we will create a container component for the header. Create a new src/containers/ConnectedHeader.jsx file with the following contents:

```
import { connect } from 'react-redux'
import { bindActionCreators } from 'redux'

import Header from '../components/Header.jsx'

const mapStateToProps = (state) => {
  return { session: state.session }
}
```

```
const ConnectedHeader = connect(mapStateToProps)(Header)

export default ConnectedHeader
```

3. **Edit** `src/components/App.jsx` **and import the** `ConnectedHeader` **component:**

```
import ConnectedHeader from '../containers/ConnectedHeader.jsx'
```

4. Then, put this component in the same place where we cut out the previous header:

```
<div><ConnectedHeader /></div>
```

The application should look exactly the same as before.

Hiding/showing components when the user is logged in

Now that we have separated the header in a `Header` component and injected the session as a property, we can make use of the session to check whether the user is logged in or not.

Edit `src/components/Header.jsx` and add checks for the `session` property:

```
const Header = ({ session }) =>
  <div>
    { !session && <div><ConnectedRegistration /></div> }
    { !session && <div><ConnectedLogin /></div> }
    { session && <div><ConnectedCreatePost /></div> }
  </div>
```

Now, you should only see the **Login** and **Register** links. Once you log in, you should only see the **New post** link.

Showing the currently loggedin user

The last thing we need to do is show the currently logged-in user in the header. We will reuse the `User` component for this feature:

1. **Edit** `src/components/Header.jsx` **and import the** `User` **component:**

```
import User from './User.jsx'
```

2. Then, pass the `session` substate to the `User` component:

```
const Header = ({ session }) =>
  <div>
    { !session && <div><ConnectedRegistration /></div> }
    { !session && <div><ConnectedLogin /></div> }
    { session &&
      <div>
        <b>Logged in as:</b>{' '}
        <User {...session} />
      </div>
    }
    { session && <div><ConnectedCreatePost /></div> }
  </div>
```

Try to log in again, and you will now see who you are logged in as:

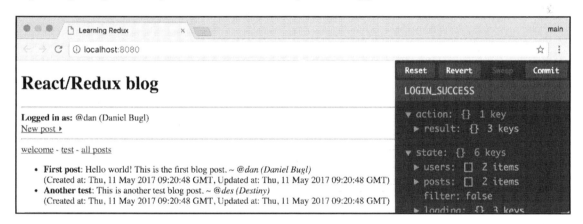

Our new header after logging in

Sending the token with certain requests

If you try to create a new post after logging in, you will get the following error:

```
Error: No authorization token was found
```

We are not sending the token with the `createPost` request yet. We are now going to do that:

1. Edit `src/actions/posts.js` and extend the `_createPost` and `createPost` functions by passing a `token` in addition to the `post`. First, we extend the `_createPost` function:

   ```
   const _createPost = (token, post) => thunkCreator({
   ```

   Then, we extend the `createPost` function:

   ```
   export const createPost = (token, post) => (dispatch) =>
     _createPost(token, post)(dispatch)
   ```

2. Next, we need to use the token in the `_createPost` function. As we have discussed before, we will need to pass an `Authorization: Bearer <token>` header:

   ```
   const _createPost = (token, post) => thunkCreator({
     types: [ CREATE_POST_REQUEST, CREATE_POST_SUCCESS,
   CREATE_POST_FAILURE ],
     promise: fetch('http://localhost:8080/api/posts', {
       method: 'POST',
       headers: {
         'Accept': 'application/json',
         'Content-Type': 'application/json',
         'Authorization': `Bearer ${token}`
       },
       body: JSON.stringify(post)
     })
     .then(response => response.json())
   })
   ```

3. Now, we need to inject the token via `connect`. Edit `src/containers/ConnectedCreatePost.jsx` and return the token from `mapStateToProps`:

   ```
   const mapStateToProps = (state, props) => {
     return {
       error: state.error && state.error.message,
       token: state.session && state.session.token
     }
   }
   ```

4. Finally, we will use the token in the `handleSubmit` method of the `CreatePost` component; edit `src/components/CreatePost.jsx`:

```
handleSubmit (evt) {
  evt.preventDefault()
  const { title, text, category } = this.state
  this.props.createPost(this.props.token, { title, text, category
})
    this.setState({ message: 'Successfully created post!' })
}
```

Now, you can log in and create a new post. The author will be automatically set as the currently loggedin user:

Creating a post via the (authenticated) API

Example code

The current state of the project can be found in the `chapter7_2.zip` attachment.

Unpack the zip file, change into the directory, run `npm install` and `npm start`, then open `http://localhost:8080` in your browser.

redux-auth

Since user authentication is such a common use case, there is a Redux library that provides a way to handle various kinds of authentication: **redux-auth**. Additionally, redux-auth provides components for various kinds of forms related to authentication. Furthermore, it supports OAuth2 for logging in with an external account (for example, loging in with Google, Facebook, and so on).

In this book, we will not cover implementing authentication with redux-auth, but it is documented well on the GitHub page of the library at `https://github.com/lynndylanhurley/redux-auth`.

Summary

In this chapter, we discussed what token authentication is and why using it instead of traditional cookie/session ID authentication makes sense. Next, we learned about an open standard for token authentication: JSON Web Token (JWT). We focused on how tokens are created and what makes them secure. Finally, we discussed how to use JWTs and implemented them in our Redux application.

In the next chapter, we will focus on how to write tests for and with Redux, as well as the pros and cons of testing in Redux. Tests can be written for all elements of Redux. Furthermore, we will discuss how to mock a Redux store for testing, which is useful for testing asynchronous actions.

8
Testing

In the preceding chapter, we discussed token authentication via **JSON Web Tokens (JWT)**. Now, users can log in to our application and their session is stored on the client side in a JWT.

In this chapter, we will focus on how to write tests for, and with, Redux. As the elements of Redux are simply JavaScript objects and functions, they will be easy to test. This chapter will cover the following topics:

- Setting up a testing engine
- Testing action creators and reducers
- Mocking a Redux store, which is useful for testing asynchronous actions

Setting up Jest

First, we need to set up a testing engine to be able to run tests. In this book, we will use Jest (https://facebook.github.io/jest/). Jest, like React, is developed by the Facebook open source team. Perform the following steps to set up Jest:

1. The first step is to install Jest via npm:

   ```
   npm install --save-dev jest
   ```

2. Since we want to use the new JavaScript syntax, we also need to install babel-jest and regenerator-runtime (which is required for babel-jest):

   ```
   npm install --save-dev babel-jest regenerator-runtime
   ```

If you use npm 3 or 4, or Yarn, you do not need to explicitly install `regenerator-runtime`.

3. Next, we create a `__tests__` directory in the project root. This is where we will put our test files.

4. Then, we create a `__tests__/example.test.js` file, with the following code:

```
test('example test', () =>
  expect(1 + 1).toBe(2)
)
```

5. Finally, we define a `test` script in our `package.json` file:

```
"scripts": {
  ...other scripts...,
  "test": "jest"
}
```

Now that we have our test engine set up, simply execute the following command to run all tests:

npm test

You should see the following output:

```
● ● ● 1. fish /Users/dan/Google Drive/Personal/LearningRedux/Code/chapter8_1 (fish)
dan@galaxy ~/G/P/L/C/chapter8_1> npm test

> chapter8_1@1.0.0 test /Users/dan/Google Drive/Personal/LearningRedux/Code/chapter8_1
> jest

 PASS  __tests__/example.test.js
  ✓ example test (5ms)

Test Suites: 1 passed, 1 total
Tests:       1 passed, 1 total
Snapshots:   0 total
Time:        0.959s, estimated 2s
Ran all test suites.
```

Output of the Jest test engine

You might notice that Jest summarized the test results. It only does this when all tests are succeeding. When a test fails, Jest will show much more detailed information, including the difference of the expected and received output. As a result, it is very easy to figure out why tests are failing:

Output of the Jest test engine with a failing test

Testing automatically on every file change

We can add another script, `test:watch`, which will run the tests every time we change and save a file.

Edit `package.json` and add a new `test:watch` script:

```
"scripts": {
  ...other scripts...,
  "test:watch": "npm test -- --watch"
}
```

Now, we can execute the following command:

```
npm run test:watch
```

This will run all tests and re-run them every time we save a file:

Output of the Jest test engine in the --watch mode

Checking code coverage

Jest also allows us to check the code coverage, which lets us know how much of our application source code is covered by tests (in percentages).

We are going to add another script, `test:cov`, which will run all tests and then print a table showing the code coverage.

Edit `package.json` and add a new `test:cov` script:

```
"scripts": {
  ...other scripts...,
  "test:cov": "npm test -- --coverage"
}
```

Now, we can execute the following command:

```
npm run test:cov
```

This command will run all tests and then display a table with the code coverage report:

Output of the Jest test engine in the `--coverage` mode

As you can see, the coverage report is empty right now. This is because we have not written any tests yet! At the end of this chapter, the coverage report will look like this:

Jest code coverage report at the end of this chapter

Example code

The current state of the project can be found in the `chapter8_1.zip` attachment.

Unpack the zip, change into the directory, and run `npm install` and `npm test` to run the tests.

Using Jest

Now that we have set up Jest, you are going to learn about its features and how to use it for testing in general. In the next section, you are going to learn how to test Redux with Jest.

Using test and describe

We have already learned that tests in Jest are written via the `test` function:

```
// example.test.js
test('example test', () =>
  expect(1 + 1).toBe(2)
)
```

Tests are grouped by putting them into separate files. However, we can also group tests *within* a file using the `describe` function:

```
// example.test.js
describe('number tests', () => {
  test('example test', () =>
    expect(1 + 1).toBe(2)
  )
})
```

If a test is failing, one of the first things you should do is check if the test still fails when it is the only test that runs. For this case, Jest provides a way to only run one test: `test.only`. All you need to do is temporarily rename the `test` function to `test.only`:

```
test.only('example test', () =>
  expect(1 + 1).toBe(2)
)
```

If the test does not fail anymore when it's run on its own, it probably means that another test is interfering with this one. This might mean that you need to clean the environment after each test. You will learn more about that later.

Matchers

Jest offers various ways to test values. Testing values is done using **matchers**. They have the following structure:

```
expect(OUTPUT).MATCHER(COMPARISON)
```

The whole preceding expression is called an **assertion**. The first part, expect (OUTPUT), returns an "expectation" object. This object offers various matchers (MATCHER), which can be called to compare the output value against a comparison value (COMPARISON). Jest tracks all failing matchers and outputs error messages for you.

In the example test from the previous section, we had the following code:

```
expect(1 + 1).toBe(2)
```

In this example, it is:

- OUTPUT = 1 + 1
- MATCHER = toBe
- COMPARISON = 2

.toBe or .not.toBe

The toBe matcher uses === to test for exact equality. This works well for primitive values such as numbers or strings.

If you want to check the value/contents of objects, you need to use toEqual instead, because two objects are never the exact same (even if they have the same contents). For example:

```
test('object example', () => {
  const data = { hello: 'world' }
  data['hi'] = 'world'
  expect(data).toEqual({ hello: 'world', hi: 'world' })
})
```

 Matchers should explain as closely as possible what you want your code to be doing. For example, after updating the username to dan, expect (username).toBe ('dan').

It is also possible to negate matchers by adding a not. prefix; for example, expect (1 + 1).not.toBe (0).

Truthiness

In JavaScript there are various kinds of truthy/falsy values. For example, an empty value could be represented as undefined, null, or false. Jest offers various matchers for these cases:

- toBeNull: This matches only null
- toBeUndefined: This matches only undefined
- toBeDefined: This is the opposite of toBeUndefined (= .not.toBeUndefined)
- toBeTruthy: This matches anything that would be considered true in an if statement
- toBeFalsy: This matches anything that would be considered false in an if statement

For example, null will pass the check for the following matchers:

```
test('null', () => {
  const n = null
  expect(n).toBeNull()
  expect(n).toBeDefined()
  expect(n).not.toBeUndefined()
  expect(n).not.toBeTruthy()
  expect(n).toBeFalsy()
}
```

On the other hand, 0 will pass for the following matchers:

```
test('zero', () => {
  const z = 0
  expect(z).not.toBeNull()
  expect(z).toBeDefined()
  expect(z).not.toBeUndefined()
  expect(z).not.toBeTruthy()
  expect(z).toBeFalsy()
})
```

Numbers

Jest also offers various matchers for comparing numbers:

- toBeGreaterThan: This expects the OUTPUT to be greater than the COMPARISON: OUTPUT > COMPARISON

- `toBeGreaterThanOrEqual`: This expects the OUTPUT to be greater than or equal to the COMPARISON:
  `OUTPUT >= COMPARISON`

- `toBeLessThan`: This expects the OUTPUT to be less than the COMPARISON:
  `OUTPUT < COMPARISON`

- `toBeLessThanOrEqual`: This expects the OUTPUT to be less than or equal to the COMPARISON:
  `OUTPUT <= COMPARISON`

Of course, you can also use `toBe` and `toEqual` for numbers (as we did in the first example).

For floating point numbers, there is a special matcher: `toBeCloseTo`. This matcher is useful when dealing with rounding errors in floating point calculations; for example:

```
test('floating point numbers', () => {
  const val = 0.1 + 0.2
  expect(value).not.toBe(0.3)
  expect(value).toBeCloseTo(0.3)
})
```

Strings

In addition to `toBe` and `toEqual`, you can match strings against regular expressions (regex) via `toMatch`. For example:

```
test('hello world contains world', () => {
  expect('hello world').toMatch(/world/)
})
```

Like any matcher, it can be negated with `.not`:

```
test('hello world does not contain hi', () => {
  expect('hello world').not.toMatch(/hi/)
})
```

Arrays

Jest provides a special matcher to check if an array contains an item: `toContain`, for example:

```
const arr = [1, 2, 3]

test('array contains 2', () => {
```

```
  expect(arr).toContain(2)
})
```

If you want to check if an array contains a certain object, you have to use `toContainEqual,`; for example:

```
const arr = [{ name: 'dan' }, { name: 'des' }]

test('array contains dan', () => {
  expect(arr).toContainEqual({ name: 'dan' })
})
```

Exceptions

It is not enough to test successful cases; sometimes you also need to test certain failing cases (for example, invalid username handled properly).

When you want to test if a function throws an error when it is called, you can use the `toThrow` matcher; for example:

```
function failingTest () {
  throw new Error('this is supposed to fail!')
}

test('failing test', () => {
  expect(failingTest).toThrow()
})
```

You can also match on the error type, which is useful if you have defined custom errors. For example, to only match an `APIError`:

```
expect(failingTest).toThrow(APIError)
```

Or, you can match on the error message; for example:

```
expect(failingTest).toThrow(/supposed to fail/)
```

All matchers

You can find a list of all matchers in the Jest API reference for `expect`: `https://facebook.github.io/jest/docs/expect.html`.

Testing asynchronous code

Sometimes, you have asynchronous code that you want to test. You can call matchers in callbacks, but then Jest needs to know when to stop the test. Depending on how you are dealing with asynchronous code (callbacks, promises, and so on), Jest offers various ways to handle it.

Callbacks

This is the oldest and most common way to deal with asynchronous code in JavaScript. You have a function that accepts a callback function as an argument; for example, `fetchPosts(callback)`. When the asynchronous request finishes, the `callback` function is executed:

```
function fetchPosts (callback) {
  // usually, we would fetch posts in an asynchronous request here
  // in this example, we simply execute the callback
  callback([ { title: 'test' }, { title: 'hello world' } ])
}
```

By default, Jest marks a test as complete when it reaches the end of the test function, which means that the following test will finish too early and not execute the matcher:

```
test('this finishes too early', () => {
  fetchPosts(posts =>
    expect(posts).toContain({ title: 'test' })
  )
})
```

For this case, Jest offers an alternative way to define tests. Instead of defining the test function with an empty argument, we can use a single argument called done. If you do this, Jest will wait until the done callback function is executed to finish the test:

```
test('fetchPosts returns array of posts', done => {
  fetchPosts(posts => {
    expect(posts).toContain({ title: 'test' })
    done()
  })
})
```

 If done() is never called, the test will time out and fail.

Promises

If you use promises instead of callbacks, like we did in our project, Jest provides an easier way to handle asynchronous tests. You can simply return a promise from the test, and Jest will wait for it to resolve. If the promise is rejected, the test will automatically fail. Let's assume our `fetchPosts` function returns a promise now. Then, our test would look as follows:

```
test('fetchPosts returns array of posts', () => {
```

We will use another matcher here, to ensure that a certain number of assertions are called during a test. This is useful when dealing with asynchronous code:

```
expect.assertions(1)
```

Then, we simply return our promise and check the result:

```
return fetchPosts()
  .then(posts => expect(posts).toContain({ title: 'test' }))
})
```

 Make sure that you `return` the promise; otherwise, your test will complete early (but still fail, because we expected one assertion).

If you want to expect a promise to fail, add a `.catch` handler:

```
test('logging in without username/password should fail', () => {
  expect.assertions(1)
  return login().catch(e =>
    expect(e).toMatch('could not login')
  )
})
```

.resolves/.rejects

Since Jest Version 20, special matchers for promises are provided. Instead of returning a promise and using `.then` to check the result, you can use `.resolves`, as follows:

```
test('fetchPosts returns array of posts', () => {
  expect.assertions(1)
  return expect(fetchPosts()).resolves.toContain({ title: 'test' })
})
```

Make sure to `return` the assertion; otherwise, the test will complete early (but still fail, because we expected one assertion).

The same also works for failing promises, via `.rejects`:

```
test('logging in without username/password should fail', () => {
  expect.assertions(1)
  return expect(login()).rejects.toMatch('could not login')
})
```

Setup and teardown

As mentioned earlier, there are cases where we need to clean up the environment after our tests run (teardown). In other cases, we might want to run some code before the tests run, like creating sample data (setup).

There are two ways to do setup and teardown in Jest:

- You can run code before/after *each* test, via `beforeEach` and `afterEach`
- Or you can run code before/after *all* tests, via `beforeAll` and `afterAll`

 `beforeEach`, `afterEach`, `beforeAll`, and `afterAll` also support asynchronous code, in the same way that tests support it. You can use the `done` argument, or return a promise.

Running every time before/after each test

Sometimes, you want to execute some code before each test runs, to setup the environment for the test. For this case, Jest provides a `beforeEach` function. After the test completes, you might want to clean up the environment, with the `afterEach` function.

For example, we might want to create some posts before each test runs and remove them again after the tests have finished:

```
let posts = []

beforeEach(() => {
  posts.push({ title: 'test' })
  posts.push({ title: 'hello world' })
```

```
})

afterEach(() => {
  posts = []
})

test('test post exists', () =>
  expect(posts).toContain({ title: 'test' })
)

test('hello world post exists', () =>
  expect(posts).toContain({ title: 'hello world' })
)
```

Running once before/after all tests

Sometimes you only need to carry out the setup once, before all your tests run. For this case, Jest provides `beforeAll` and `afterAll` functions. They work the same way as `beforeEach` and `afterEach`, but only run once for the whole test file:

```
let posts = []

beforeAll(() => {
  posts.push({ title: 'test' })
  posts.push({ title: 'hello world' })
})

test('test post exists', () =>
  expect(posts).toContain({ title: 'test' })
)

test('hello world post exists', () =>
  expect(posts).toContain({ title: 'hello world' })
)
```

Scoping

By default, the `before` and `after` functions apply to every test in a file. However, Jest also provides a way to group tests, via `describe`:

```
let posts = []

beforeAll(() => {
  posts.push({ title: 'test', user: 'dan' })
  posts.push({ title: 'hello world', user: 'dan' })
```

```
  })

  test('test post exists', () =>
    expect(posts).toContain({ title: 'test' })
  )

  describe('resolving users for posts', () => {
    let users = []

    beforeAll(() => {
      users.push({ username: 'dan', realname: 'Daniel Bugl' })
    })

    test('getting realname of author', () =>
      expect(getAuthorRealname(posts[0])).toMatch('Daniel Bugl')
    )
  })
```

In the preceding example, the second `beforeAll` function only gets called for the tests in the `describe` block.

Mocking

There are cases where your application would make requests to the outside world, such as fetching posts from an API. When running our tests, we still want to be able to see if the request would succeed, but not actually make the request. This is where mocking comes in handy.

There are two ways you can define mock functions with Jest:

- Creating a mock function by calling `jest.fn()`
- `require()` a mocked component via `jest.mock('moduleName')`

.mock property

All mock functions have a special `.mock` property, which stores data about how the function has been called:

```
const getUser = jest.fn()
getUser('dan')
getUser('des')
console.log(getUser.mock.calls)
```

The preceding example would print the following output:

```
[ ['dan'], ['des'] ]
```

The `.mock` property also keeps track of the value of `this` for each call:

```
const mockTest = jest.fn()

const a = new mockTest()
const b = {}
const bound = mockTest.bind(b)
bound()

console.log(mockTest.mock.instances)
```

The preceding example would print an array with the context `a` and the context `b`, like this:
`[ <a>, <b> ].`

Return values

Mock functions can also mock return values. For example, let's say we want to mock the result of a `getPosts` function:

```
const getPosts = jest.fn()

getPosts.mockReturnValueOnce([ { title: 'test' } ])

console.log(getPosts())
// output: [ { title: 'test' } ]
console.log(getPosts())
// output: undefined
```

If we want to return the same value every time, we need to use a mock implementation.

Implementations

Let's rewrite the previous example, with a mock implementation that *always* returns posts:

```
const getPosts = jest.fn(() => {
  return [ { title: 'test' } ]
})

console.log(getPosts())
// output: [ { title: 'test' } ]
console.log(getPosts())
```

```
// output: [ { title: 'test' } ]
```

Mock implementations also allow us to implement more complicated behavior, such as simulating a callback function:

```
const getPosts = jest.fn(cb => cb([ { title: 'test' } ]))
```

Or even a promise:

```
const getPosts = jest.fn(() =>
  Promise.resolve([ { title: 'test' } ])
)
```

It is also possible to define multiple implementations so that the function returns a separate result for different calls, via `.mockImplementationOnce`:

```
const getPosts = jest.fn()
  .mockImplementationOnce(() => Promise.resolve([]))
  .mockImplementationOnce(() => Promise.resolve([ { title: 'test' } ]))
```

When the mocked function is called, implementations will be called in the order of their declaration.

Once the mocked function runs out of implementations to run once, it will run the default implementation (if it is defined):

```
const getPosts = jest.fn(() => [])
  .mockImplementationOnce(() => [ { title: 'test' } ])
  .mockImplementationOnce(() => [ { title: 'hello world' } ])

console.log(getPosts(), getPosts(), getPosts(), getPosts())
```

The preceding example would output: `[ { title: 'test' } ], [ { title: 'hello world' } ], [], []`

Special matchers

Jest provides special matchers for mock functions:

- `expect(mockFunc).toBeCalled()`: This asserts that the mock function was called at least once
- `expect(mockFunc).toBeCalledWith(arg1, arg2)`: This asserts that the mock function was called at least once with the specified arguments
- `expect(mockFunc).lastCalledWith(arg1, arg2)`: This asserts that the last call to the mock function was passed the specified arguments

- `expect(mockFunc).toHaveBeenCalledTimes(number)`: This asserts that the mock function has been called exactly `number` times

Testing Redux

Because Redux reducers and action creators are just functions, and actions are simply objects, they are easy to test. Furthermore, many of those functions are pure, which means they have no side effects. Pure functions only use their arguments and constants to produce the output. This is why we only need to pass certain arguments and check the output to test the function. If there are side effects involved (which is the case for asynchronous action creators), we need to do some mocking.

Synchronous action creators

We start by writing tests for our synchronous action creators. Remember: *action creators are functions which return action objects*. To test them, we need to call the action creator and check if it returns the expected action object.

We are going to implement tests for the filter action creators, as they are the only synchronous ones in our application:

1. Create a new directory, which will contain all action creator related tests: `__tests__/actions/`.
2. Create a new file: `__tests__/actions/filter.test.js`.
3. Import the filter related action creators and action types:

   ```
   import { setFilter, clearFilter } from '../../src/actions'
   import { SET_FILTER, CLEAR_FILTER } from
   '../../src/actionTypes'
   ```

4. We start by writing the test for the `setFilter` action creator:

   ```
   test('setFilter should create an action to set the filter', ()
   => {
   ```

5. Then, we define an example category to be used as a filter and our expected action:

```
const category = 'test'
const expectedAction = {
  type: SET_FILTER,
  filter: category
}
```

6. Finally, we use `expect()` to ensure that the action creator behaves as expected:

```
expect(setFilter(category)).toEqual(expectedAction)
})
```

Let's see if our test succeeds, by running:

npm test

You should see the new test file being executed and the `setFilter` test passing:

Jest running two test files, including our new filter test

Now that we know how writing tests for synchronous action creators works, we can write a similar test for the `clearFilter` action creator:

```
test('clearFilter should create an action to clear the filter', () => {
  const expectedAction = {
    type: CLEAR_FILTER
  }
  expect(clearFilter()).toEqual(expectedAction)
})
```

Reducers

Just like synchronous action creators, reducers are pure functions. They accept the current state and an action object as arguments and return a new state. As a result, they are very easy to test—we simply compare the expected state after an action with the actual result of the reducer.

For simplicity, we are going to start with the `filterReducer`:

1. Create a new directory, which will contain all reducer-related tests: `__tests__/reducers/`.
2. Create a new file: `__tests__/reducers/filter.test.js`.
3. Import the filter-related action creators and the reducer:

    ```
    import { setFilter, clearFilter } from '../../src/actions'
    import filterReducer from '../../src/reducers/filter'
    ```

Note that we cannot import the `filterReducer` directly from the reducers folder (like we did with the action creators) because we are only exporting the root reducer from there.

Testing initial state

We start by writing a test for the initial state:

1. Edit `__tests__/reducers/filter.test.js` and define the test function:

    ```
    test('initial state should be false (no filter)', () => {
    ```

2. To initialize the reducer, we pass `undefined` as the state (first argument) and an empty object as the action (second argument):

    ```
    const state = filterReducer(undefined, {})
    ```

3. Now, we check the initial state of the reducer:

    ```
    expect(state).toBe(false)
    })
    ```

Initializing state with beforeEach()

Because we do not want to initialize the state manually in each test, we can use the
beforeEach() helper to reset the state before each test runs:

1. First, we store the state in a variable outside of all the functions so that we can
   access it across our test functions and beforeEach. Edit
   __tests__/reducers/filter.test.js and add the following code after the
   import statements:

   ```
   let state
   ```

2. Next, we use the beforeEach() helper to initialize the state the same way we
   did before:

   ```
   beforeEach(() => {
     state = filterReducer(undefined, {})
   })
   ```

3. Now, we can adjust the initial state test to look as follows:

   ```
   test('initial state should be false (no filter)', () => {
     expect(state).toBe(false)
   })
   ```

Testing the setFilter action

After setting up our initial state, we can dispatch any actions by passing them to the reducer
function:

1. We are going to write a test to ensure the setFilter action actually changes the
   filter. Edit __tests__/reducers/filter.test.js and add the following
   code:

   ```
   test('setFilter action should change filter state', () => {
   ```

2. We start by creating the action object with the action creator:

   ```
   const category = 'test'
   const action = setFilter(category)
   ```

3. Now, we call the reducer with the current `state` and our `action`, then save the new state:

```
state = filterReducer(state, action)
```

4. Finally, we test if the state was changed to the category we set the filter to:

```
    expect(state).toBe(category)
})
```

Testing the clearFilter action

Because the initial state is `false` (which is also the result of the `clearFilter` action), we first need to *dispatch* a `setFilter` action and ensure the state was changed. Then, we *dispatch* the `clearFilter` action and ensure the state is `false` again:

1. We start by setting a filter, just like in the previous test. Edit `__tests__/reducers/filter.test.js` and add the following code:

```
test('clearFilter action should reset filter state', () => {
  const category = 'test'
  state = filterReducer(state, setFilter(category))
  expect(state).toBe(category)
```

2. Then, we create the `clearFilter` action, pass it to the reducer function, and ensure the state is `false` again:

```
  const action = clearFilter()
  state = filterReducer(state, action)
  expect(state).toBe(false)
})
```

Reducers with async actions

To be able to test reducers with asynchronous actions, we need to create a store with the thunk middleware. Furthermore, we also need to mock HTTP requests via `nock`;

1. We start by installing nock via npm:

```
npm install --save-dev nock
```

2. Then, we import the required functions to create a store with the thunk middleware, as well as nock to mock HTTP requests. Create a new `__tests__/reducers/users.test.js` file with the following contents:

```
import { createStore, applyMiddleware } from 'redux'
import thunk from 'redux-thunk'
import nock from 'nock'
```

3. We also import the `fetchUser` action creator and the `usersReducer` (which we want to test):

```
import { fetchUser } from '../../src/actions'
import usersReducer from '../../src/reducers/users'
```

4. Instead of creating the initial state, this time we create a full Redux store from the `usersReducer`. We use the `beforeEach` helper to do this before each test:

```
const middlewares = [ thunk ]
let store

beforeEach(() => {
    store = createStore(usersReducer, applyMiddleware(thunk))
})
```

5. The nock library requires us to call `nock.cleanAll()` after each test, which cleans up the side effects from mocked HTTP requests:

```
afterEach(() => {
  nock.cleanAll()
})
```

6. We start by writing a test for the initial state. This time, we need to call `store.getState()` to get the state:

```
test('initial state should be empty array (no users)', () => {
    expect(store.getState()).toEqual([])
})
```

7. Now, we write a test for the `fetchUser` action:

```
test('fetchUser action should add user object to state', () =>
{
```

8. First, we create the user object, which we will use to mock the result of the API. We will also use this object to compare the results:

```
const username = 'dan'
const realname = 'Daniel Bugl'
const userObj = { username, realname }
```

9. The nock library lets us define APIs, which will be mocked when we call `fetch` in the action creator later. In this case, we want to mock our backend (`http://localhost:8080/`):

```
nock('http://localhost:8080/')
```

10. We define the `GET /api/users/dan` route and reply with the user object whenever our application makes a request to that route:

```
.get(`/api/users/${username}`)
.reply(200, userObj)
```

11. Because we will be dealing with asynchronous code and promises, we need to tell Jest to expect some assertions. In this test function, we are only going to have one assertion:

```
expect.assertions(1)
```

12. Now, all that's left to do is to create and dispatch the action:

```
const action = fetchUser(username)
return store.dispatch(action)
```

13. The `store.dispatch(action)` function returns a promise. We use `.then()` to check the state after the action has been processed. The state should now contain the user object:

```
.then(() =>
  expect(store.getState()).toContainEqual(userObj)
)
})
```

Asynchronous action creators

To be able to test asynchronous action creators, we need to mock the Redux store via `redux-mock-store`. The mock store will create an array of dispatched actions, which serves as an action log for our tests. Like in the previous section, we also mock the HTTP requests via `nock`:

1. As always, we start by installing the required library via `npm`:

   ```
   npm install --save-dev redux-mock-store
   ```

2. We import the mocking libraries and `redux-thunk` middleware and create a new `__tests__/actions/users.test.js` file with the following contents:

   ```
   import configureMockStore from 'redux-mock-store'
   import thunk from 'redux-thunk'
   import nock from 'nock'
   ```

3. Then, we import the `fetchUser` action creator and all action types into an `actionTypes` object:

   ```
   import { fetchUser } from '../../src/actions'
   import * as actionTypes from '../../src/actionTypes'
   ```

4. We create a function to mock a store and pass the `thunk` middleware to it:

   ```
   const middlewares = [ thunk ]
   const mockStore = configureMockStore(middlewares)
   let store
   ```

5. Now, we define the `beforeEach` helper. In this case, we create a new mock store with an initial state for every test:

   ```
   beforeEach(() => {
     store = mockStore({ users: [] })
   })
   ```

6. Like in the previous section, we have to call `nock.cleanAll()` after each test:

   ```
   afterEach(() => {
     nock.cleanAll()
   })
   ```

7. We are going to use a `describe` block to group all `fetchUser` related tests together:

```
describe('fetching user', () => {
```

Testing successful requests

The first test will be the success case—we are going to mock the API and then call the `fetchUser` action creator. Afterwards, we check if the FETCH_USER_REQUEST and FETCH_USER_SUCCESS actions were dispatched to our mock store:

1. We start by defining the successful test. Edit `__tests__/actions/users.test.js` and add the following code to the `describe('fetching user')` block:

```
test('dispatches FETCH_USER_SUCCESS when fetching succeeds',
() => {
```

2. As we did in the previous section, we start by defining the user object and mocking the API:

```
const username = 'dan'
const realname = 'Daniel Bugl'
const userObj = { username, realname }

nock('http://localhost:8080/')
  .get(`/api/users/${username}`)
  .reply(200, userObj)
```

3. Then we define the actions we expect to be dispatched:

```
const expectedActions = [
  { type: actionTypes.FETCH_USER_REQUEST },
  { type: actionTypes.FETCH_USER_SUCCESS, result: userObj }
]
```

4. Because we will be dealing with asynchronous code and promises, we need to tell Jest to expect some assertions. In this test function, we are only going to have one assertion:

```
expect.assertions(1)
```

5. Now all that's left to do is to create and dispatch the action. Then we ensure the expected actions were dispatched:

```
return store.dispatch(fetchUser(username))
  .then(() =>
    expect(store.getActions()).toEqual(expectedActions)
  )
})
```

Testing failing requests

We also have to test another case - when the request fails. This happens, for example, when the user does not exist:

1. Edit __tests__/actions/users.test.js and add the following code to the describe('fetching user') block:

```
test('dispatches FETCH_USER_FAILURE when fetching fails', ()
=> {
```

2. We have to mock the API again. However, this time we return a 404 status code with an error message:

```
const username = 'nonexistant'
const errorMsg = 'user not found'

nock('http://localhost:8080/')
  .get(`/api/users/${username}`)
  .reply(404, { error: errorMsg })
```

3. As before, we define our expected actions. This time, the second action should be FETCH_USER_FAILURE:

```
const expectedActions = [
  { type: actionTypes.FETCH_USER_REQUEST },
  { type: actionTypes.FETCH_USER_FAILURE, error: new
Error(errorMsg) }
]
```

4. We also have to tell Jest to expect one assertion:

```
expect.assertions(1)
```

5. Then we dispatch the action, as we did in the success case. However, this time we use `.catch` instead of `.then` because the promise is supposed to fail:

```
return store.dispatch(fetchUser(username))
  .catch(() =>
    expect(store.getActions()).toEqual(expectedActions)
  )
})
})
```

Example code

The current state of the project can be found in the `chapter8_2.zip` attachment.

Unpack the zip, change into the directory, and run `npm install` and `npm test` to run the tests.

Other tests

Now that we have implemented our tests, we can run them via `npm test`. They should all pass:

All of our implemented tests are passing!

We can also view the coverage report by running `npm run test:cov`. You will see that we have fully covered the filter-related actions and reducers. For the other features, we still need to implement some tests:

```
● ● ●    1. fish  /Users/dan/Google Drive/Personal/LearningRedux/Code/chapter8_2 (fish)
dan@galaxy ~/G/P/L/C/chapter8_2 [1]> npm run test:cov

> chapter8_2@1.0.0 test:cov /Users/dan/Google Drive/Personal/LearningRedux/Code/chapter8_2
> npm test -- --coverage


> chapter8_2@1.0.0 test /Users/dan/Google Drive/Personal/LearningRedux/Code/chapter8_2
> jest "--coverage"

 PASS  __tests__/actions/users.test.js
 PASS  __tests__/reducers/users.test.js
 PASS  __tests__/reducers/filter.test.js
 PASS  __tests__/actions/filter.test.js
 PASS  __tests__/example.test.js

Test Suites: 5 passed, 5 total
Tests:       11 passed, 11 total
Snapshots:   0 total
Time:        2.232s
Ran all test suites.
----------------|----------|----------|----------|----------|-------------------|
File            | % Stmts  | % Branch | % Funcs  | % Lines  |Uncovered Lines    |
----------------|----------|----------|----------|----------|-------------------|
All files       |   68.67  |   76.92  |   30.3   |   74.32  |                   |
 src            |   100    |   100    |   100    |   100    |                   |
  actionTypes.js|   100    |   100    |   100    |   100    |                   |
 src/actions    |   53.7   |   50     |   25.81  |   60     |                   |
  filter.js     |   100    |   100    |   100    |   100    |                   |
  index.js      |   100    |   100    |   100    |   100    |                   |
  posts.js      |   28     |   0      |   0      |   33.33  |... 50,52,56,64    |
  users.js      |   46.15  |   100    |   22.22  |   55.56  |   17,18,33,48     |
  utils.js      |   100    |   100    |   100    |   100    |                   |
 src/reducers   |   90     |   88.89  |   100    |   90     |                   |
  filter.js     |   100    |   100    |   100    |   100    |                   |
  users.js      |   83.33  |   80     |   100    |   83.33  |              11   |
----------------|----------|----------|----------|----------|-------------------|
```

Test coverage report after implementing our tests

 Note that the coverage report only shows files that are imported in any of the test cases. If you do not import anything in your tests, the coverage report will be empty (as we have seen at the beginning of this chapter).

Up to now, we have learned how to write the rest of the tests for this application (and various other applications). Implementing the rest of the tests will work similarly to the ones we have already covered and is left as an exercise for the reader.

Testing React components

In addition to testing our reducers and action creators, you might want to also test your components. Because React components usually only rely on their props and do not have a lot of internal states, they are also easy to test.

However, testing React components would push the boundaries of this Redux-focused book. For more information, check out https://facebook.github.io/jest/docs/tutorial-react.html.

Summary

In this chapter, you learned how to use Jest, a testing engine, to write tests for applications. Afterwards, you learned how to test all the elements of Redux. Make sure to write tests for all features so that whenever you make a change, you can be sure that you do not break anything else.

In the next chapter, you are going to learn how to implement multiple pages in a Redux application—through routing. We will start by manually implementing a simple router in Redux. Then, you are going to learn how to handle more complicated routing by using existing routing libraries.

9
Routing

In the previous chapter, you learned how to write tests with Jest for all the elements of our Redux application.

Until now, our application only consisted of a single page. Most growing applications, however, use multiple pages to ensure the user interface does not get too cluttered. For example, let's assume we want to add some information about the blog, like an *About* section. As this information is not always important to the user, it would not make sense to always display it on the main page. Hiding the information with our `HiddenContent` component would work, but be a bit clumsy if we wanted to add other kinds of content/pages later. To be able to use multiple pages, we are going to implement a router in our application. Furthermore, the router can provide separate pages for the post category filters.

In this chapter, you are going to learn how to implement multiple pages/screens via routing in our application:

- We are going to start by manually implementing basic routing with Redux
- Afterwards, we will extend our simple router by using a library, which can handle more advanced routing
- Finally, you are going to learn about deeply integrating the routing library and Redux

Creating a simple router

To get a feeling for how routing works with Redux (and React), we are going to start by manually implementing a simple router for our application. To be able to implement routing, we first need to split our application into separate pages: the main page and the about page.

Our simple router will work as follows:

- Our Redux store gets a new `route` sub-state, which contains the name of the current page as a string.
- A `Router` component decides which page to show based on the `route` sub-state.
- A `Navigation` component provides links that trigger a `navigate(pageName)` action creator, which changes the state to the new page.
- When the state changes, the `Router` component gets the new state as a property, re-renders and shows the new page.

You can use the code in `chapter8_2.zip` as a starting point for this section.

Defining the action types and action creator

We start by defining a `NAVIGATE` action and `navigate(pageName)` action creator. Dispatching this action will change the current page/route of our application. To define action types and action creators, perform the following steps:

1. Edit `src/actionTypes.js` and add the following lines:

```
// ...other action types...

// router
export const NAVIGATE = 'NAVIGATE'
```

2. Now we create a new `src/actions/router.js` file, and import the action type:

```
import { NAVIGATE } from '../actionTypes'
```

3. We implement the (very simple) action creator:

```
export const navigate = (pageName) => {
  return {
    type: NAVIGATE,
    page: pageName
  }
}
```

4. Finally, we export the action creator in the `src/actions/index.js` file:

```
export * from './users'
export * from './posts'
export * from './filter'
export * from './router'
```

Creating the reducer

The next step is handling the action in a reducer. To create a reducer, perform the following steps:

1. As mentioned before, we are going to add a `route` sub-state, which contains the current page. Create a new `src/reducers/route.js` file. We start by importing the action type:

```
import { NAVIGATE } from '../actionTypes'
```

2. Next, we define our reducer function. The default state will be the main page:

```
export default function routeReducer (state = 'main', action) {
```

3. Then, we handle the `NAVIGATE` action type, and store the new page in the `route` sub-state by returning it from the reducer:

```
const { type, page } = action
if (type === NAVIGATE) {
  return page
}
return state
}
```

4. Finally, we need to import and use our `routeReducer` in the root reducer. Edit `src/reducers/index.js`, import it:

```
import routeReducer from './route'
```

5. Then, pass it to the `combineReducers` helper function:

```
const appReducer = combineReducers({
  users: usersReducer,
  posts: postsReducer,
  filter: filterReducer,
  loading: loadingReducer,
  error: errorReducer,
  session: sessionReducer,
  route: routeReducer,
})
```

Creating the page components

Now that we have the routing logic set up, we split our current main page up into multiple components, one for each subpage of the app.

Creating the MainPage component

We are going to start with the main page. To create the `MainPage` component, perform the following steps:

1. Create a new folder `src/components/pages/` and a file `src/components/pages/MainPage.jsx`. In this file, we import the `ConnectedPostList` and `ConnectedFilterList`:

```
import React from 'react'

import ConnectedPostList from
'../../containers/ConnectedPostList.jsx'
import ConnectedFilterList from
'../../containers/ConnectedFilterList.jsx'
```

2. Then, cut out the following code from the `src/components/App.jsx` file:

```
<div><ConnectedFilterList /></div>
<div><ConnectedPostList /></div>
```

3. Use these two components to create a `MainPage` component, by inserting the following code in `src/components/pages/MainPage.jsx`:

```
const MainPage = () =>
  <div>
    <div><ConnectedFilterList /></div>
    <div><ConnectedPostList /></div>
  </div>

export default MainPage
```

4. Now, we import the `MainPage` component in our `src/components/App.jsx` component:

```
import MainPage from './pages/MainPage.jsx'
```

5. Put the following code in the place where we cut out code earlier, in the `src/components/App.jsx` file:

```
<MainPage />
```

Open the application; it should look and work the same way as before. We simply put our main page into a separate component.

Creating the AboutPage component

Now, we are going to create another page component that shows information about the blog. To create the `AboutPage` component, perform the following steps:

1. Create a new file `src/components/pages/AboutPage.jsx`, we first import `React`:

```
import React from 'react'
```

2. Then, we create the component, which will simply display some text:

```
const AboutPage = () =>
  <div>
    <h2>Learning Redux blog</h2>
    <p>This is a blog application written to teach Redux and React.
It is built throughout the Learning Redux book.</p>
  </div>

export default AboutPage
```

This page component won't be displayed yet. In the next step, we are going to create the `Router` component that allows navigation between the main and the about page.

Creating the Router component

It's time to create the actual `Router` component, which will take the `route` state as a property and decide which page to show based on it. To create the `Router` component, perform the following steps:

1. Create a new file `src/components/Router.jsx` and import the two-page components we created earlier:

   ```
   import React from 'react'

   import MainPage from './pages/MainPage.jsx'
   import AboutPage from './pages/AboutPage.jsx'
   ```

2. Then define the `Router` component, which takes the current `route` as property:

   ```
   const Router = ({ route }) => {
   ```

3. We use a `switch` statement to decide which page to show:

   ```
   switch (route) {
     case 'about':
       return <AboutPage />
     default:
     case 'main':
       return <MainPage />
   }
   }
   ```

4. Do not forget to export the component:

   ```
   export default Router
   ```

Connecting the Router component to Redux

We still need to connect the Router component to Redux, in order to pass the `route` sub-state as a property to it. To connect the `Router` component to Redux, perform the following steps:

1. Create a new file `src/containers/ConnectedRouter.jsx` and import the `Router` component:

   ```
   import { connect } from 'react-redux'

   import Router from '../components/Router.jsx'
   ```

2. Next, we define the `mapStateToProps` function, in which we return the `route` part from the state:

   ```
   const mapStateToProps = (state, props) => {
     const { route } = state
     return { route }
   }
   ```

3. Finally, we connect and export the container component:

   ```
   const ConnectedRouter = connect(mapStateToProps)(Router)

   export default ConnectedRouter
   ```

Using the Router component

After creating the `Router` component, we still need to use it in our `App` component. To use the Router component, perform the following steps:

1. Edit `src/components/App.jsx` and import the `ConnectedRouter` component (the `MainPage` import can be removed now):

   ```
   import ConnectedRouter from '../containers/ConnectedRouter.jsx'
   ```

2. Replace the following code:

   ```
   <MainPage />
   ```

   With our router:

   ```
   <ConnectedRouter />
   ```

Again, when you open the application, everything should work the same as before. As we do not have any way to change the route yet, the main page will always be displayed.

Creating the Navigation component

All that's left to do is creating a component that shows a navigation bar and allows us to change the route by clicking on links. To create the Navigation component, perform the following steps:

1. Create a new file `src/components/Navigation.jsx` and import React:

   ```
   import React from 'react'
   ```

2. First, we create a small helper function, which decides if a link is clickable or not. If the current route equals the route that the link is supposed to navigate to, we do not set the `href` attribute, thus rendering the link as non-clickable:

   ```
   const isClickable = (route, currentRoute) =>
     route === currentRoute ? null : 'javascript:void(0)'
   ```

3. Next, we create the Navigation component, which takes the navigate action creator and the current route as properties:

   ```
   const Navigation = ({ navigate, route }) =>
   ```

4. Then, we simply render a list of links, using the isClickable helper function and the navigate action creator:

   ```
   <div>
     <a href={isClickable('main', route)} onClick={() =>
   navigate('main')}>main</a>
     {' - '}
     <a href={isClickable('about', route)} onClick={() =>
   navigate('about')}>about</a>
   </div>
   ```

5. Do not forget to export the component:

   ```
   export default Navigation
   ```

Connecting the Navigation component to Redux

Similarly to the Router component, we are going to connect the Navigation component to Redux by passing the route sub-state as a property to it. Additionally, we use mapDispatchToProps to pass the navigate action creator to the Navigation component. Perform the following steps to connect the Navigation component to Redux:

1. Create a new file src/containers/ConnectedNavigation.jsx and import the Navigation component and the navigate action creator:

   ```
   import { connect } from 'react-redux'
   import { bindActionCreators } from 'redux'

   import Navigation from '../components/Navigation.jsx'
   import { navigate } from '../actions'
   ```

2. Next, we define the mapStateToProps function, in which we return the route part from the state:

   ```
   const mapStateToProps = (state, props) => {
     const { route } = state
     return { route }
   }
   ```

3. Then, we define the mapDispatchToProps function, where we return the navigate action creator:

   ```
   const mapDispatchToProps = (dispatch, props) =>
     bindActionCreators({ navigate }, dispatch)
   ```

4. Finally, we connect and export the container component:

   ```
   const ConnectedNavigation = connect(mapStateToProps,
   mapDispatchToProps)(Navigation)

   export default ConnectedNavigation
   ```

Using the Navigation component

After creating the `Navigation` component, we still need to use it in our `App` component. To use the `Navigation` component, perform the following steps:

1. Edit `src/components/App.jsx` and import the `ConnectedNavigation` component:

   ```
   import ConnectedNavigation from
   '../containers/ConnectedNavigation.jsx'
   ```

2. Add the following code after the ConnectedErrorMessage and before the first `<hr />`:

   ```
   <div><ConnectedNavigation /></div>
   ```

Open the application; this time you should see the navigation bar:

Our simple router in action - you can see the navigation bar, with the "main" page currently selected

Click on the **about** link to navigate to our AboutPage component:

Application state after clicking on the **about** link - showing the AboutPage component

Code example

The current state of the project can be found in the chapter9_1.zip attachment.

Unpack the zip, change into the directory, run npm install and npm start, then open http://localhost:8080 in your browser.

Using a routing library

In the previous section, you learned how to manually implement routing with Redux and React *without* using a library. While this approach works, there are a couple issues with our solution:

- When creating a new route, we have to adjust the code in multiple parts of our project:
  - In the Router component, where we decide which route shows which page.
  - In the Navigation component, where we have to add a link to the new route.
- It is not possible to create more complicated routes, like a separate page for each post.

- It is not possible to link to a certain page via a URL. The current route is only stored in the Redux store.
- Route changes are not reflected in the browser history. This means that the user can't go back and forth between pages with browser features.

In this section, we are going to use two libraries to implement routing: **react-router** and **react-router-redux**. The first library, react-router, allows us to define routes and links to certain routes. It works similar to our `Router` and `Navigation` components. The second library, react-router-redux, connects the routing state to the Redux store, allowing us to use routing information anywhere in our application.

You can use the code in `chapter9_1.zip` as a starting point for this section.

Introducing react-router

Since version 4, react-router uses a model called **Dynamic Routing**, which is different from **Static Routing**—the model you are probably more familiar with.

Static routing

Many libraries and frameworks, like Express, Rails, Ember, or Angular use static routing. With static routing, you declare your routes during the initialization stage of the app, before any rendering happens.

For example, configuring a route in express would look as follows:

```
app.get('/', handleMainPage)
app.get('/posts', handlePostsPage)
app.get('/posts/:id', handlePostPage)

app.listen()
```

All routes are (statically) declared before the app listens.

Dynamic routing

In contrast to the static declaration of routes, react-router uses a more dynamic approach, where you can use `<Route>` components anywhere in your app.

For example, we could make a simple page with a navigation bar and the main container that changes depending on the route/path:

```
const App = () =>
  <Router>
```

With the `<Link>` component, we can define links to certain paths/routes. In this example, we are going to define links to the main page and a posts page:

```
<nav>
  <Link to="/">Main</Link>
  <Link to="/posts">Posts</Link>
</nav>
```

Then, we can use the `<Route>` component to display certain other components (our page components) when the path matches a certain route:

```
<div>
  <Route path="/" component={MainPage} />
  <Route path="/posts" component={PostsPage} />
</div>
</Router>
```

Nested routes

With dynamic routing, nesting can simply be done by nesting the `Route` components.

For example, if we wanted to implement a `/posts/:id` page, we could define the sub-route in the `PostsPage`, as follows:

```
const PostsPage = ({ match }) =>
  <div>
    <Route path={match.url + '/:id'} component={PostPage} />
  </div>
```

We need to use `match.url` here to get the relative path from the previous route (in this case, `/posts`).

More routing

Dynamic routing also allows for other concepts, like responsive routing. However, going deeper into this is beyond this books' scope. You can find more information on the official react-router documentation: `https://reacttraining.com/react-router/`.

Specifically, the web section (react-router also works with React Native): `https://reacttraining.com/react-router/web/guides/philosophy`.

Using react-router

Now that you learned about react-router, we are going to implement it in our app and connect it to Redux!

Installing react-router

First of all, we need to install `react-router` via npm:

```
npm install --save react-router-dom
```

Defining the <Router> and <Route>

The next step is wrapping our `App` in a `<Router>` component and defining some `<Route>` components. Perform the following steps:

1. Edit `src/components/App.jsx` and import the `Router` (specifically, `BrowserRouter`) and `Route` components:

   ```
   import { BrowserRouter as Router, Route } from 'react-router-dom'
   ```

2. Next, we need to import our page components:

   ```
   import MainPage from './pages/MainPage.jsx'
   import AboutPage from './pages/AboutPage.jsx'
   ```

3. Then, wrap the whole `App` component's contents with the `<Router>` component:

   ```
   const App = ({ store }) =>
     <Provider store={store}>
       <Router>
         <div>
           <h1>React/Redux blog</h1>
           <div><ConnectedLoading /></div>
           <div><ConnectedErrorMessage /></div>
           <hr />
           <div><ConnectedHeader /></div>
           <hr />
   ```

4. And replace the `<ConnectedRouter>` component with our routes:

```
<Route exact path="/" component={MainPage} />
<Route path="/about" component={AboutPage} />

{ (process.env.NODE_ENV !== 'production') && <DevTools /> }
</div>
</Router>
</Provider>
```

Defining the <Link>

Perform the following steps, to define `<link>` links to the sub-pages:

1. Edit `src/components/Navigation.jsx` and import the `Link` component:

```
import { Link } from 'react-router-dom'
```

2. Then, replace the current `Navigation` component with the following code, defining two `<Link>` components:

```
const Navigation = () =>
  <div>
    <Link to="/">main</Link>
    {' - '}
    <Link to="/about">about</Link>
  </div>
```

Trying out the router

Now that we have react-router set up, let's try it out by starting our app via:

```
npm start
```

Then, go to `http://localhost:8080/` and the routes should work similarly to how they did with our own router! Our application now looks as follows:

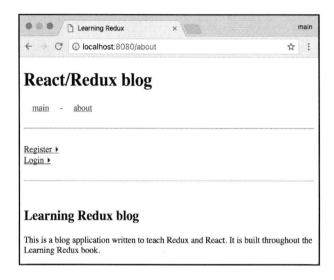

React-router in action, state after clicking the "about" link

Note how the URL changes to `/about` now. Furthermore, you can now use the browser history to go back and forth between pages in our Redux/React application.

Marking the currently selected link

React-router offers a special version of the `<Link>` component. It is called `<NavLink>` and adds styling attributes to the link.

By default, the currently active link is given the `active` class. The `activeClassName` property can be used to change that behavior.

Furthermore, the `activeStyle` property can be used to define a style object for active links. This is what we are going to use in this section:

1. Edit `src/components/Navigation.jsx` and change the import from `Link` to `NavLink`:

   ```
   import { NavLink } from 'react-router-dom'
   ```

2. Now, we define a style object for active links:

   ```
   const activeLink = {
     textDecoration: 'none',
     color: 'black'
   }
   ```

3. Then, replace all `<Link>` components with `<NavLink>` and pass the previously defined object as the `activeStyle` property:

   ```
   const Navigation = () =>
     <div>
       <NavLink to="/" activeStyle={activeLink}>main</NavLink>
       {' - '}
       <NavLink to="/about" activeStyle={activeLink}>about</NavLink>
     </div>
   ```

4. We also need to use the `exact` property to ensure the first link does not always get matched and marked as active. Without this property, / would match the main *and* all subpages and the link would always get marked as active:

   ```
   const Navigation = () =>
     <div>
       <NavLink to="/" exact activeStyle={activeLink}>main</NavLink>
       {' - '}
       <NavLink to="/about" activeStyle={activeLink}>about</NavLink>
     </div>
   ```

Just like in the simple router we implemented at the beginning of this chapter, the active page is now marked in the navigation bar:

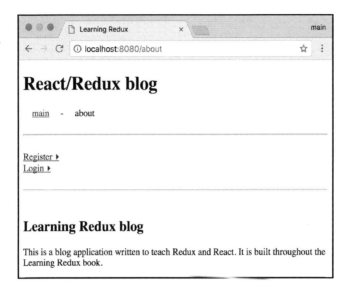

State after clicking the "about" link, it is now marked as active

Using react-router with Redux

Up to now, you have learned how routing works in general. Then, you learned how to use react-router to implement more complicated routing in our application. Now, we are going to learn how to deeply integrate react-router with Redux.

Do I need to connect my router to Redux?

No. React-router and Redux work fine together, even without a deep integration.

However, there is sometimes an issue that a component doesn't update when the location changes. This issue happens if:

- the component is connected to Redux via `connect`; and
- the component is *not* a `Route` component, which means it is not rendered via
  `<Route component={ComponentName} />`

The problem here is that Redux implements the `shouldComponentUpdate` React lifecycle hook, and Redux does not know that anything changed if it isn't receiving props from the router.

This issue can be fixed by wrapping the component with the `withRouter` helper after wrapping it with `connect`, like this:

```
import { withRouter } from 'react-router-dom'
export default withRouter(connect(mapStateToProps)(ComponentName))
```

In our application, we are going to need to wrap the following components with the `withRouter` helper (because they are connected and not a `Route` component):

- `ConnectedLoading`
- `ConnectedErrorMessage`
- `ConnectedHeader`

Why deeply integrate my router with Redux?

Deeply integrating your router with Redux has some advantages, such as:

- synchronizing the routing data with the store, and being able to access it from there in other parts of our Redux application
- being able to navigate by dispatching actions, like we did in our custom router
- having support for time traveling debugging for route changes via Redux DevTools

Note that you do not *need* this deep integration in every application, because:

- routing data is already passed as properties to route components
- instead of dispatching actions to navigate, we can navigate using the `history` object passed as a property to `Route` components
- route changes are unlikely to matter for time traveling debugging

Example code

The current state of the project can be found in the `chapter9_2.zip` attachment.

Unpack the zip, change into the directory, run `npm install` and `npm start`, then open `http://localhost:8080` in your browser.

Using react-router-redux

If, considering the concerns in the previous section, you decide you want to deeply integrate react-router with Redux: That is what we are going to do in this section!

Installing react-router-redux

As always, we first need to install the libraries via npm:

```
npm install --save react-router-redux@next
npm install --save history
```

Using the routerMiddleware

Next, we need to make react-router use the Redux store. This is done by applying the routerMiddleware provided by react-router-redux when creating the Redux store. Perform the following steps:

1. Edit `src/store/middleware.js` and import the `routerMiddleware`:

   ```
   import { routerMiddleware } from 'react-router-redux'
   ```

2. The middleware requires us to pass a history object to it. So we also import the `createHistory` helper from the **history** library:

   ```
   import createHistory from 'history/createBrowserHistory'
   ```

3. Now, we use this helper function to create a new `history` object and export it:

   ```
   export const history = createHistory()
   ```

4. Then, pass the `middleware` as another argument to the `applyMiddleware` helper function:

   ```
   const middleware = applyMiddleware(
     thunkMiddleware,
     routerMiddleware(history)
   )
   ```

Using the routerReducer

After setting up the middleware, react-router-redux still needs us to place their reducer in our Redux store so that the routing state can be stored there. Perform the following steps:

1. Edit `src/reducers/index.js` and import the `routerReducer` from `react-router-redux`:

   ```
   import { routerReducer } from 'react-router-redux'
   ```

2. Then, pass it to the `combineReducers()` function:

   ```
   const appReducer = combineReducers({
     ...other reducers...,
     route: routerReducer,
   })
   ```

Using the ConnectedRouter

Instead of using the `BrowserRouter` component from react-router-dom, we now need to use the `ConnectedRouter` component from `react-router-redux`. This component also requires us to pass a `history` property, which means we need to import that from our `middleware.js` file. Perfom the following steps:

1. Edit `src/components/App.jsx` and adjust the import statement from `react-router-dom`, remove the `BrowserRouter as Router` part:

   ```
   import { Route } from 'react-router-dom'
   ```

2. Import the `ConnectedRouter` component from `react-router-redux`:

   ```
   import { ConnectedRouter } from 'react-router-redux'
   ```

3. Import the `history` object:

   ```
   import { history } from '../store/middleware'
   ```

4. Replace the `Router` component with `ConnectedRouter` and pass the `history` object to it:

```
const App = ({ store }) =>
  <Provider store={store}>
    <ConnectedRouter history={history}>
      ...app structure...
    </ConnectedRouter>
  </Provider>
```

Testing out the router

The router should work the same way as it did before. However, if you look at the Redux DevTools, you can see a `@@router/LOCATION_CHANGE` action being dispatched when a link in the navigation bar is clicked and the route/page is changed:

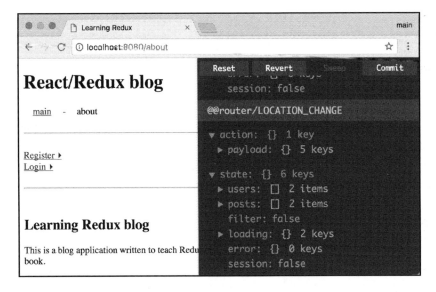

State of our application after clicking on **about**—you can see the action being dispatched in the DevTools (dark sidebar)

Navigating by dispatching actions

Because our router is now connected to Redux, we can dispatch an action to navigate to another page/route.

To do this, simply import the `push` action creator from the library:

```
import { push } from 'react-router-redux'
```

You can dispatch this action like any other, using `store.dispatch`:

```
store.dispatch(push('/about'))
```

Or pass it to a connected component via `mapDispatchToProps`:

```
const mapDispatchToProps = (dispatch, props) =>
  bindActionCreators({ push }, dispatch)
```

Example code

The current state of the project can be found in the `chapter9_3.zip` attachment.

Unpack the zip, change into the directory, run `npm install` and `npm start`, then open `http://localhost:8080` in your browser.

Summary

In this chapter, you learned how to implement routing with Redux and React. Routing allows us to make more complex applications with multiple pages. We started by implementing our own simple router. In the second and third part of this chapter, you learned how to implement routing by using libraries like react-router and react-router-redux.

In the next chapter, you are going to learn how to render a React/Redux application on the server to be able to provide the user with a fully rendered application on the first request. Server-side rendering will speed up the initial load time and allow search engines to parse the application. Furthermore, when using server rendering, users with JavaScript disabled can still use the basic functionality of our application (reading blog posts).

10
Rendering on the Server

In the preceding chapter, we discussed implementing routing into our Redux/React application.

In this chapter, we will discuss how to render a Redux/React application on the server to provide the user with a fully rendered application on the first request. This will speed up the initial load time of the application and allow search engines to view the application content (in our case, blog posts).

Why render on the server?

Before we start implementing server-side rendering in our application, let's take a moment to think about why it would be useful.

Current process to load the page

At the moment, users have to wait for the following process to be completed until the page is loaded:

1. The client makes a request to our server, which serves the initial HTML.
2. The initial HTML is loaded and parsed.
3. CSS and JS are imported from the HTML file gets that requested and parsed.
4. The JS code is loaded and React is initialized.
5. React draws the initial state (no data yet).
6. Data is fetched and pulled into the Redux store.
7. React rerenders using the data from the Redux store.
8. The app is fully loaded now.

As you can imagine, this process can take quite long, especially on slower connections. Furthermore, when the client has JavaScript disabled, nothing will be rendered at all.

Using server-side rendering

Server-side rendering shortens this process immensely:

1. The initial HTML loads with the data already prerendered by React on the server.
2. CSS is imported from the HTML file that gets requested and parsed.
3. The app is fully visible now (with all the data).
4. JS is imported from the HTML file that gets requested and parsed.
5. The app is fully loaded and usable now.

In comparison with not using server-side rendering, this process presents the user with the full app, including all data, on the first request (when the initial HTML is loaded). Then, the style (CSS) and logic (JavaScript) load to make the app fully usable.

In addition to the speed improvement, server-side rendering has a couple more advantages:

- The app can be loaded without JavaScript enabled:
- This means that browsers with JavaScript disabled can still view the page, just not interact with it
- Furthermore, crawlers (for example, search engines indexing your website) can read all the information on your page, as it is part of the initial HTML
- The user does not need to wait for data to load after the initial request; it is already there
- Fewer requests are required, as data for initializing the Redux store does not need to be fetched one by one by the client since it is already a part of the initial request
- It allows for further performance improvements, such as caching the initial Redux state on the server so that we do not need to make multiple database requests every time a user visits our application

Preparing for server-side rendering

With server-side rendering, we always need to keep in mind that our React code will be executed in the browser *and* on the server:

- Ensure that you do not use the `window`, `location`, `history`, and `document` objects—it is not possible to access these on the server.
- Use the best practices of Redux/React—do not use the global scope, keep your components self-sustaining, and do not directly manipulate the DOM.
- Ensure that your code does not have any memory leaks. This is already a problem, even without server-side rendering, but having a memory leak in the server, with potentially limited resources and high load, will be an even bigger problem.
- Ensure that the third-party libraries you use work on the server. Libraries that work on both the client and the server are called *universal* or *isomorphic*.

Using the isomorphic-fetch library

In *Chapter 6*, *Interfacing with APIs*, we used `fetch` to make the API requests. Unfortunately, this function does not work on the server side without importing it from the `isomorphic-fetch` library.

Perform the following steps to replace `fetch` with `isomorphic-fetch`:

1. Install the `isomorphic-fetch` library using `npm`:

   ```
   npm install --save isomorphic-fetch
   ```

2. Edit `src/actions/posts.js` and import the following isomorphic `fetch` function at the start of the file:

   ```
   import fetch from 'isomorphic-fetch'
   ```

3. Edit `src/actions/users.js` and add the same import statement, as follows:

   ```
   import fetch from 'isomorphic-fetch'
   ```

Implementing server-side rendering

Now that we know why server-side rendering is useful, let's implement it in our application. First, we will need to think about what we need to do to implement this functionality:

1. Figure out which (sub)page was requested.
2. Gather all the data required to render the page.
3. Render the HTML using this data.
4. Send this HTML to the client.

For this section, we will use the template code from `chapter10_1.zip`. This template adds a file on the server where we can implement server-side rendering without having to deal with the rest of the server code.

Handling the request/routing

In order to be able to render any page on the server, we need to make use of react-router on the server. First, we will emulate a Redux store, browser history, and location. Then, we can make use of the `match` helper function of `react-router` to decide which page to display.

Emulating the Redux store and browser history

First, we need to create a Redux store and history object (for the router):

1. Open `server/render.js` and import React. This is required because we are going to use JSX:

   ```
   import React from 'react'
   ```

2. Then, we need to import the `renderToString` function from `react-dom/server` to be able to render DOM/HTML on the server side:

   ```
   import { renderToString } from 'react-dom/server'
   ```

3. Next, we need to create a `MemoryHistory` (to emulate the `BrowserHistory`) for `react-router`:

   ```
   import createHistory from 'history/createMemoryHistory'
   ```

4. We also import the `configureStore` and `initStore` functions:

```
import configureStore from '../src/store'
import initStore from '../src/initStore'
```

5. The file already defines a `serverSideRendering` function, which we will fill in now:

```
const serverSideRendering = (req, res) => {
  // TODO
  return res.render('index')
}
```

 With express, we will use this function as follows:
`server.get('*', serverSideRendering)`

6. Replace the highlighted lines in the code in step 5 with the following code; we start by logging some debug output:

```
console.log('server-side rendering started for', req.url)
```

7. Then, we create the memory history and call `configureStore(initialState, history, serverRendering)`:

```
const history = createHistory()
```

```
const store = configureStore({}, history, true)
```

Initializing the Redux store

Now, we will initialize the Redux store to be able to use it when rendering our components:

1. First, we need to import the `Provider` component from `react-redux` to be able to connect our application to the Redux store:

```
import { Provider } from 'react-redux'
```

2. We call the `initStore` function and pass the `store` variable to it:

```
return initStore(store)
```

3. The `initStore` function returns a promise, so we can use `.then()` to define a handler function:

```
.then(() => {
```

4. Now that the Redux store is initialized, we can use the `renderToString` function to render our application:

```
const markup = renderToString(
```

5. Finally, we use the `<Provider>` component and pass the `store` variable to it in order to make the store available to our application:

```
<Provider store={store}>
  {/* TODO */}
</Provider>
)
```

Using react-router to decide which page to render

Next, we will use `react-router` to decide which page to render:

1. We import the `StaticRouter` component from `react-router-dom`:

```
import { StaticRouter } from 'react-router-dom'
```

2. We also import our `App` component:

```
import App from '../src/components/App.jsx'
```

3. Then, we replace the `{/* TODO */}` part with the `<StaticRouter>` component:

```
<StaticRouter location={isIndexPage ? '/' : req.url}>
```

4. Finally, we render our `<App>` component:

```
  <App />
</StaticRouter>
```

Handling react-router redirects

We still need to handle `redirect` components on the server side. In the client, the browser history changes state, and we get a new screen. On the server, we pass a `context` property to the `StaticRouter` component. If `context.url` exists, we know that the app has redirected, so we send a redirect response.

We are now going to adjust the code in `server/render.js`:

1. Before rendering using `renderToString`, create a `context` variable:

```
return initStore(store)
  .then(() => {
    let context = {}
    const markup = renderToString(
```

2. Pass this `context` variable as a property to the `<StaticRouter>` component:

```
        <StaticRouter location={isIndexPage ? '/' : req.url}
context={context}>
```

3. After rendering the `StaticRouter` component using `renderToString`, we check whether `context.url` exists and redirect accordingly:

```
let context = {}
const markup = renderToString(
  ...
)

if (context.url) {
  return res.redirect(301, context.url)
}
```

Injecting rendered React components into the index.html template

In the template code, the server now renders a `server/views/index.ejs` file instead of the `index.html` file from the `root` folder. We will use **Embedded JavaScript** (**EJS**) to inject our rendered React components into the HTML template. Later, we will inject the initial Redux store state the same way.

For now, let's inject the rendered components using EJS:

1. To use EJS templates, we will install `ejs` via npm:

   ```
   npm install --save ejs
   ```

   EJS offers the following ways to inject JavaScript code into `.ejs` template files:

   - `<% code %>`: Code is evaluated but not printed out
   - `<%= code %>`: Code is evaluated and printed out (escaped)
   - `<%- code %>`: Code is evaluated and printed out (not escaped)

2. In our case, we will need the third variant (evaluate, and print out without escaping), as we will inject raw HTML code. Edit `server/views/index.ejs` and inject a `markup` variable into the main container:

   ```
   <div id="root"><%- markup %></div>
   ```

We will pass this variable to `res.render()` later.

Injecting the preloaded Redux store state

We now want to inject the preloaded Redux store state so that the Redux store will already be initialized once the page loads.

We will continue where we left off in the `serverSideRendering` function in the `server/render.js` file, after calling the `renderToString()` function:

1. First, we convert the Redux store state to JSON:

   ```
   const storeState = JSON.stringify(store.getState())
       .replace(/</g, '\\u003c')
   ```

 For security reasons, we are escaping the < characters. This ensures that no HTML can get injected into the page via the contents of the Redux store.

2. Now, we inject the store state into the template file using a `<script>` tag. Edit `server/views/index.ejs` and add the following highlighted code:

   ```
   <body>
     <div id="root"><%- markup %></div>
   ```

```
  <script>
  window.__PRELOADED_STATE__ = <%- storeState %>
  </script>
  <script src="main.js"></script>
</body>
```

Rendering the template file

Finally, we need to render the template file, passing the two variables (markup and storeState) to it:

1. We log a debug message and respond to the request by rendering the index.ejs template file:

```
console.log('server-side rendering done')
return res.render('index', { markup, storeState })
```

2. We still need to handle the error case of the promise. In this case, we will log the error and load the template file (without passing variables to it) as a fallback:

```
})
.catch(err => {
  console.error('server-side rendering error:', err)
  return res.render('index')
})
```

Using the preloaded Redux store state

Now that we have defined the window.__PRELOADED_STATE__ variable, all that's left to do is to use it when creating the store on the client side.

Open src/index.js and pass window.__PRELOADED_STATE__ to the configureStore() function:

```
const store = configureStore(window.__PRELOADED_STATE__)
```

 In this case, we do not care that the code will not work on the server side, so it is fine to use window.

Caching the index page

Since the index page gets accessed very frequently, we can cache its HTML markup and store its state in memory to be able to immediately serve the index page to clients. This further improves the performance of our application.

We are now going to implement a very simple caching technique:

1. In the `server/render.js` file, define the `cachedResult` variable above the function definition:

   ```
   let cachedResult = false
   ```

2. Add a check to see if the index page was requested to the `serverSideRendering` function:

   ```
   const isIndexPage = req.url === '/' || req.url === '/index.html'
   ```

3. If the index page was requested, and the `cachedResult` variable is filled in (not `false`), we can immediately send the cached result:

   ```
   if (isIndexPage) {
     if (cachedResult) return res.render('index', cachedResult)
   }
   ```

4. Finally, we change the bottom of our `.then()` handler function to store the result of the index page once it finishes rendering:

   ```
   if (isIndexPage) {
     cachedResult = { markup, storeState }
     console.log('server-side rendering done, cached result')
     return res.send(cachedResult)
   } else {
     console.log('server-side rendering done')
     return res.send({ markup, storeState })
   }
   ```

Now, when the first client requests the index page, it will be rendered and cached on the server. Subsequent requests to the index page will be served with the cached result, decreasing the load time of the application immensely.

The server code also requests the index page when it starts. That way, not even the first client needs to wait for the index page to be rendered. In `server/serveFrontend.js`, add the following line:

```
serverSideRendering({ url: '/' }, { render: () => {} })
```

However, there are issues with this simple caching technique. When new blog posts are created, the cached index page currently does not get updated. To work around this, we could update the cache periodically using timers.

Performance improvements

Now that we have server-side rendering with a simple caching method set up, let's check how much the performance of our application has improved.

We will start by taking a look at the old application, without the server-side rendering (`chapter10_1.zip`):

Network performance of the chapter10_1 application (no server-side rendering)

Note that these tests were done by making a local request. On a live application, it would take much longer to make requests because network latency affects each request that is made.

As you can see, it makes the following requests (in sequence, because they depend on each other):

1. Request to the main page.
2. Request for `main.js` (Redux store initializes).
3. Request for `/posts`.
4. Request for `/dan`.
5. Request for `/des`.

With server-side rendering, we can reduce this to the first two requests and immediately show the page after the first request, before JavaScript even loads:

Network performance of the chapter10_2 application (with server-side rendering)

Summary

In this chapter, we discussed why server-rendering makes sense and what benefits we get from using this technique. Then we learned how to implement server-side rendering in our Redux/React application. We did this by using react-router on the server to figure out which page to render. Furthermore, we used `ReactDOMServer` to render React components to a string. Finally, we discussed how to inject a preloaded Redux store state into our application.

In the upcoming chapters, we will start diving deeper into how Redux works, and cover how to extend Redux. In the next chapter, we will cover how to solve generic problems with higher-order reducers. We will focus on how to make our own abstractions on top of Redux to generalize behavior such as undo/redo. This means that you do not have to re-implement this kind of behavior every time. You can even package these abstractions into a library to for example, you could allow undo/redo for any Redux (sub)state.

11
Solving Generic Problems with Higher-Order Functions

In the preceding chapter, you learned how to render your Redux/React application on the server side to be able to provide the user with a fully rendered application at the first request.

After understanding how to use Redux and seeing how powerful its libraries can be through the previous chapters, in this chapter, we will discuss how to make our own abstractions on top of Redux. These abstractions can generalize behavior, such as undo/redo, meaning that you do not have to re-implement such features for each part of the application that makes use of them. Furthermore, these generic abstractions can be packaged as libraries and used in *any* Redux application.

In this chapter, we will cover the following topics:

- Making functions pure
- Creating higher-order functions
- Solving generic problems with Redux
- Implementing generic undo/redo with Redux

Making functions pure

Before we learn how to make generic abstractions for our reducers, we will take a closer look at pure functions. We have already learned a bit about them in the previous chapters. Pure functions have no side effects; they always return the same output, given the same input. The following is what makes Redux so predictable:

- Reducers take the current state and an action and return the new state
- All reducers are pure functions
- Given the same input, pure functions return the same output
- As a result, given the same state and action, reducers will always return the same new state

When writing abstractions on top of our reducers, we need to make sure that they are also pure functions, otherwise we will lose the benefits of Redux and introduce unpredictable behavior.

Simple side effects

Let's take a look at an impure function. The following example has a side effect:

```
let i = 0
function counter () {
  return i++
}
```

In this case, the function is modifying a global variable, which causes a side effect. This means that with the same input, this function will *not* return the same output:

- `counter():0`
- `counter():1`
- `counter():2`

No side effects

A pure counter function would look like this:

```
function counter (i) {
  return i + 1
}
```

With the same input, it will always return the same output:

- `counter(0)`: 1
- `counter(0)`: 1

If we want to count, we will need to call the counter function multiple times or pass the result of a previous call to `counter()` to it:

- `counter(counter(0))`: 2
- `counter(1)`: 2

Other side effects

However, there are many more versions of side effects that are not related to modifying the state outside of the function. In fact, any effect that does not contribute to the return value is considered a side effect. That includes functions such as this:

```
function counter (i) {
  console.log('i =', i)
  return i + 1
}
```

Calling `console.log` in the preceding function causes a side effect. Technically speaking, all functions have some side effects (such as taking time and consuming memory). Usually when we talk about side effects, we are most concerned with IO and modifying the external state.

Side effects and Redux

For Redux reducers, side effects such as logging the debug output are alright because they do not affect how the new state is computed. We just have to ensure that when we pass the same state and action, it will always return the same new state. Furthermore, we have to make sure that we never modify the current state directly.

The following reducer and side effect (highlighted) would be okay in a Redux application, as it does not affect the new state:

```
function counterReducer (state = 0, action) {
  console.log('action', action)
  const { type } = action
  switch (type) {
    case 'PLUS': return state + 1
```

```
      case 'MINUS': return state - 1
      default: return state
  }
}
```

A reducer with a side effect that *does* affect the new state, however, is a problem:

```
// DO NOT DO THIS
let i = 0
function counterReducer (state, action) {
  const { type } = action
  switch (type) {
    case 'PLUS': return ++i
    case 'MINUS': return --i
    default: return i
  }
}
```

In the preceding code, the reducer modifies the global state outside of the function instead of computing the new state from the existing state. This means that we will not get the same new state if we call the reducer with the same state and action.

All reducer functions have to be pure. This ensures that Redux remains predictable. If we want to extend our reducer with a higher-order reducer, we also need to ensure that this higher-order reducer function is pure.

Creating higher-order functions

There are two kinds of higher-order functions:

- Functions that take a function as an argument (for example, a callback pattern)
- Functions that return a function as their result

So, higher-order functions are simply functions that deal with functions. Higher-order reducer functions (also called higher-order reducers) are functions that wrap (take and return) reducer functions. We will talk more about these later.

Functions as arguments

The first type of higher-order functions are functions that take other functions as arguments:

```
function someFn (fn) { ... }
```

You might be familiar with this from the callback pattern, which used to be very common when working with asynchronous JavaScript. We pass a `callback` function that takes an error object as the first argument and the data as the second. If no error happens, the first argument will be `null`:

```
function requestAndDo (callback) {
  return fetch('http://localhost:1234')
    .then(data => callback(null, data))
    .catch(err => callback(err))
}
```

A function like this can be called by passing a callback function to it:

```
requestAndDo((err, data) => {
  if (err) throw err
  // ...handle data...
})
```

Similarly, we could write a higher-order function that executes another function and logs its result with a message:

```
function doAndLog (fn, msg) {
  const result = fn()
  console.log(msg, result)
  return result
}
```

It would be used like this:

```
doAndLog(() => 1 + 1, 'result:')
```

This will print the following output to the console: `result: 2`.

Functions as results

The other type of higher-order functions are functions that return functions:

```
function someFn (someArg1, someArg2, ...someArgs) {
  return function someOtherFn (someOtherArg1, ...someOtherArgs) { ... }
}
```

Higher-order functions can be written in a more concise way by using arrow function syntax:

```
const someFn = (someArg1, someArg2, ...someArgs) => (someOtherArg1,
...someOtherArgs) => { ... }
```

For example, we could create a function that creates a `logger` function:

```
function createLogger (name) {
  return function logger (message) {
```

This `logger` function can now access the `name` string from the broader scope (`createLogger` scope), as well as the `message` string from the closer scope (`logger` scope):

```
    console.log(name + ': ' + message)
  }
}
```

This type of higher-order function can be written in an especially elegant way using arrow functions, as follows:

```
const createLogger = (name) => (message) =>
  console.log(name + ': ' + message)
```

The `createLogger` function can be used like this:

```
const log = createLogger('my-app')
```

It returns a `log` function, which will execute `console.log` with our defined `name` as a prefix of the message:

```
log('started')
```

This would print out: `my-app: started`.

Solving generic problems with Redux

You may noticed that as your application grows, there will be common patterns in your application logic. For example, you may be doing the same kind of work for different kinds of data. With the techniques you have learned in this chapter, you can reduce code duplication by reusing the common logic by putting it into a higher-order function.

There are multiple ways to extend a Redux/React application:

- Higher-order reducers (such as `redux-undo`)
- Higher-order action creators (such as generic data fetching from an API)
- Higher-order components (such as `<Provider>`)
- Middleware (such as `redux-logger`)

The last concept, middleware, extends the Redux store directly, and will be discussed in the next chapter (Chapter 12, *Extending the Redux Store using Middleware*). The other concepts all use higher-order functions to extend Redux/React concepts, such as reducers, action creators, and components.

Higher-order reducers

As we discussed in the previous chapters, Redux reducers are simply functions. This means that we can apply the same pattern to them and create higher-order reducer functions (or, in short, higher-order reducers).

A higher-order function is a function that returns a function (and/or takes a function as an argument). A higher-order *reducer* is a reducer that returns a reducer (and/or takes a reducer as an argument).

For example, a higher-order reducer that simply calls the reducer (effectively not doing anything special) will look like this:

```
function doNothingWith (reducer) {
  return function (state, action) {
    return reducer(state, action)
  }
}
```

In fact, the preceding example is both types of higher-order function: It takes a `reducer` function as an argument *and* returns a reducer function.

We have actually already discussed a powerful higher-order reducer: the `combineReducers` helper function provided by the Redux library. It allows you to pass multiple reducers (in an object) and create a root reducer function from it. A simple implementation of this helper function would look like this:

```
function combineReducers (reducers) {
  return function (state = {}, action) {
```

We will loop through all of the keys in the `reducers` object by using `reduce` on them:

```
    return Object.keys(reducers).reduce((nextState, key) => {
```

Then, we would call every reducer (using `reducers[key]`) with the part of the state it manages (using `state[key]`) and store the result in `nextState[key]`:

```
        nextState[key] = reducers[key](state[key], action)
        return nextState
    }, {})
  }
}
```

There are various other use cases for higher-order reducers, such as:

- Generic routing (`react-router-redux`)
- Generic undo/redo (`redux-undo`)
- Ignoring certain actions for certain reducers, for example, for performance reasons (`redux-ignore`)
- Resetting the state on certain actions (`redux-recycle`)

There are many more implementations for Redux applications.

Higher-order action creators

Redux action creators are also simply functions. This means that we can create higher-order action creator functions.

Consider having the following asynchronous action creator function:

```
const fetchPosts = () => (dispatch) => {
  dispatch({ type: FETCH_POSTS_REQUESTED })
  return fetch('http://localhost:8080/api/posts')
    .then(result => {
      dispatch({ type: FETCH_POSTS_RESOLVED, result })
      return result
    })
    .catch(error => {
      dispatch({ type: FETCH_POSTS_REJECTED, error })
    })
}
```

Now, let's say that we need a similar function, `fetchUsers`. We could simply copy and paste the code and change the action types and the URL, but that would duplicate the code and make it harder to maintain. If we copy and paste the code, then every time we modify the behaviour of one of the functions to fix a bug, it still,be fixed in the other function.

The best way to solve this is to put the common code into a higher-order function, then use that function to create the `fetchUsers` and `fetchPosts` action creators. In a previous chapter (Chapter 6, *Interfacing with APIs*), we created a `thunkCreator` utility function that creates `action creator` functions from a `promise`:

```
export const thunkCreator = (action) => {
  const { types, promise, ...rest } = action
  const [ REQUESTED, RESOLVED, REJECTED ] = types

  return (dispatch) => {
    dispatch({ ...rest, type: REQUESTED })
    return promise
      .then(result => {
        dispatch({ ...rest, type: RESOLVED, result })
        return result
      })
      .catch(error => {
        dispatch({ ...rest, type: REJECTED, error })
        throw error
      })
  }
}
```

The `thunkCreator` function is essentially a generic version of the `fetchPosts` action creator. The `thunkCreator` function takes some information about the action (`types`, a `promise`, and other action data) and creates an action creator function:

- `types`: An array defining three action types, the first one being dispatched when the request starts, the second one when it successfully completes, and the third one when it fails
- `promise`: The JavaScript promise to use--in our case, a request to the backend server
- **Other action data**: The rest of the object properties will be used to create the action objects

We can make use of it to (re)create the `fetchPosts` and `fetchUsers` action creators:

```
const fetchPosts = () => thunkCreator({
  types: [ FETCH_POSTS_REQUEST, FETCH_POSTS_SUCCESS, FETCH_POSTS_FAILURE ],
  promise: fetch('http://localhost:8080/api/posts')
            .then(response => response.json())
})
```

We could even create another function to create the promise, further reducing code duplication:

```
const fetchAPI = (path, options) =>
  fetch('http://localhost:8080/api' + path, options)
    .then(response => response.json())
```

Making use of the `fetchAPI` utility function, our `fetchPosts` action creator now looks like this:

```
const fetchPosts = () => thunkCreator({
  types: [ FETCH_POSTS_REQUEST, FETCH_POSTS_SUCCESS, FETCH_POSTS_FAILURE ],
  promise: fetchAPI('/posts')
})
```

The `fetchUsers` action creator will look very similar:

```
const fetchUsers = () => thunkCreator({
  types: [ FETCH_USERS_REQUEST, FETCH_USERS_SUCCESS, FETCH_USERS_FAILURE ],
  promise: fetchAPI('/users')
})
```

As you can see, there are various ways to extract common logic using (higher-order) functions. You have to use common sense to decide when to create a generic pattern instead of implementing something specifically for a certain use case. Usually, you start with a specific use case (such as fetching posts, as shown in the example), then you realise that you need to implement a similar use case. Instead of copy and pasting your code, extract the common logic into a generic (higher-order) function and make use of it to create the other functions.

Higher-order components

As React components are also just functions, we can create higher-order components to reuse component logic, similar to how we reused reducer logic with higher-order reducers.

The signature of a higher-order component looks as follows:

```
const EnhancedComponent = higherOrderComponent(WrappedComponent)
```

A component transforms properties into the UI, and a higher-order component transforms a component into another (enhanced) component; for example, we could define a higher-order component `logProps`, which logs property changes in the wrapped component:

```
function logProps (WrappedComponent) {
```

We return a new React class component:

```
return class extends React.Component {
```

Using a class component, we can define a `componentWillReceiveProps` lifecycle method to listen to property changes:

```
componentWillReceiveProps (nextProps) {
  console.log('current props:', this.props)
  console.log('next props:', nextProps)
}
```

Finally, we would need to render the wrapped component (in this case, without mutating it):

```
  render () {
    return <WrappedComponent {...this.props} />
  }
  }
}
```

Now, we can use this higher-order component to turn an existing component into a logged component:

```
const Counter = ({ count }) => <span>{count}</span>
const LoggedCounter = logProps(Counter)
```

Note that higher-order components should add features to components; they should not drastically alter them. This means that the component returned from a higher-order component should have a similar interface to the wrapped component.

Higher-order components should pass through *all* properties that do not concern them. In our example, we would simply pass all properties to it, as our higher-order component does not make use of any of them. However, we could also make use of some properties in the higher-order component and pass the rest of the properties to the wrapped component:

```
render () {
  const { extraProp, ...restProps } = this.props
  const injectedProp = calculateSomething(extraProp)
  return <WrappedComponent injectedProp={injectedProp} {...restProps} />
}
```

We have already used a higher-order component, the `connect` function, provided by react-redux. It turns a normal component into a Redux-connected (container) component:

```
const ConnectedComponent = connect(mapStateToProps,
mapDispatchToProps)(WrappedComponent)
```

Implementing generic undo/redo Redux

Before we implement generic undo/redo functionality, we will look at a simple Redux application that has a counter:

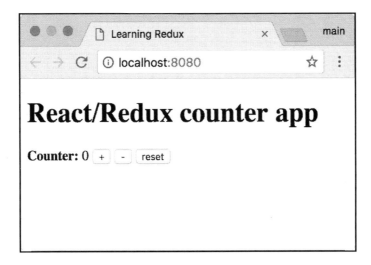

Counter application from chapter11_1.zip

Setting up the counter application

First, let's set up the counter application example:

1. Unzip the counter application example in `chapter11_1.zip`.
2. Then, run the following command to install all dependencies:

   ```
   npm install
   ```

3. Afterward, we can start the application using the following command:

   ```
   npm start
   ```

   This will start the `webpack-dev-server` on `http://localhost:8080`.

4. Open `http://localhost:8080/` in your browser, and you should see the application from the screenshot given in the preceding section.

Looking at the counter reducer

The counter is controlled by a `counterReducer` in `src/reducers/counter.js`:

```
import { INCREMENT, DECREMENT, RESET } from '../actionTypes'

export default function counterReducer (state = 0, action) {
  switch (action.type) {
```

Its logic is quite simple:

- On an `INCREMENT` action, increase the state by 1:

    ```
    case INCREMENT:
       return state + 1
    ```

- On a `DECREMENT` action, decrease the state by 1:

    ```
    case DECREMENT:
       return state - 1
    ```

- On a `RESET` action, set the state to 0:

    ```
    case RESET:
       return 0
    ```

- For unhandled action types, simply return the current state:

    ```
    default:
       return state
    }
    }
    ```

Implementing undo/redo in the counter application

The goal is to have a way to undo/redo actions that happened on the counter. Consider the following example:

- Initial state - state: 0
- After `INCREMENT`: state: 1
- After `INCREMENT`: state: 2
- After `DECREMENT`: state: 1

- After UNDO: state: 2
- After UNDO: state: 1
- After UNDO: state: 0
- After REDO: state: 1

Defining the action types

We want to implement undo/redo behavior in our counter application. This means that we need to define the following new action types in `src/actionTypes.js`:

```
export const UNDO = 'UNDO'
export const REDO = 'REDO'
```

Defining the action creators

Next, we define action creators for these two action types:

1. Create a new file `src/actions/undo.js`.
2. Edit the `src/actions/undo.js` file and import the previously defined action types:

   ```
   import { UNDO, REDO } from '../actionTypes'
   ```

3. Then, define the undo function:

   ```
   export const undo = () => {
     return { type: UNDO }
   }
   ```

4. Similarly, define the redo function:

   ```
   export const redo = () => {
     return { type: REDO }
   }
   ```

5. Finally, re-export the action creators in `src/actions/index.js`:

   ```
   export * from './undo'
   ```

Defining the new state

We want to be able to undo/redo actions, so we will need to store a history of states (instead of just storing the current state). Consider the following:

```
state = 0
```

Instead of the preceding code, our initial state might look something like this:

```
state = [0]
```

After a few actions, the state might look like this:

```
state = [0, 1, 2, 3, 2]
```

This will show 2 on the counter (as it is the latest state).

However, in addition to the history, we will also need to store a pointer to the current state. Otherwise, after some undo/redo actions, we have no way to tell which state in the history is the current state.

Let's turn our state into an object, storing the history array and the currentState index:

```
state = {
  history: [0],
  currentState: 0
}
```

This means we can access the current state by accessing the currentState index from the history array:

```
state.history[state.currentState]
```

After three decrement actions, our state will look as follows:

```
state = {
  history: [0, -1, -2, -3],
  currentState: 3
}
```

After an undo action, the state will look like this:

```
state = {
  history: [0, -1, -2, -3],
  currentState: 2
}
```

Rewriting the counter reducer

Now that we have defined the new state, let's rewrite the counter reducer.

1. We start by changing the default state--edit `src/reducers/counter.js` and replace the function with the following code:

```
const initialState = {
  history: [0],
  currentState: 0
}

export default function counterReducer (state = initialState,
action) {
```

2. Then, we unwrap the state object:

```
const { history, currentState } = state
```

3. We store the current count in a separate variable:

```
const count = history[currentState]
```

Handling the counter-related actions

Now, we need to handle all counter-related actions:

1. Let's start with the increment action:

```
switch (action.type) {
  case INCREMENT:
```

2. We return a new state object based on the current `state` object:

```
return {
  ...state,
```

3. Then, we replace the current `history` array with our new state inserted at the end:

```
history: [ ...history, count + 1 ],
```

4. We also need to set the `currentState` index to the last element in the array:

```
currentState: history.length
}
```

5. Similarly, we handle the decrement action:

```
case DECREMENT:
  return {
    ...state,
    history: [ ...history, count - 1 ],
    currentState: history.length
  }
```

6. Then, we handle the reset action, where we add a new 0 state to the history and jump to it:

```
case RESET:
  return {
    ...state,
    history: [ ...history, 0 ],
    currentState: history.length
  }
```

7. Finally, we return the current state by default (for all unhandled action types):

```
    default:
      return state
  }
}
```

Handling the undo/redo actions

Now all that's left to do is handling the undo/redo actions:

1. First, we import the UNDO and REDO action types:

```
import { INCREMENT, DECREMENT, RESET, UNDO, REDO } from
'../actionTypes'
```

2. Then, we define some new cases in the `switch` statement, starting with the UNDO action type:

```
case UNDO:
```

3. Again, we return a new state object based on the current `state` object:

```
return {
  ...state,
```

4. However, this time, we only replace the `currentState` part, reducing the index by 1, if possible:

```
currentState: currentState <= 0
  ? currentState
  : currentState - 1
}
```

5. Similarly, we handle the `redo` action, increasing the index by 1, if possible:

```
case REDO:
  return {
    ...state,
    currentState: currentState >= history.length - 1
      ? currentState
      : currentState + 1
  }
```

Creating undo/redo buttons

Next, we need to create some buttons so that the user can trigger undo/redo actions in the application:

1. Edit `src/components/Counter.jsx` and pull the `undo` and `redo` action creators from the properties:

```
const Counter = ({ count, increment, decrement, reset, undo,
redo }) =>
```

2. Then, create two new buttons after the reset button--one for undo, and one for redo:

```
<span>
  <b>Counter:</b> {count}
  {' '}
  <button onClick={increment}>+</button>
  {' '}
  <button onClick={decrement}>-</button>
  {' '}
  <button onClick={reset}>reset</button>
  {' '}
  <button onClick={undo}>undo</button>
  {' '}
  <button onClick={redo}>redo</button>
</span>
```

3. We need to inject those two action creators as properties using `connect` and `mapDispatchToProps`. Edit `src/containers/ConnectedCounter.jsx` and import the undo and redo actions:

```
import { increment, decrement, reset, undo, redo } from
'../actions'
```

4. Then, we inject them as properties using `mapDispatchToProps`:

```
const mapDispatchToProps = (dispatch, props) =>
  bindActionCreators({ increment, decrement, reset, undo, redo
}, dispatch)
```

5. We also need to modify `mapStateToProps` to access the current count from the `history` array:

```
const mapStateToProps = (state, props) => {
  const { counter } = state
  const { history, currentState } = counter

  return { count: history[currentState] }
}
```

Trying out undo/redo

Start the application using `npm start` and open `http://localhost:8080` in your browser; you should see the following state:

After clicking on the **+** button three times, you should see the following state:

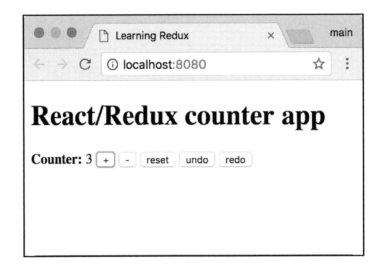

After clicking the **undo** button two times, you should see the following state:

After clicking the **redo** button once, you should see the following state:

When you try this out yourself, make sure that you open the console window in the browser inspector to see the state changes happen.

Example code

The current state of the project can be found in the `chapter11_2.zip` attachment.

Unpack the zip, move it into the directory, run `npm install` and `npm start`, and then open `http://localhost:8080` in your browser.

Implementing a generic undo/redo higher-order reducer

Although the undo/redo feature we implemented in the previous section works well, it only works with the counter state. If we had a different use case, such as undo/redo in a text field, we would have to re-implement the whole undo/redo logic.

Furthermore, our counter reducer is now dealing with much more than just counting--it is also dealing with undo/redo behavior. This is an indicator for refactoring potential--in this case, we can refactor the undo/redo behavior into a generic undo/redo higher-order reducer.

Defining the undoable higher-order reducer

Our goal is to create a generic undo/redo higher-order reducer, which we will call `undoable` (because it makes a reducer function undoable):

1. Create a new file `src/undoable.js`.

2. We start with the function definition. It is a higher-order function that takes a reducer function as an argument:

   ```
   export default function undoable (reducer) {
   ```

3. Then, we need to return a new reducer function, which means we will need to think of the initial state of our higher-order reducer. For now, let's define a constant `initialState` and set it to `{}`:

   ```
   const initialState = {} // TODO
   ```

4. Now, we can return the (to-be enhanced) reducer function:

   ```
   return function enhancedReducer (state = initialState,
   action) {
       // TODO
   }
   }
   ```

Defining the initial state

Now, we need to think about the state object of the undoable higher-order reducer. You may think that it would be easier to simply store the history in local variables in the function. If we did that, we could retain the state structure in our enhanced reducer, and we would not need to adjust our application to access the state using `state.history[state.currentState]`.

However, as we discussed earlier, we should not cause side effects that affect the calculated state of the reducer. This also applies to higher-order reducers. This is why we need to store all undo/redo data in the Redux state, not just in a local variable. If we did store the state in a local variable, it would cause unpredictable behavior when combining our generic reducer with other libraries, such as Redux DevTools.

Problems with our previous solution

While our simple solution with the array and the index worked fine for a simple undo/redo implementation, it will have undesired behavior in more complex situations.

For example, if we do three increment actions, our state would be this:

```
{
  history: [0, 1, 2, 3],
  currentState: 3
}
```

Then, we undo it two times:

```
{
  history: [0, 1, 2, 3],
  currentState: 1
}
```

Now, when we do another increment action, the new state will get pushed to the end, messing up the history:

```
{
  history: [0, 1, 2, 3, 2],
  currentState: 4
}
```

If we undo this again now, we will switch the counter from 2 to 3, not back to 1 (which would be the expected behavior). By simply going through the history by index, we are losing track of the past and future states.

A new kind of history

However, there is a different way we can store the history, that is, by tracking the past and future states in arrays and storing the present state beside them:

```
{
  past: [...],
  present: ...,
  future: [...]
}
```

A nice bonus of using this history structure is being able to simply access the present state through state.present instead of having to select it from the array by index using, for example, state.history[state.currentState]

If we try the same scenario with this kind of history, we will have the following state after three increment actions:

```
{
  past: [0, 1, 2],
  present: 3,
  future: []
}
```

Each undo action pushes the present state to the beginning of the future array and removes the last element from the past array, setting the present state to it:

```
{
  past: [0, 1],
  present: 2,
  future: [3]
}
```

We will now undo it one more time (twice in total):

```
{
  past: [0],
  present: 1,
  future: [2, 3]
}
```

Now, when we do another increment action, we discard the future state (set it to an empty array) and set the new present state accordingly. The previous present state gets added to the end of the past array, as follows:

```
{
  past: [0, 1],
  present: 2,
  future: []
}
```

When we undo again now, we will go from 2 to 1, which is the expected behavior:

```
{
  past: [0],
  present: 1,
  future: [2]
}
```

Defining a generic initial state

Now that we know what our history object will look like, all that's left to do is creating the initial state:

1. Consider the following line:

    ```
    const initialState = {} // TODO
    ```

    Replace it with our new history object:

    ```
    const initialState = {
      past: [],
      present: ..., // TODO
      future: []
    }
    ```

2. There is still a problem--how do we set a generic initial state as `present`? We do not know what the reducer's internal state looks like. However, we can simply call the `reducer` (which was passed as an argument to our `undoable` higher-order function) with an `undefined` state and an empty action to trigger it to populate its initial state. Update the `initialState` definition:

    ```
    const initialState = {
      past: [],
      present: reducer(undefined, {}),
      future: []
    }
    ```

Now that we have a generic history object, it does not matter anymore what the reducer state looks like.

It could be a simple counter reducer, which would make the state look as follows:

```
{
  past: [0, 1],
  present: 2,
  future: [3]
}
```

Alternatively, it could be a user reducer, having an object of the currently logged-in user as the state:

```
{
  past: [{ username: 'des', realname: 'Destiny' }],
  present: { username: 'dan', realname: 'Daniel Bugl' },
  future: []
```

```
}
```

It could also be a `todos` reducer that handles an array of `todo` items as its state:

```
{
  past: [
    [],
    [{ text: 'Read "Learning Redux" book' }],
    [{ text: 'Read "Learning Redux" book', complete: true }]
  ],
  present: [
    { text: 'Read "Learning Redux" book', complete: true },
    { text: 'Implement Undo/Redo' }
  ],
  future: [
    [
      { text: 'Read "Learning Redux" book', complete: true },
      { text: 'Implement Undo/Redo', complete: true }
    ]
  ]
}
```

No matter how simple or complex the state is, our generic `undoable` higher-order reducer can handle it.

Handling generic undo/redo actions

For our new history object, we will need a new undo/redo algorithm. It should be generic that is work on all data types `T` with the following state structure:

```
{
  past: Array<T>,
  present: T,
  future: Array<T>
}
```

There will be three cases that our higher-order reducer needs to handle:

- An undo action
- A redo action
- All other actions (in this case, we need to update the present state)

Defining the action types

First, we define the undo and redo action types:

1. Edit `src/undoable.js` and add the following definitions to the top of the file (outside of the function):

```
export const actionTypes = {
  UNDO: 'UNDO',
  REDO: 'REDO'
}
```

2. Get rid of the old non-generic action types by removing them from the `src/actionTypes.js` file (delete the highlighted lines):

```
export const INCREMENT = 'INCREMENT'
export const DECREMENT = 'DECREMENT'
export const RESET = 'RESET'

export const UNDO = 'UNDO'
export const REDO = 'REDO'
```

Defining the action creators

Next, we define action creators for our action types in `src/undoable.js`:

```
export const undo = () => {
  return { type: actionTypes.UNDO }
}

export const redo = () => {
  return { type: actionTypes.REDO }
}
```

Remove the old non-generic action creators by doing the following:

1. Delete the `src/actions/undo.js` file.
2. Remove the re-export from `src/index.js` (delete the highlighted lines):

```
export * from './counter'
export * from './undo'
```

3. Adjust the imports in `src/containers/ConnectedCounter.jsx`:

```
import { increment, decrement, reset } from '../actions'
import { undo, redo } from '../undoable'
```

Implementing the enhanced reducer

We now implement the enhanced reducer function, which will contain the main undo/redo logic. Edit the following function:

```
return function enhancedReducer (state = initialState, action) {
  // TODO
}
```

Replace the `// TODO` line by doing the following:

1. We start by destructuring the `state` into `past`, `present`, and `future` constants:

```
const { past, present, future } = state
```

2. Next, we make a `switch` statement to handle multiple action types:

```
switch (action.type) {
  case actionTypes.UNDO: {
    return state // TODO
  }
  case actionTypes.REDO: {
    return state // TODO
  }
  default: {
    return state // TODO
  }
}
```

Handling the undo action

On an undo action, we want to do the following steps:

- Remove the *last* element from the `past`
- Insert the current `present` state at the *beginning* of the `future`
- Set the `present` to the element we removed from the `past` in the first step

Replace the `return state // TODO` line following case `actionTypes.UNDO`, by doing the following:

1. First, we check whether there are elements in the `past` array. If not, we simply return the current `state`:

```
if (past.length <= 0) return state
```

2. Next, we store the last element from the `past`, because we will need it in the last step:

```
const previous = past[past.length - 1]
```

3. Then, we create a new array from the `past` array, with the last element excluded:

```
const newPast = past.slice(0, past.length - 1)
```

4. Next, we create a new future array, where we insert the current `present` at the beginning:

```
const newFuture = [present, ...future]
```

5. Finally, we return the new state, setting the new `present` state to the last element of the old `past` array (which we stored in the `previous` constant in the second step):

```
return {
    past: newPast,
    present: previous,
    future: newFuture
}
```

Handling the redo action

On a redo action, we want to do the following steps:

- Remove the first element from the `future`
- Insert the current `present` state at the *end* of the `past`
- Set the `present` to the element we removed from the `future` in the first step

Replace the `return state // TODO` line below `case actionTypes.REDO:` by doing the following:

1. First, we check whether there are elements in the `future` array. If not, we simply return the current `state`:

```
if (future.length <= 0) return state
```

2. Next, we store the first element from the `future` because we will need it in the last step:

```
const next = future[0]
```

3. Then, we create a new array from the `future` array, with the first element excluded:

```
const newFuture = future.slice(1)
```

4. Next, we create a new `past` array, where we insert the current `present` at the end:

```
const newPast = [...past, present]
```

5. Finally, we return the new state, setting the new `present` state to the first element of the old `future` array (which we stored in a `next` constant in the second step):

```
return {
  past: newPast,
  present: next,
  future: newFuture
}
```

Handling other actions (updating the present state)

This is the tricky part--now we need to delegate handling the action to the reducer that we got as an argument. Then, we will use its result to insert a new present state.

Replace the `return state // TODO` line below `default:` by doing the following:

1. First, we call the `reducer` function with the current `present` state and the `action` we received. The result is stored in a `newPresent` constant:

```
const newPresent = reducer(present, action)
```

2. Next, we compare the new `present` to the old `present`; if they are the same, we simply return the current state. This prevents unnecessary additions to the history:

```
if (present === newPresent) {
  return state
}
```

3. Otherwise, we create a new `past` array from the current one, where we insert the current `present` at the end. Furthermore, we set the `present` state to `newPresent` and clear the `future` state by setting it to an empty array:

```
return {
  past: [...past, present],
  present: newPresent,
  future: []
}
```

Whenever an action other than an undo or redo action comes in, we delegate it to the wrapped `reducer` function, which calculates the new state. Then, this new state is added to the undo/redo history.

Removing undo/redo logic from the counter reducer

Now that we have implemented a generic higher-order reducer that can make our counter reducer undoable, we can remove the undo/redo logic completely from the reducer.

Replace the contents of the `src/reducers/counter.js` file with the following code:

```
import { INCREMENT, DECREMENT, RESET } from '../actionTypes'

export default function counterReducer (state = 0, action) {
  switch (action.type) {
    case INCREMENT:
      return state + 1

    case DECREMENT:
      return state - 1

    case RESET:
      return 0

    default:
      return state
  }
}
```

Wrapping the counter reducer with undoable

All that's left to do is wrapping the counter reducer with our `undoable` higher-order reducer:

1. Edit `src/reducers/index.js` and import the `undoable` higher-order reducer:

   ```
   import undoable from '../undoable'
   ```

2. Then, wrap the `counterReducer` with `undoable()`:

   ```
   const appReducer = combineReducers({
     counter: undoable(counterReducer),
   })
   ```

3. Now, we need to adjust the selector in `mapStateToProps` to access the state using `state.counter.present`. Edit `src/containers/ConnectedCounter.jsx` and modify the `mapStateToProps` function:

   ```
   const mapStateToProps = (state, props) => {
     const { counter } = state

     return { count: counter && counter.present }
   }
   ```

Start the application using `npm start` and open `http://localhost:8080` in your browser; it should work the same way as it did before, but now we have a generic `undoable` higher-order reducer that we can reuse.

Furthermore, we have a much better history object structure now, avoiding any problems that might arise where the history gets messed up when doing normal actions after undo/redo actions.

Open the browser console to see the state changing as you use the application:

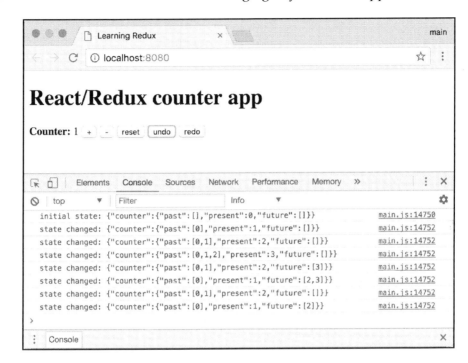

Application state (chapter11_3.zip) after three increment actions, then two undo actions, then another increment action, and another undo action

Problems with our simple undoable higher-order reducer

Although our `undoable` higher-order reducer works fine, it only supports very basic undo/redo behavior. For example, when we have multiple reducers that are wrapped in undoable and we trigger an `undo` action, all wrapped reducers do an `undo` operation. You may also want to include only certain actions in the undo/redo history by defining a filter function.

We could extend our higher-order reducer to accept an object of options as an argument, where we can define separate undo/redo action types and a filter function.

Example code

The current state of the project can be found in the `chapter11_3.zip` attachment.

Unpack the ZIP, move it into the directory, run `npm install` and `npm start`, and then open `http://localhost:8080` in your browser.

Implementing redux-undo

All the custom behavior mentioned in the previous section is already possible if you use the `undoable` **higher-order reducer** from the `redux-undo` library:

```
import undoable from 'redux-undo'
undoable(reducer, options)
```

For example, you can define a custom action type for undo/redo actions:

```
import undoable from 'redux-undo'
undoable(reducer, {
  undoType: 'CUSTOM_UNDO',
  redoType: 'CUSTOM_REDO'
})
```

Alternatively, you can filter certain actions:

```
import undoable, { includeAction, excludeAction } from 'redux-undo'

undoable(reducer, { filter: includeAction(SOME_ACTION) })
undoable(reducer, { filter: excludeAction(SOME_ACTION) })

undoable(reducer, { filter: includeAction([SOME_ACTION, SOME_OTHER_ACTION])
})
undoable(reducer, { filter: excludeAction([SOME_ACTION, SOME_OTHER_ACTION])
})
```

There are more functionalities that redux-undo provides. Feel free to check out the GitHub page for more information:

```
https://github.com/omnidan/redux-undo
```

Installing redux-undo

We install `redux-undo` using npm:

```
npm install --save redux-undo@beta
```

Wrapping our reducer with undoable

Now, we wrap our reducer with the `undoable` higher-order reducer from the redux-undo library.

Consider the following import statement:

```
import undoable from '../undoable'
```

Replace it with the `redux-undo` import:

```
import undoable from 'redux-undo'
```

We have already wrapped our reducer with the `undoable` function in the preceding section:

```
const appReducer = combineReducers({
  counter: undoable(counterReducer),
})
```

Ensure that the highlighted code in the preceding code is present.

Adjusting the state selector

Next, we need to adjust the state selector. In our case, we have already done that. In `src/containers/ConnectedCounter.jsx`, we would have to adjust our selector in the `mapStateToProps` function:

```
const mapStateToProps = (state, props) => {
  const { counter } = state
  return { count: counter && counter.present }
}
```

Ensure that the highlighted code in the preceding code is present.

Importing the undo/redo actions

Now all that's left to do is to import and inject the undo/redo action creators from the redux-undo library.

Edit `src/containers/ConnectedCounter.jsx` and take a look at the following import statement:

```
import { undo, redo } from '../undoable'
```

Now, replace it with this:

```
import { ActionCreators } from 'redux-undo'
const { undo, redo } = ActionCreators
```

We have already injected the action creators using `mapDispatchToProps` earlier in this chapter:

```
const mapDispatchToProps = (dispatch, props) =>
  bindActionCreators({ increment, decrement, reset, undo, redo }, dispatch)
```

Ensure that the highlighted code in the preceding code is present.

Debug mode

Start the application using `npm start` and open `http://localhost:8080` in your browser; it should work the same way as it did before, but now we are using the generic redux-undo library.

If you want to see what's going on in the background, enable debug mode by passing the option to `undoable`.

Edit `src/reducers/index.js` and pass an `option` object as the second argument of `undoable` with the `debug` property set to `true`:

```
const appReducer = combineReducers({
  counter: undoable(counterReducer, { debug: true }),
})
```

Now, every time an action happens, redux-undo will print some information about it in the console:

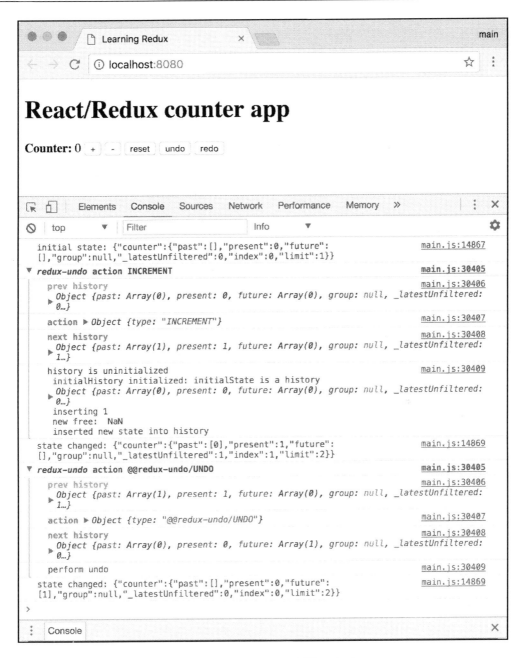

The counter application with redux-undo (debug mode on)

Example code

The current state of the project can be found in the `chapter11_4.zip` attachment.

Unpack the ZIP, move it into the directory, run `npm install` and `npm start`, and then open `http://localhost:8080` in your browser.

Summary

In this chapter, we discussed advanced patterns when developing JavaScript, Redux, and React applications. We started by learning about basic concepts, such as pure functions, and then moved on to higher-order functions. Next, we learned how to use these concepts in a Redux/React application through higher-order reducers and higher-order action creators. Then, we focused on how to implement generic undo/redo behavior in a Redux application by creating a higher-order reducer. Finally, we used the redux-undo library to achieve the same undo/redo behavior, as well as more customized behavior.

In the next chapter, we will cover how to directly extend the Redux store using middleware by providing an example of implementing logging in the Redux store.

12
Extending the Redux Store via Middleware

In the preceding chapter, we discussed how to solve generic problems in Redux/React with higher-order reducers/action creators/components. We extended the elements of Redux by creating their higher-order versions.

In this chapter, we will directly extend the Redux store by creating middleware for it. Finally, we will wrap up the book by giving some general tips and tricks on developing Redux applications.

In this chapter, we will cover the following topics:

- Learning about the middleware pattern
- Using Redux store middleware to implement logging
- Learning final tips and tricks for developing Redux applications

What is middleware?

Middleware is a JavaScript pattern, similar to the **Chain of Responsibility (CoR)** pattern, where a chain of functions is used to handle an incoming event, often in the form of a request.

This pattern is especially useful in libraries that deal with events (such as requests in express or actions in Redux). The middleware pattern has several benefits:

- It allows us to do the following:
    - Use several functions to handle the event and process the data
    - Have functions act as a filter for certain kinds of data
- It doesn't require explicit knowledge between sender and receiver
- The chain of functions can be changed during runtime, acting as an event pipeline

Certain libraries, such as express, allow you to extend their functionality using middleware. This is usually done using .use() on the instance (in express, the instance will be the app object). We pass a middleware function to the .use() function. The middleware function gets a next function as the last argument, which is called when our middleware is done dealing with our data:

```
const instance = someLibraryFn()

function middlewareFn (next) {
  console.log('middleware was called')
  next()
}

instance.use(middlewareFn)
```

Express middleware

The HTTP library, express, allows us to extend the server by executing middleware on every request; for example, consider this:

```
const app = express()

function middlewareFn (req, res, next) {
  console.log('requested url:', req.originalUrl)
  next()
}

app.use(middlewareFn)
```

The preceding middleware function logs the requested URL for each request, then continues with the rest of the request. If we want our middleware to reject the request, we can simply throw an error instead of calling `next()`.

Creating our own middleware pattern

Now that we know what middleware is and how it works in practice, let's create our own middleware pattern.

Sketching out the API

First, we need to sketch out what the API will look like:

1. First, we create an instance of our `Middleware` library:

```
const instance = new Middleware()
```

2. Next, we load some middleware functions, which call the `next()` function after they are done:

```
instance.use(next => ...)
```

3. Finally, we start our instance and let it run through all middleware functions. We can pass a function to the `run` method, which will be called after all middleware functions are done:

```
instance.run(() => ...)
```

Creating the Middleware class

Now, we define the `Middleware` class, which will contain our middleware chain functionality:

1. Define a `Middleware` class:

```
class Middleware {
```

2. Initially, we set the middleware function to a function that simply calls `next()` (essentially doing nothing); this is the default behavior of our `Middleware` library:

```
constructor () {
  this.middleware = (next) => next()
}
```

Defining the run method

Next, we define the `run` method, which takes a function as an argument. This function will be called after the `middleware` function finishes running:

1. Define the `run` method:

```
run (fn) {
```

2. In this function, we call `this.middleware()` and pass a `next` function to it:

```
this.middleware(
```

3. The `next` function will end up calling the passed function, `fn`, with the `this` context of our library:

```
  () => fn.call(this)
  )
}
```

Every non-arrow function (this includes the `function` and `class` definitions) has its own `this` context. Arrow functions, however, can access the `this` context from the upper scope, meaning that they inherit the `this` context from the parent scope (defined by { } brackets).

Up to now, we have not dealt with `this` context much, as it's usually used for direct mutation of a state. Such a direct mutation of a state would make our application unpredictable, and go against the Redux principles.

However, it is fine to use `this` in the context of this example, and there are perfectly valid use cases for the `this` context.

Defining the use method

Now, we need to define the `use` method, which takes a `middleware` function as an argument and adds it to the middleware chain:

1. Define the `use` method:

```
use (fn) {
```

2. First, we store a reference to the preceding `middleware` function:

```
const previousFn = this.middleware
```

3. Next, we overwrite `this.middleware` with a new middleware function:

```
this.middleware = (next) =>
```

4. In this `middleware` function, we first call the previous `middleware` function via `.call(this, next)` so that the `this` context is retained:

```
previousFn.call(this, () =>
```

5. In the passed function, we call the current `middleware` function and pass the `next` argument to it:

```
    fn.call(this, next)
  )
}
```

Using our own middleware pattern

Now we can make use of our middleware pattern:

1. First, we create an instance:

```
const instance = new Middleware()
```

2. Then, we define a `Middleware` that waits 500 milliseconds and sets some value on the instance:

```
instance.use(function (next) {
  setTimeout(() => {
    console.log('first')
    this.firstMiddlewareLoaded = true
    next()
```

```
  }, 500)
})
```

 Note that we use the `function () { }` syntax to define the `middleware` function. Using this syntax ensures that the function gets its own `this` context (which, in this case, will be the instance). An arrow function, however, inherits the `this` context from the upper scope.

3. We define another `Middleware` that waits `250` milliseconds and sets some value on the instance:

```
instance.use(function (next) {
  setTimeout(() => {
    console.log('second')
    this.secondMiddlewareLoaded = true
    next()
  }, 250)
})
```

4. Before we start the chain, we will store the current timestamp to see how long it takes in total:

```
const start = new Date()
```

5. Now, we can start the chain by calling the `.run()` method:

```
instance.run(function () {
  console.log('first middleware loaded:', this.firstMiddlewareLoaded)
  console.log('second middleware loaded:', this.secondMiddlewareLoaded)
  console.log('time passed:', new Date() - start)
})
```

The output will be as follows (or similar to this; `time passed` may vary):

```
first
second
first middleware loaded: true
second middleware loaded: true
time passed: 777
```

As you can see, more than 750 milliseconds have passed and the values on the instance were set, which means that both middleware were "loaded" properly.

Example code

The current state of the project can be found in the `chapter12_1.zip` attachment.

Unpack the zip, change it into the directory, and run `npm install` and `npm start`. It should print some messages to the console.

Using the Redux store middleware

After learning about middleware in general, let's focus more on a specific implementation of the middleware pattern: the Redux store middleware.

While using a similar concept of middleware, Redux middleware solves different problems than, for example, express middleware. It provides a third-party extension point between dispatching an action and the moment it reaches the reducer.

Redux middleware can be used for logging, crash reporting, asynchronous APIs, routing, and much more.

Implementing logging

Let's say we want to log every action that happens in our application together with the new state after the action. Right now, we have already subscribed to the store to log state changes. However, this method does not include information about the action.

Manual logging

The first approach would be manually logging all actions:

```
const action = addPost('hello world')

if (console.group) console.group(action.type)

console.info('dispatching', action)
store.dispatch(action)
console.log('new state', store.getState())

if (console.groupEnd) console.groupEnd(action.type)
```

We need to check whether `console.group` exists, because it only does on some browsers, and it does not exist in Node.js (which is problematic for server-side rendering).

However, it would be a lot of work to put this kind of logging all over our application.

Wrapping the dispatch function

A better approach would be to write a function that will dispatch and log an action:

```
function dispatchAndLog (store, action) {
  if (console.group) console.group(action.type)
  console.info('dispatching', action)
  store.dispatch(action)
  console.log('new state', store.getState())
  if (console.groupEnd) console.groupEnd(action.type)
}
```

Then, we could use it like this:

```
dispatchAndLog(store, addPost('hello world'))
```

However, it's still not very convenient to use this function instead of `dispatch` everywhere.

Monkeypatching the dispatch function

With JavaScript, we can simply overwrite the `dispatch` implementation of Redux with our own, as we did with the `this.middleware` function earlier in this chapter:

```
// DO NOT DO THIS
const next = store.dispatch
store.dispatch = function dispatchAndLog (action) {
  if (console.group) console.group(action.type)
  console.info('dispatching', action)
  const result = next(action)
  console.log('new state', store.getState())

  if (console.groupEnd) console.groupEnd(action.type)
  return result
}
```

However, this is a bad solution, as it might break on future Redux updates. Furthermore, it is simply not a good API. It also does not work well when you want to combine multiple plugins, possibly causing conflicts.

Assume that we have another middleware to report errors (in our case, we simply will log them):

```
// DO NOT DO THIS
const next = store.dispatch
store.dispatch = function dispatchAndReportErrors (action) {
  try {
    return next(action)
  } catch (err) {
    console.error('error:', err)
    throw err
  }
}
```

As you can see in the preceding code, we are using the middleware pattern to monkeypatch `store.dispatch`. Although combining those two simple middleware functions would work fine, it is still a hack, not an official Redux API, and it might cause conflicts with more complicated middleware.

Hiding monkeypatching

Let's try to put our monkeypatching into a nicer solution. Instead of replacing the `store.dispatch` function directly, we will create a higher-order function that returns our `dispatchAndLog` function:

```
// DO NOT DO THIS
function logger (store) {
  const next = store.dispatch
  return function dispatchAndLog (action) {
    if (console.group) console.group(action.type)

    console.info('dispatching', action)
    const result = next(action)
    console.log('new state', store.getState())

    if (console.groupEnd) console.groupEnd(action.type)
    return result
  }
}
```

Now, we could provide a helper function that applies the monkeypatching as an implementation detail. This allows us to apply multiple middleware like the preceding one:

```
// DO NOT DO THIS
function applyMiddlewareByMonkeypatching (store, middlewares) {
```

First, we copy and reverse the array so that the first middleware in the array ends up being applied first:

```
const m = middlewares.slice()
m.reverse()
```

Then, we monkeypatch `store.dispatch` with each middleware, one at a time:

```
m.forEach(middleware =>
  store.dispatch = middleware(store)
)
}
```

However, we are still monkeypatching. It is still a hack, not an official Redux API, and it might cause conflicts with more complicated middleware--we just hid the ugliness.

Getting rid of monkeypatching

The problem in our previous attempts of implementing middleware was the chaining--we keep replacing the (enhanced) dispatch function with a new one that calls the preceding one.

There is a different way to implement chaining--the middleware could get the `next()` function as a parameter instead of directly accessing `store.dispatch`:

```
function logger (store) {
  return function wrapDispatchWithLogger (next) {
    return function dispatchAndLog (action) {
      if (console.group) console.group(action.type)

      console.info('dispatching', action)
      const result = next(action)
      console.log('new state', store.getState())

      if (console.groupEnd) console.groupEnd(action.type)
      return result
    }
  }
}
```

Since we are nesting a lot of higher-order functions here, we can use arrow functions to make our code look more readable:

```
const logger = store => next => action => {
  if (console.group) console.group(action.type)
```

```
console.info('dispatching', action)
const result = next(action)
console.log('new state', store.getState())

if (console.groupEnd) console.groupEnd(action.type)
return result
}
```

This, in fact, is exactly what Redux middleware looks like.

Now our middleware takes the `next()` dispatch function and returns a dispatch function, which serves as the next `next()` function--the next middleware does the same and it keeps going like that through the whole middleware chain. You may still want to access some store methods such as `getState()`, so `store` is available as the top-level argument.

Instead of monkeypatching, we will now use multiple levels of higher-order functions. This pattern is very useful when you want to partially process a function throughout your application/library. At each level of our application/library, the function is applied with one of the arguments, and the returned function is passed on to the next level. This continues until the whole function is processed, and we get data out at the end.

Applying middleware

Instead of applying middleware by monkeypatching, we can now take a store object, create the enhanced dispatch function by applying the middleware functions, and then return a *new* store object:

```
function applyMiddleware (store, middlewares) {
  const m = middlewares.slice()
  m.reverse() // reverse array, so that the first middleware in the array
ends up being applied first

  const dispatch = store.dispatch
  m.forEach(middleware =>
    dispatch = middleware(store)(dispatch)
  )

  return Object.assign({}, store, { dispatch })
}
```

This is not the official implementation of `applyMiddleware()` that ships with Redux. However, it is pretty similar, but different in three important aspects. The official implementation has the following features:

- It only exposes a subset of the store API to the middleware: `dispatch(action)` and `getState()`.
- It ensures that if you call `store.dispatch(action)` from your middleware instead of `next(action)`, the action will travel through the whole middleware chain again, including the current middleware. This is useful for asynchronous middleware.
- To ensure that you only apply middleware once, it operates on `createStore()` rather than the store itself. Instead of `(store, middlewares) => store`, the signature is `(...middlewares) => (createStore) => createStore`.

Additionally, `createStore()` accepts an optional last argument to specify enhancer functions, such as `applyMiddleware()`.

Implementing Redux middleware

We have already implemented a perfectly valid Redux middleware function at the end of the preceding section. For the sake of completeness, let's go through the implementation again. This time, we will implement middleware in our blog application.

You can use `chapter10_2.zip` as a template for this section. Unzip the folder and run `npm install`, and then run `npm start` or `npm run start:dev`.

Creating a middleware folder

We start by creating a folder for our middleware functions--do not confuse this with `src/store/middleware.js`, which is responsible for applying existing middleware to the store:

1. Create a new folder: `src/middleware/`.
2. Create a new file for our logging middleware: `src/middleware/logger.js`.
3. Create a new file for our error reporting middleware: `src/middleware/error.js`.
4. Create a new file to re-export our other middleware functions from: `src/middleware/index.js`.

5. Edit the `src/middleware/index.js` file and re-export the functions from the other files:

```
import loggerMiddleware from './logger'
import errorMiddleware from './error'

export { loggerMiddleware, errorMiddleware }
```

Logging middleware

Edit `src/middleware/logger.js` and define the logging middleware:

1. We start by defining the `logger` middleware function:

```
const logger = store => next => action => {
```

2. First, we start a logging group based on the action type:

```
if (console.group) console.group(action.type)
```

3. Next, we log the action:

```
console.info('dispatching', action)
```

4. Then, we apply the next middleware function (or the dispatch function) and store the result:

```
const result = next(action)
```

5. After applying the next function, we log the new state of the store:

```
console.log('new state', store.getState())
```

6. Finally, we end the logging group and return the result we stored earlier:

```
if (console.groupEnd) console.groupEnd(action.type)
return result
}
```

7. Do not forget to export the function:

```
export default logger
```

Error reporting middleware

Edit `src/middleware/error.js` and define the error reporting middleware:

1. Again, we start with the function definition. This time, we will log something after the first argument is applied:

```
const errorReporter = store => {
    console.log('error reporter active')
```

2. Afterward, we simply return the other functions:

```
return next => action => {
```

3. Then, we catch errors with a `try`/`catch` statement:

```
try {
```

4. Here, we call the next middleware function (or the dispatch function):

```
return next(action)
```

5. If an error happens, we log and rethrow it:

```
} catch (err) {
    console.error('error:', err)
    throw err
    }
  }
}
```

6. Finally, we export the middleware function:

```
export default errorReporter
```

Applying our middleware to the Redux store

Edit `src/store/middleware.js`:

1. Import the two middleware functions we created:

```
import { loggerMiddleware, errorMiddleware } from
'../middleware'
```

2. Then, add them as arguments to the `applyMiddleware` function:

```
return applyMiddleware(
  thunkMiddleware,
  routerMiddleware(history || createHistory()),
  loggerMiddleware,
  errorMiddleware
)
```

3. We can now get rid of our state change logging via `store.subscribe()`. Edit `src/index.js`, and take a look at the following lines:

```
console.log('initial state:', JSON.stringify(store.getState(),
null, 2))
store.subscribe(() =>
  console.log('state changed:', store.getState())
)
```

Replace the preceding lines with this code:

```
console.log('initial state', store.getState())
```

Example code

The current state of the project can be found in the `chapter12_2.zip` attachment.

Unpack the ZIP, change it into the directory, and run `npm install` and `npm start` (or `npm run start:dev`). Then, open `http://localhost:8080` in your browser.

Open your browser console and perform some actions in the application. You should see them getting logged to the console:

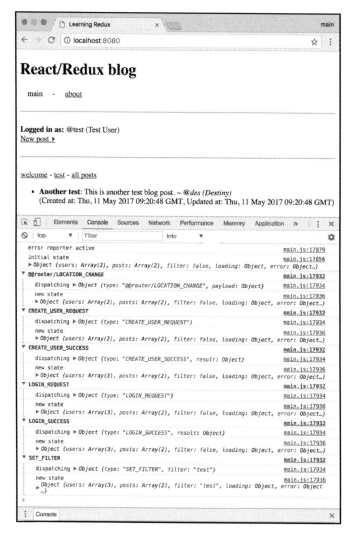

Our Redux application with our custom middleware functions loaded (logger and error reporter)

In the preceding screenshot, you can see the first log message from the error reporter middleware. This is triggered when Redux initializes and the middleware gets applied to the store. Then, you can see the initial state being logged manually. Finally, you can see all our actions being logged in separate groups for each action.

Thunk middleware

You may wonder what exactly the thunk middleware does. In fact, it is a very short function that checks whether an action is a function (that means whether we returned a function from an action creator). If that is the case, we call the function with `dispatch` and `getState`; otherwise, we simply call `next`:

```
const thunk = store => next => action =>
  typeof action === 'function'
    ? action(store.dispatch, store.getState)
    : next(action)
```

It looks pretty simple, huh? Middleware is a simple, but powerful concept.

Final tips and tricks

In the final section of this book, we will walk through some general tips and tricks that we need to keep in mind when we develop Redux applications:

- Designing the application state
- Updating application state

Designing the application state

In many applications, you will deal with nested or relational data. For example, our blog had posts--each post could have many comments, and both comments and posts are written by a user.

Using indices

We have already discussed this previously--you may prefer to store your data in objects with their database ID as the key, and the data entry as the value. Such an object is called an index, and structuring the state as an index makes it easy to select and update the data.

For example, we could store our posts as follows:

```
{
  posts: {
    "post1": {
      id: "post1",
      author: "dan",
      text: "hello world",
      comments: ["comment1"]
    },
    "post2": { ... },
    ...
  }
}
```

We can access a single post via `state.posts[postId]`. Using an array, we would have to use `.find()` to loop through all posts and find the one with the correct `id`.

Normalized state

When designing the Redux state, you should make sure that you keep the following in mind:

- Try not to duplicate data, as it becomes harder to ensure that all data is up to date and synchronized.
- Nested data means that the reducer logic has to be more nested or more complex. Ensure that each reducer only handles a certain kind of data, stored in its state subtree.
- Deeply nested data also brings performance issues--when our state updates, all ancestors in the state tree need to be copied and updated, and the new object references will cause connected components to re-render, even if the data hasn't actually changed.

To avoid most of these issues, you need to make sure that you design Redux state in a normalized way. The concepts of normalized data (from database architecture) are as follows:

- Each type of data gets its own *table* in the state
- Each *data table* should store the individual items in an object, with the IDs of the items as keys and the items themselves as values
- Any references to individual items should be done by storing the item's ID
- Arrays of IDs should be used to indicate ordering

A normalized state for our example could look as follows:

```
{
  posts: {
    byId: {
      "post1": {
        id: "post1",
        author: "dan",
        text: "hello world",
        comments: ["comment1"]
      },
      "post2": { ... }
    },
    allIds: ["post1", "post2"]
  },
  users: {
    byUsername: {
      "dan": { ... },
      "des": { ... }
    },
    allUsernames: ["dan", "des"]
  },
  comments: {
    byId: {
      "comment1": {
        author: "des",
        text: "nice work!"
      },
      "comment2": { ... }
    },
    allIds: ["comment1", "comment2"]
  }
}
```

Generally, we can apply knowledge from the database table/relationship design when designing the Redux state.

Organizing data in the application state

An application might have a mixture of relational data and nonrelational data. There are no hard rules on how to design state, but a common pattern is to organize data by putting it into separate subobjects of the state. For example, we could put data from the backend and UI state into separate subobjects:

```
{
  data: {
```

```
      posts: { ... },
      users: { ... },
      comments: { ... }
    },
    editedData: {
      posts: { ... },
      users: { ... },
      comments: { ... }
    },
    ui: {
      route: { ... },
      ...
    },
    otherData: { ... }
}
```

When existing data is edited, we temporarily store the changes in `state.editedData`, then synchronize them to the server. Once we get the updated data as a response from the server, we can update the entry in `state.data`.

Updating an application state

As we discussed, we should never modify the state object directly, and instead return a *new* state object by copying data from the old one. We will now cover common patterns when updating data in an immutable way like that.

Updating nested objects

The key in this pattern is to copy and update *every* level of nesting appropriately. We will first discuss some common mistakes when updating nested objects. Afterwards, we will take a look at the correct approach.

Common mistake 1 - New variables that point to the same objects

When you define a new variable from an object, it does not create a new object--it only creates another reference to the same object.

Consider the following example:

```
const brokenReducer = (state, action) = {
  let posts = state.posts
  posts[action.id].text = action.text
  return { ...state, posts }
```

```
  }
```

The preceding highlighted line directly modifies the existing state object. *Do not do this.*

Common mistake 2 - Only making a shallow copy

A very common mistake is only copying one level of a nested object.

Consider the following example:

```
const brokenReducer = (state, action) => {
  let newState = { ...state }
  newState.nestedState.nestedField = action.data
  return newState
}
```

In this case, the preceding highlighted line modifies the original state.nestedState object because we only made a shallow copy of the root object.

Correct approach - Copying all levels of nested data

The correct way to update nested data is to copy all levels, as follows:

```
const workingReducer = (state, action) => {
  return {
    ...state,
    nestedState: {
      ...nestedState,
      nestedField: action.data
    }
  }
}
```

It is very useful to use rest/spread syntax (. . .) for this pattern.

Updating arrays

Normally, we would modify an array via functions such as push, unshift, and splice. However, we cannot directly use these on the state in a reducer, as it would mutate the previous state directly.

To work around this, we can use `slice` to create copies of the array and create a new array based on these slices.

Inserting items

Let's say, we want to insert an `item` at the index `i`. First, we create two slices:

- The beginning of the array (from `0` to `i`)
- The end of the array (from `i`)

Then, we create a new array from the first slice, our new item, and the second slice:

```
const insertItem = (state = [], action) => {
  const i = action.index
  const item = action.item

  return [
    ...state.slice(0, i),
    item,
    ...state.slice(i)
  ]
}
```

Removing items

This works similar to how we insert items, except that we only create two slices and merge them together (with no item in-between). For the second slice, we skip one item after `i` to "delete" it:

```
const removeItem = (state = [], action) => {
  const i = action.index

  return [
    ...state.slice(0, i)
    ...state.slice(i + 1)
  ]
}
```

Updating items

To update items, we can use `Array.map` to loop through all items, and then only edit certain items:

```
const updateItem = (state = [], action) => {
  const i = action.index
```

```
const editedData = action.item

return state.map((item, index) => {
  // we do not care about this item, skip
  if (index !== i) return item

  // we want to edit this item
  return { ...item, ...editedData }
})
}
```

Mutating copies

Note that we just need to ensure that the original reference to the state is not modified. As long as we make a copy first, we can safely mutate the copy. This means that we can do the following:

```
let copiedState = state.slice()
```

We can do any operations we want on the `copiedState` variable.

Using libraries

There are various utility libraries that help us to deal with immutable updates. The folowing is a short (incomplete) list of them:

- `dot-prop-immutable`: Provides helper functions that allow us to modify data via string paths; for example, `state = dotProp.set(state, `todos.${index}.complete`, true)`
  https://github.com/debitoor/dot-prop-immutable
- `immutability-helper`: Uses objects with special operations to modify a state; for example, `state = update(['x'], { $push: ['y'] })`
  https://github.com/kolodny/immutability-helper.
- `immutable.js`: If you want, you can use an immutable data structure altogether for your Redux store state; `immutable.js` data structures always return new instances instead of modifying data directly; for example,
  https://facebook.github.io/immutable-js/

Summary

In this chapter, we first covered what middleware is. Then, we specifically focused on Redux store middleware and how it can be used. Finally, we covered how to directly extend the Redux store by creating our own middleware. To wrap up, we ended the book with a section on general tips and tricks for developing Redux applications.

In this book, we started out focusing on why and how Redux works. Afterward, we dove deeper into how to use Redux in combination with a UI library, such as React or Angular. Then, we moved on to implement common functionalities in our Redux application--user authentication, interfacing with APIs, writing tests, and routing. Finally, we discussed extending Redux itself, by solving common problems with state management (such as undo/redo functionality) through higher-order reducers and middleware.

Index

A

action creators
  about 19, 30
  arrow functions 30, 31
  defining 83, 84
  exporting 31
  filter action creators 86
  importing 31
  multiple actions, dispatching 163
  post action creators 85
  user actions 84
action types
  defining 83
  exporting 29
  importing 29
  separating 29
actions
  about 19
  application state, modifying 12
  code example 32
  defining 11
  dispatching 12
  implementing 28
  URL 28
AJAX (Asynchronous JavaScript and XML) 165
Angular 1
  actions, dispatching from user interface 112
  application, creating 107
  code example 107, 109, 112
  controller, defining 108
  controller, redefining 111
  module, defining 108
  ng-redux, setting up 109
  Redux 105
  setting up 106
Angular 2+

@angular-redux/store, setting up 115
  code example 118
  Redux 113
  setting up 113
application state, designing
  data, organizing 339
  indices, using 337
  normalized state 338
  tips 337
application state, updating
  arrays, updating 341
  libraries, using 343
  nested objects, updating 340
  tips 340
application state
  defining 10, 11
  filter state 83
  modifying, with actions 12
  posts state 82
  users state 82
arrays
  copies, mutating 343
  items, inserting 342
  items, removing 342
  items, updating 342
  updating 341
Asynchronicity 7
asynchronous action creators
  about 238
  posts, creating via API 189
  requests fails, testing 240
  successful requests, testing 239
  users, creating via API 186
asynchronous code
  callbacks 224
  promises 225
  testing 224

asynchronous operations
  action types, defining 164
  asynchronous action creator, creating 164
  asynchronous action creators, handling via
    middleware 167
  handling, with Redux 163
  multiple actions, dispatching from action creator
    163
  redux-thunk middleware, setting up 167
Awesome Redux
  URL 17

B

Babel
  setting up 25
  URL 22, 25
backend
  backend API 156
  example code 158
  example output 159, 160, 161, 162, 163
  example request 159, 162, 163
  GET /api/posts 157
  GET /api/posts/ id 158
  GET /api/users 160
  GET/api 157
  POST /api/posts 159
  POST /api/posts/ id 160
  POST /api/users 161
  POST /api/users/ username 162
  setting up 155
blog application
  action creators, defining 83
  action types, defining 83
  application state, defining 82
  building, with Redux and React 79
  code example 92, 102
  goal 80
  project structure 81
  reducers, implementing 87
  Redux store, setting up 91
  user interface, implementing 92
boilerplate code
  extracting 169

C

ChartMonitor
  about 150
  properties 152
  references 152
  setting up 151
  URL 150
claims 195
code examples
  executing 22
  project, setting up 22
  template code 28
container components
  ConnectedFilterList component 98
  ConnectedPostList component 97
  creating, with React-Redux 77
  creating, with React-Redux bindings 76
  example code 76, 79
  implementing 73
  selectors, using 78
  versus presentational components 68
  writing 73
Cross-Origin Resource Sharing (CORS) 197
custom middleware pattern
  API, sketching 323
  creating 323
  example code 327
  Middleware class, creating 323
  using 325

D

DevTools component
  connecting, to Redux 124
  creating 123
  DevTools.instrument() store enhancer, using 125
  multiple store enhancers, using 128
  persistState() store enhancer, implementing 127
  re-dispatch, avoiding 129
  simple session key provider, implementing 129
  store enhancer, using 130
DockMonitor
  about 141
  properties 142
  setting up 142

URL 141
Document Object Model (DOM) 51
dumb and smart components 68
dynamic React components
  about 61
  coding 67
  dynamic class component, creating 62
  initial state, setting 62
  life cycle methods 63
  state, updating 64
  static class component, creating 61
  with timer 64
dynamic routing
  about 256
  nested routes 257
  responsive routing 257

E

Embedded JavaScript (EJS) 275
error state
  component, implementing 183
  component, using 184
  handling 182
  reducer, implementing 182

F

fetch
  URL 166
filter reducer
  writing 40
functional components 58
fundamental principles
  about 13
  read-only state 14
  single source of truth 13
  state changes, processing with pure functions 14

G

generic problems, solving
  higher-order action creators, creating 290
  higher-order components, creating 292
  higher-order reducers, creating 289
  tips 288
generic Undo/Redo functionality
  action creators, defining 296, 309

action types, defining 296, 309
actions, handling 299, 308
counter application, setting up 294
counter reducer, rewriting 298
counter reducer, viewing 295
counter reducer, wrapping with undoable 314
counter-related actions, handling 298
enhanced reducer, implementing 310
example code 303, 315
generic initial state, defining 307
higher reducer, implementing 303
history 305
implementing 294
implementing, in counter application 295
initial state, defining 304
present state, updating 312
problems, with previous solution 305
redo action, handling 311
redux-undo, implementing 316
state, defining 297
undo action, handling 310
undo/redo buttons, creating 300
undo/redo logic, removing from counter 313
undo/redo, trying out 301
undoable higher-order reducer, defining 304
undoable higher-order reducer, problems 315

H

higher-order action creators
  creating 290
higher-order components
  creating 292
higher-order functions
  as arguments 286
  as results 287
  creating 286
higher-order reducers
  creating 289
Hot Module Replacement (HMR) 137, 140, 155
hot reloading
  for React components 136
  setting up 136
  testing 139
  used, in Redux reducers 139
  webpack, configuring 136

I

Inspector
  about 145
  properties 148
  references 148
  setting up 146
  usage 147

J

Jest
  asynchronous code, testing 224
  code coverage, checking 216
  code, executing 226
  describe, using 219
  example code 218
  file change, testing 216
  matchers 219
  mocking 228
  scoping 227
  setting up 213, 226
  teardown 226
  test, using 219
  tests, executing 227
  using 219
JSON Web Tokens (JWT)
  about 213
  header 195
  payload 195
  signature 196
  structure 194
  token 197
  URL 194
  using 197
JSX
  rendering with 54
  setting up 55
  using 55

L

libraries
  @angular-redux/router 17
  @angular-redux/store 16
  ng-redux 16
  react-redux 16
  react-router-redux 17
  redux-auth 16
  redux-devtools 16
  redux-logger 17
  redux-promise 16
  redux-ui-router 17
  redux-undo 17
  URL 16, 17
loading state
  component, implementing 179
  component, using 181
  handling 178
  reducer, implementing 178
logging, Redux store middleware
  dispatch function, monkeypatching 328
  dispatch function, wrapping 328
  implementing 327
  manual logging 327
LogMonitor
  about 143
  properties 145
  setting up 144
  URL 143
  usage 144

M

matchers
  .not.toBe 220
  .toBe 220
  about 219
  arrays 222
  exceptions 223
  numbers 221
  reference 223
  strings 222
  truthy/falsy values 221
Middleware class
  creating 323
  run method, defining 324
  use method, defining 325
middleware
  about 321
  applying, to Redux store 335
  custom middleware pattern, creating 323
  error reporting middleware 334

example code 335
express middleware 322
folder, creating 332
implementing 332
logging 333
thunk middleware 337
mocking, Jest
.mock property 228
implementations 229
matchers 230
return values 229
Mozilla Developer Network (MDN) 98
Mutation 8

N

Navigation component
connecting, to Redux 253
creating 252
using 254
nested objects
all levels, copying 341
level, copying 341
updating 340
variable, defining 340
Node.js
setting up 22
URL 22
notifications
asynchronous action creators, using 185
example code 192
sending, to API via Redux 185

P

package.json file
URL 22
page components
AboutPage component, creating 249
creating 248
MainPage component, creating 248
performance optimization 279
posts reducer
creating, with CREATE_POST 36, 37
destructuring, using 35
editing, with EDIT_POST 37, 39
main structure 34

parsing, with rest operator 35
testing 39
writing 34
presentational components
code 72
Post component 69
PostList components 71
versus container components 68
writing 69
project
Babel, setting up 25
entry files, setting up 25
initializing 22
Node.js, setting up 22
Redux, setting up 28
setting up 22
webpack, executing 26
webpack, setting up 23, 24
promise 166
pure functions
creating 284
other side effects 285
side effects 284
side effects, avoiding 285
without side effects 284

R

React components
testing 243
React, connecting to Redux
about 67
container components, writing 73
presentational component, versus container
component 68
presentational components, writing 69
React-Redux bindings
setting up 77
used, for creating container component 77
using, to create container component 76
react-router-redux
action dispatch, navigating 266
ConnectedRouter, using 265
example code 267
installing 264
router, testing 266

routerMiddleware, using 264
routerReducer, using 265
using 264
react-router
about 256
installing 258
Link, defining 259
redirects, handling 275
references 258
Route, defining 258
router connection, determining 262
Router, defining 258
router, integrating 263
router, using 259
selected link, marking 260
used, for determining page render 274
using 258
using, with Redux 262
React
components, using 59
dynamic React components 61
principles 52
rendering, with JSX 54
setting up 52
simple React element, creating 56
simple text, rendering 53
static React component, creating 57
using 51
ReactDOM 52
reduce
URL 99
reducers
about 12, 15, 19, 233
action creators, defining 33
action types, defining 33
action types, importing 33
clearFilter action, testing 235
combining 40
creating 247
filter reducer 89
filter reducer, writing 40
implementing 32, 87
initial state, testing 233
posts reducer 88
posts reducer, writing 34

root reducer 90
setFilter action, testing 234
state, initializing with beforeEach() 234
testing 41, 42
users reducer 87
with async actions 235
Redux cycle
action, dispatching 20
data flow 20
main reducer function, executing 21
new state, saving 21
strictly unidirectional data flow 21
Redux DevTools Extensions
URL 122
Redux DevTools
build scripts, adding for production and
development 132
ChartMonitor 150
configureStore(), importing 134
configureStore(), using 134
development store, implementing 133
DevTools component, creating 123, 124
DevTools component, loading in development
mode 135
DevTools, connecting to Redux 124
DevTools, rendering 125
DevTools.instrument() store enhancer, using 125
DockMonitor 141
example code 135
excluding, in production 131
Inspector monitor 145
installing 123
integrating 122
LogMonitor 143
NODE_ENV environment variable, injecting with
webpack 131
other monitors 152
production store, implementing 134
production store, separating from development
store 133
references 124
SliderMonitor 148
store, importing 134
URL 122
using 141

Redux ecosystem
  about 16
  reference 17
Redux store middleware
  logging, implementing 327
  middleware, applying 331
  monkeypatching, avoiding 330
  monkeypatching, hiding 329
  using 327
Redux store
  boilerplate code, extracting 169
  data, pulling from API 169
  emulating 272
  error state, handling 182
  example code 185
  initializing 273
  loading state, handling 178
  posts, pulling from API 170
  single user, fetching 172
  users, fetching 174
  users, pulling from API 172
Redux, testing
  about 231
  asynchronous action creators 238
  example code 241
  reducers 233
  reducers, with async actions 235
  synchronous action creators 231
  tests, executing 241
redux-auth 212
redux-thunk 167
redux-undo
  debug mode 318
  example code 320
  implementing 316
  reducer, wrapping with undoable 317
  reference 316
  state selector, adjusting 317
  undo/redo actions, importing 317
Redux
  asynchronous operations, handling 163
  notification, sending to API 185
  setting up 28
  with Angular 2+ 113
Router component

connecting, to Redux 251
creating 250
using 251
router
  action creator, defining 246
  action types, defining 246
  code example 255
  creating 245
  Navigation component, creating 252
  page component, creating 248
  reducer, creating 247
  Router component, creating 250
routing library
  example code 263
  react-router 256
  react-router, using with Redux 262
  using 255

S

selectors
  using 78
server-side rendering
  advantages 269
  browser history, emulating 272
  implementing 272
  index page, caching 278
  isomorphic-fetch library, using 271
  preloaded Redux store state, injecting 276
  preloaded Redux store state, using 277
  preparing 271
  process, page loading 269
  react-router redirects, handling 275
  react-router, used for determining page render 274
  Redux store, emulating 272
  Redux store, initializing 273
  rendered React components, injecting into index.html template 275
  routing, handling 272
  template file, rendering 277
  using 270
SliderMonitor
  about 148
  properties 150
  setting up 149

URL 148
usage 150
static React component
creating 57
functional components 58
Static Routing 256
store enhancers 125
store
about 19, 43
actions, dispatching 45, 46
creating 44, 45
state changes, subscribing 45
user interface, rendering 46, 47
strictly unidirectional data flow 21

T

template strings 173
thunk middleware 337
token authentication
action creator, defining 202
action types, defining 202
backend API 199
components, displaying when user is logged in 208
components, hiding when user is logged in 208
example code 211
example output 199, 200, 201
example request 199, 200, 201
header, separating 206
implementing 198
logged in user, displaying 208
login action, dispatching in component 204
login, testing 205
POST /api/login 199
POST /api/posts 200
POST /api/users 200

reducer, creating 203
secured routes 201
token, sending with curtain requests 209
token, storing in Redux store 202
user login, checking 206

U

User Interface (UI)
about 7
App component, implementing 100
App component, rendering 101
container components, implementing 96
Filter component 95
FilterList component 95
implementing 92
post component 93
PostList component 94
presentational components, implementing 92
Provider component, using 100
timestamp component 94
user component 93
user interface, store
rendering 46, 47
sample data, creating 47
user input, handling 47
utility libraries
reference 343

W

webpack-dev-server (WDS) 140
webpack
configuring, with hot reloading 136
executing 26
setting up 23, 24
URL 24

Made in the USA
Lexington, KY
08 August 2018